MONTREAL

THE UNKNOWN CITY

MONTREAL

THE UNKNOWN CITY

Kristian Gravenor
and
John David Gravenor

ARSENAL PULP PRESS

VANCOUVER

MONTREAL: THE UNKNOWN CITY
Copyright © 2002 by Kristian Gravenor and John David Gravenor
"Dining" chapter copyright © 2002 by Maria Francesca LoDico

ARSENAL PULP PRESS
103-1014 Homer Street
Vancouver, B.C.
Canada V6B 2W9
arsenalpulp.com

The publisher gratefully acknowledges the support of the Government of
Canada through the Book Publishing Industry Development Program for its
publishing activities.

Book design by Lisa Eng-Lodge
Production assistance by Judy Yeung
Cover photograph: Yves Marcoux/Getty Images
Printed and bound in Canada

NATIONAL LIBRARY OF CANADA CATALOGUING IN PUBLICATION DATA:
Gravenor, Kristian
   Montreal: the unknown city / Kristian Gravenor and John David Gravenor.

   Includes index.
   ISBN 1-55152-119-9

   1. Montréal (Quebec)—Guidebooks. I. Gravenor, John David. II. Title.
   FC2947.18G73 2002   917.14'28044   C2002-91150-1
   F1054.5.M83G73 2002

c o n t e n t s

acknowledgments

Four out of five know-it-alls surveyed say writing a book is the proverbial life of Riley. All right, what of it? So what if we spent the better part of a year under the linden tree, getting feet tickled, grapes peeled, and chugging amphetamines. We had to and you would too, if you spent every night in bed wearing thick leather brogues just in case your informants called in with hot leads to chase down. Remember, our sacrifices are for you, Dear Reader (but we really mean, Dear Book-Buyer). Truth be told, our crucial supply of bennies, cola, and aspirin would have dried up months ago if it weren't for the dedication of some of these alphabetically-ordered folks. Without them, it wouldn't have been possible. (Well, okay, it might have been possible. But it wouldn't have been as incredible.)

So thanks go to: Fred Angus, Chris Barry, Arthur "God of Hellfire" Brown, Dan Burke, Rhonda Chung, Bernard de Neeve, Mike Fish, Galine and Jeannie and Livia and Annika and Owen and Tyra, Patrick Gélinas, Billy Georgette, Barry Henderson, Alan Hustak, Jimmy Kalafatidis, Ibolya Kaslik, James Martin, Peter McQueen, Mom and family, Norman Olson, Pablo Palacios, Daniel Sanger, Jim Schneider, Craig Segal, Frederic Serre, Carol Sheehan, Robert Silverman, Mark Stachiew and the cats at *canada.com*, Alastair Sutherland and Peter Vavaro Sr. of The Main.

introduction

Geography is the most sentimental of sciences. For those who've spent a long time on this island, practically every square inch packs an emotional punch. There's the store you got lost in when you were five, the basement where you experienced your first kiss, the redeveloped block where once stood your favourite all-night café, and the sublime park corner you somehow never wandered into.

Don't think you're holding some ordinary guidebook with your obvious attractions and predictable tips on how you're supposed to *parlez français* with Metro ticket attendants. (Forget it! They're locked in there for a reason.) Nope, we're gunning for something bigger: to sneak you into a world most Montrealers don't even know; to slather your subconscious with a weathered patina of the living-city vibe; to give you inside scoop like a fedora-wearing wiseguy in the alley. Our job is to dole out the kind of dope that makes you feel like you've been here at least since they sold tomatoes in paper bags where skyscrapers now stand.

This island city comes in 29 different borough flavours, from places where there's a chicken in every pot to others where you'll find a syringe in every sandbox; from neighbourhoods where Welfare Day arrives like rain in the desert to others where SUVs choke traffic in front of private schools as parents pick up their brats. From the hidden surprises of the Old Port and the sari-clad saffron shoppers of Park Extension, to the cold comfort of the humid concrete masterpiece known as the Olympic Stadium, we'll endow you with intimate facts about this greatest of all possible cities.

Think of this book as a slice of the Montreal melon – a once-common fruit that went extinct, despite the fact people were willing to fork over big money for a slice. Well, that story always seemed a bit bogus to us (especially after the melon made its "miraculous" comeback in 1996), which is why we make no other mention of it in this text. Same goes for any local legend we found dodgy or overly speculative. Nevertheless, let us hand you a juicy slice of our burgh – juicy with flavours bitter, outrageous, shocking, insane, and uplifting (Okay, we're a little short on that uplifting stuff).

This is the island city that's impossible not to love. Think of the ubiquitous sweethearts who walk leisurely across the path of your waiting car long after your light turns green. A street encounter that elsewhere might end in conflict is resolved with a grin and a wink in Montreal. No mere text can completely capture the spirit of the world's largest inland port – the crossroads of English, French, Cambodian and Mohawk. But let us serve you up the very best, and for this your eyes shall be rewarded.

– Kristian Gravenor and John David Gravenor

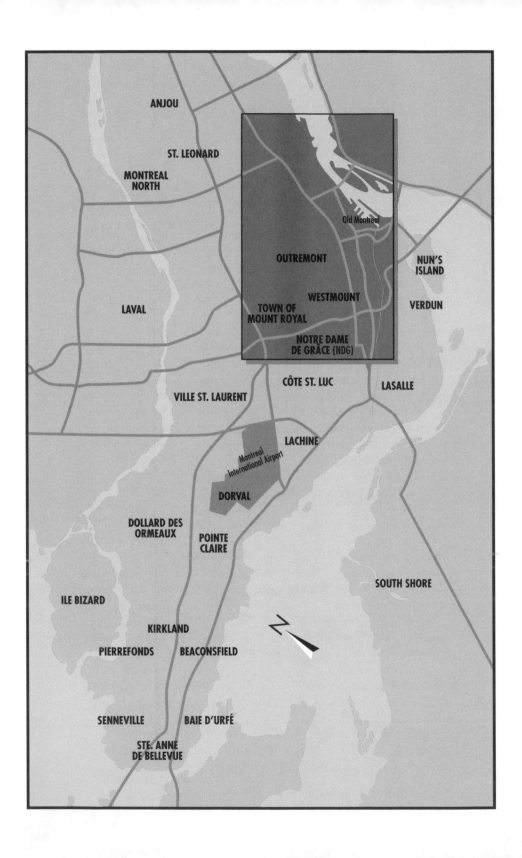

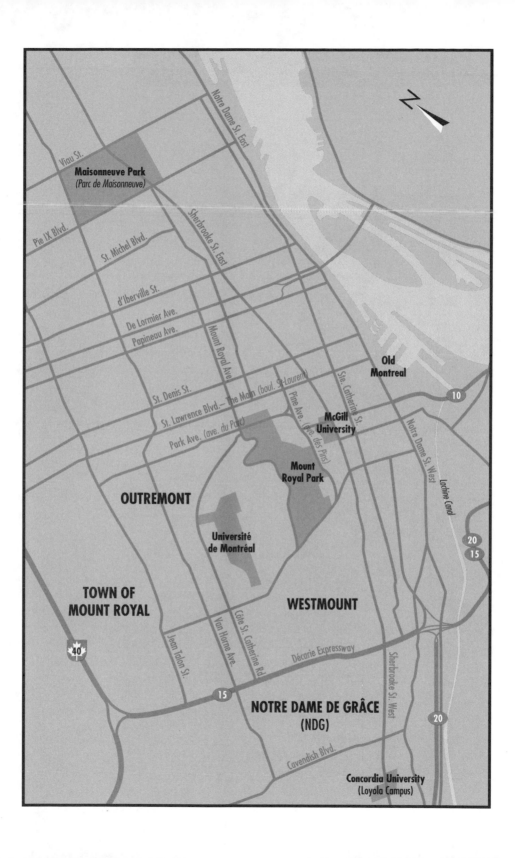

From the building where midget royalty gave way to towel-wearing men to the secret door where detail freaks worship tiny locomotives beneath the tracks of the real deal, we've got all the nooks and crannies for all you crooks and nannies.

The Disco Cross

The cross on top of Mount Royal isn't the same one that Jacques Cartier planted when he jumped off his boat in 1534. Nor is it the one that Governor de Maisonneuve hauled up there to thank the Lord after a flood receded on Christmas Day, 1642. Our 103-foot metal skeleton of a cross was planted in 1924 with cash raised by the St. Jean Baptiste Society by getting 85,000 school kids to sell 25 stamps each at a nickel apiece. The cross was supposed to be souped up with a granite covering that nobody got around to putting on.

When Pope Paul VI died in 1978, officials decided to honour him by having the lights shine purple. The problem was that, back then, purple lights weren't being manufactured. Someone was enlisted to handpaint the bulbs so they would cast a purple glow. After John Paul I was annointed that August, a storage problem led to the purple-painted bulbs being thrown out; what was the likelihood of needing them again anytime soon? Well, barely a month later, John Paul I was dead, and the painting started anew.

To help celebrate Montreal's 350th anniversary in 1992, the city spent $300,000 to replace the incandescent bulbs with cheaper-to-run fiber-optics. Since then, the cross can be made to turn red, white, blue, or even purple. But other than a one-off test in the spring of '92, Montrealers have never seen the cross in its proud plumage. The company that made the renovations explains that Catholic authorities vetoed the notion of having the cross lit in any colour but white. Church officials deny this, and now welcome the colouring of the cross. Current wisdom blames the media for the repression. Indeed, some pundits mocked former Mayor Jean Doré's colourful intentions by calling it "the disco cross." When asked why he never lit it up after succeeding Doré, Mayor Bourque said that he didn't even know it was capable of being lit in different colours.

• Nelson's column in Old Montreal was originally made of baked clay. When a worker tightened a screw too much during the 1970s, the likeness of the Hero of Trafalgar shattered. The original was removed, and the column stood empty for a long time. Some hoped Nelson would stay away: one sculptor begged for a contract to replace the tribute to the British hero with a monument to Jacques Cartier instead. Meanwhile the nationalist Societé St. Jean Baptiste wanted it to remain Nelson's column – but in honour of Wolfred Nelson, an old-time mayor with a face that could would scare a small child, and who favoured the rebellion of 1837.

• For 10 years nobody knew – at least nobody admitted knowing – where the Giants of St. James disappeared to. The four huge limestone figures that originally stood outside an Old Montreal bank finally surfaced in a bus repair depot and now loom in the Montreal Archives Centre at 535 Viger East.

• The bronze likeness of Canada's first prime minister was always a popular spot for seagulls on the south side of Dominion Square (now Dorchester Square). But in

later years, the foundling federalist attracted separatists wielding cans of spray paint. One day the city awoke to find that somebody had decapitated Sir John A. McDonald, and his statue had to be hauled away for repairs. It was returned, with a new head, in 1994. Whoever used a torch to make away with the original noggin still isn't talking.

ISLAND WITHIN AN ISLAND

Until 1980, the east-end insane asylum known as the Louis H. Lafontaine Hospital (adjacent to the entrance to the eponymously named tunnel) was once known as St. Jean de Dieu, where the local poet Emile Nelligan died, and where Premier Duplessis was, according to one biographer, treated for alcoholism. But in a strange urban arrangement, the hospital was also its own separate municipality called Gamelin until 1980. For almost its entire history the Catholic-run hospital-cum-city was equipped with its own municipal administration, fire squad, and police. Other than their psychologically-troubled patients, the town of Gamelin had no residents or elections. As well as being one of the places normal children were interned as mental patients in the Duplessis Orphan scandal, the hospital was also the site of a grisly discovery. In later years unexplained graves were found in an area known as the "pigsty cemetery" located in the fields behind the SAQ's serve-yourself wine and alcohol warehouse. No municipal records have ever been made available to the public, and officials have offered no explanation for the origin of the graves.

LOSER TAKES ALL

A local tale describes how an old geezer who lost his dentures went to the lost-and-found department at the Berri métro station, only to be presented with a box containing a half dozen similar-looking sets of teeth. Without a second thought, the intrepid old-timer casually shoved each set of dentures in his mouth until he found the one that fit. The lost-and-found attendants won't confirm the story, but they invite you to the city's largest lost-and-found resource. It receives 500 lost items a week and fields 200 calls a day, of which about 40 strike pay-dirt. People have been known to claim they lost "a black umbrella" to keep dry on a rainy day. Call 514/280-4637.

Churchill's Stash

The Sun Life building was long the tallest structure in the Commonwealth after it was built in 1909 and might have played a role in the destiny of Britain. In July 1940, Winston Churchill, risking a huge loss at the hands of German U-Boats, shipped a massive government fortune to the third sub-basement of the Montreal skyscraper, which was reinforced with metal beams for the occasion. Churchill wanted the cash here in case he had to set up a Canadian-based resistance should Hitler have taken Britain. Other curiosities of this building include the peregrine falcon that nested on its roof between 1936 and '52, where it raised 22 young. (For a few years subsequent, the rare bird returned to the downtown area, nesting on the 32nd floor of the Stock Market tower.) The Sun Life building deserves a peek for its elaborate elevator doors alone, which contain fantastic detail of squirrels and coats of arms created in 1930 at great expense.

Photo: John David Grovenor

The Birth of Smoked Meat

Photo: John David Gravenor

Ben's restaurant was named after Benjamin Kravitz, a Lithuanian who came to the city with $2 and by 1908 had opened a restaurant on the Main, introducing a recipe from his homeland involving a marinated and smoked beef brisket on rye. So now you know who brought smoked meat to Montreal. As well as becoming a downtown institution since moving to de Maisonneuve and Metcalfe in 1929, Ben's also became a sort of museum for obscure stars of the '50s. Long-forgotten celebs cling to their last bit of notoriety in hundreds of framed 8 x 10 photo glossies that cover the walls.

Walk of Obscurity

You could live your whole life in this city and never notice the Promenades des Stars. Not that you'd really be missing anything. But since 1995, you can walk by the corner of Alexandre DeSève and Ste. Catherine and stub your toe on any of two dozen brass plaques embedded in the sidewalk. Honouring fine local entertainers – such as Gilles Latulippe, Alys Robi, Béatrice Picard, and Réal Giguere – they also include names you've actually heard of, like Celine Dion. Popular French-language singer Mitsou, in spite of her ample talents, didn't earn a star (although her uncle, theatre legend and playwright Gratien Gelinas, did).

Monuments Quietly Removed

Tramway Arches

Somewhere in a provincially-owned field near Henri Bourassa sit the ornate arches from the old Craig Tramway Terminus. When the provincial government chose to knock the old building down in favour of the Palais des Congrès, planners reluctantly agreed to integrate the old colonnade, complete with arches. They reneged on the plan after conveniently misplacing some of the pieces.

Elmhurst Cows

For years three massive cow heads affixed to the wall of Sealtest Dairy thrilled and delighted passers-by on St. Jacques West. Shock, sadness, and bitter disappointment greeted their disappearance a couple of years ago, although we could be overstating the public response. The dairy, now called Parmalat, has the fiberglass heads in a storage area and, according to brass, they should be back in place by the time this book is in your hands, although they've been making this same promise for a few years now.

Five Roses Flour

Among the signature signs lost to the city was a huge, weeping neon bull near Guy and Ste. Catherine touting Oxo with the caption, "Alas my poor brother." Another, near the Victoria Bridge in the Point, featured a gargantuan neon show horse representing Dawes Black Horse Brewery. But unlike those, the "Farine Four Roses Flour" sign survived. Sort of. Somewhere along the line, the word Flour, for reasons too depressing to explain (something about a ban on English signs), was quietly extinguished.

Queen's Façade

Many heritage types had hoped that at least the façade of the old Queen's Hotel on Peel, a landmark demolished in the '80s and '90s, would be reused in a future development. Sadly, the ornate redstone rubble now sits forgotten in city yards near the Turcot highway interchange.

Saddam's Pied-à-Terre?

Saddam's not doing any explaining but locals have been curious as to why the stately mansion at 100 Somerville in Ahuntsic that once housed the Iraqi consulate was suddenly abandoned. Ever since one night during the Iran-Iraq War, the residence near the picturesque Back River (so nicknamed because it is at the back of downtown; the actual name is Rivière des Prairies) has been left totally unattended. Drifters who've dropped in over the years included one who took to mowing the grass on occasion. The Iraqis have rebuffed attempts to purchase the fenced-off property, for which they pay over $10,000 a year in municipal taxes.

Leonard Cohen's Last Stand

Over the last few years, dumbstruck tourists (many of whom are Scandinavian, for some reason) have been known to gawk at a certain building right near Portugal Park at Marie Anne and the Main. Their notion is that Leonard Cohen lives there, but in fact the bagel-loving Buddhist has barely set foot in 4316 St. Dominique (a.k.a. "St. Dump") since '95, although he remains the owner. By happenstance, another musician inhabited the digs during Cohen's absence. Much-loved bilingual rocker Michel Pagliaro bedded down at that address until 2001.

Fossils in the City

Three buildings built from Tyndall limestone from the town of Garson, Manitoba form some of the city's best archaeological collections. Tyndall limestone, which was also used in the Parliament buildings at Ottawa, was favoured in construction because it has a beautiful, swirling grain that resembles knotty pine. The costly stone also contains countless fossils in its surface that can be seen and touched, as animals were pressed into the living stone way back when southern Manitoba was covered in a tropical sea. See it for yourself at the Château Apartments (pictured; *1321 Sherbrooke St.*; the building where author Mordecai Richler lived for 20 years), the old Eaton's building (*Ste. Catherine St. and University St.*; now Ailes de la Mode), and the Alcan Building (*1188 Sherbrooke St. W.*).

Photo: John David Gravenor

They Didn't Have Squatters Then

According to a story in the *Montreal Standard* of September 4, 1937, a downtown home at a Sherbrooke Street address that's suspiciously unspecified, had been sealed shut since 1912. People with nothing better to think about would often wonder why nobody ever entered or exited the place. It seems that the owner's will insisted that the home remain closed for 25 years after his death. "Odd-style clothes" and $5,000 in loose change were found when the home was finally opened.

Photo: John David Gravenor

COMPLETE WITH NIHON SIGN

Penny-conscious Belgian multi-millionaire Alexis Nihon bought up huge swaths of the island in the 1950s, including a baseball field on Atwater and what's now de Maisonneuve. Before retiring to play golf in the Bahamas, Nihon sold the property to developers who built a mall on the site. The mall — Plaza Alexis-Nihon — now bears the Nihon name in tribute to his impressive list of virtues. Plus there's the fact that one of the conditions of the sale was that the new owners name the mall after him.

Forgotten Hockey Shrine

Photo: John David Gravenor

Stare at this site and you'll see a nondescript car-rental company parking lot. Now blink hard and you might see the Victoria Rink, opened in 1865, that had a major influence on our official clutch'n'grab winter sport. The International Ice Hockey Federation recognizes it as the scene of the earliest account of an ice hockey game, on March 3, 1875. Today's standard hockey rinks duplicate the dimensions of the Victoria's ice surface, a length that was dictated by the distance between Drummond and Stanley streets. In spite of being home to many great moments in early hockey, by the 1920s the magnificent rink began its new vocation as a parking lot. The local city council has supported a plan proposed by veteran jazz pianist Billy Georgette to return the Hockey Hall of Fame to the site. Montreal was home to the Hall until weasely NHL sneaks moved it to Toronto following the Rocket Richard riots.

BUT HE DIED HAPPY

If you rode the bus up Ridgewood in the sixties you might have noticed pious-looking women crossing themselves when the bus passed a certain building near the bottom of the hill. The unspoken gesture was in honour of Premier Duplessis who was believed by many to have died in the building while making love to his mistress. According to the story the premier, who had previously been scolded by church authorities for his libidinous ways, was quickly shuttled up north to give the impression he died in a country shack.

Sweeping Beauty

Photo: John David Gravenor

Amazement and flabbergastation are the usual reactions elicited when people are informed that the clock at the Grand Séminaire (the building on the south side of Place d'Armes, right next to the Notre Dame Basilica) is the oldest public clock in North America. Since it was ordered in Paris and slapped up in 1701, the big hand has gone around 2,638,566 times – although that statistic gets more outdated every hour. The clock underwent major renovations in 1751 and 1801 and, like Bob Dylan, went electric in the mid '60s. Unlike most of this city's fast-disappearing public clocks, this one tells the correct time.

Photo: John David Gravenor

Benito Mussolini wasn't just an Italian dictator who warmed the hearts of many an Italo-Montrealer who trained in local fascist camps, marched in black-shirt parades, and sat around a wartime detainment camp in Petawawa, Ontario. In 1936, Il Duce shelled out for the Casa d'Italia *(505 Jean Talon E.)*, which remains the spiritual centre for many locals with roots in that Beatle boot of the Mediterranean. Inside the door of the building sits a marble plaque commemorating the Italian leader. For more fascist fun, check out the Madonna Della Difesa Church at the eastern tip of Dante, where you can also see Mussolini on the ceiling riding a horse and chit-chatting with the pope. The work was painted by the great Guido Nincheri, who was reportedly reluctant to place the Bald Boss among the deities. One Italian Montrealer named Frank reports that he has frequently spray-painted over Mussolini's marble inscription and also objects to seeing Mussolini in church. "I even had to walk out on my grandmother's funeral," he says. For decades, local socialist Joseph Spada battled with fascist rival Dieni Gentile for the hearts of the local Italians, and although Gentile died in 1995, his old restaurant sits across from the church. According to Gentile's son-in-law, Joe Frantino, president of Casa d'Italia, hidden in the back room of that restaurant opposite the church sits a bust of Mussolini and other commemorative fascistic relics. "It used to make me mad when people would criticize it, but now I realize that the fascist memorabilia brings people to Little Italy and that's a good thing."

TOURISM BOOMING

Today it's the site of a McDonald's but it's also the corner of Central Station where a bomb ripped through lockers September 3, 1984, killing three French tourists. Thomas Brigham, a 65-year-old American known for babbling about religion and conspiracy, was convicted of the misdeed that took place just prior to a visit by Pope John Paul II. Brigham, a U.S. citizen and father of 11, was twice found guilty of the crime and sentenced to life. However, a psychologist and a United States vice-consul, among others, insisted that Brigham was too harmless and disorganized to pull off such a bombing. Later, a CN railway police constable described a young blond man, and not Brigham, covering his ears just before the blast and celebrating after it went off. The mysterious blond man was never found and Brigham died of a heart attack while serving his sentence in 1991.

Photo: John David Gravenor

NOW YOU SEE IT ...

As you gently flip these pages, workmen might be quietly transporting one of the city's oldest and cheesiest landmarks. That's because the e-commerce development at René Lévesque and Mountain will likely swallow up the spot occupied since the 1930s by the giant Guaranteed Pure Milk bottle, actually a five-storey water tower. The tower is well known around the world since Dusan Makavejev's 1975 Serbian-language anarcho-drama *Sweet Movie* (more about that later).

Photo: John David Gravenor

In January 1988, construction workers stumbled across three ancient underground chambers beneath a burnt-out Woolworth's store at 363 St. Jacques. Historians suggested the creepy spaces were used to store munitions, or as a place for soldiers to snooze. Maybe they served as cold storage, or as a gateway under the old city walls. Nobody seemed quite ready to admit that they hadn't the slightest idea what the vaults were used for. You can see them in the sub-basement of the Chez Plume restaurant in the Intercontinental Hotel (they have a reception room they call The Vaults). Similar subterranean vaults can be found in the old Silver Dollar Saloon (now a tourist info building at Jacques Cartier Square and Notre Dame) or in the basement of the Vieux Séminaire on Place d'Armes.

The Cinéma de Paris might be home base to our annual film fest, but it's also identified as the spot of the Princess Theatre, where the great magician and escape artist Harry Houdini suffered the injury that killed him. On October 22, 1926, Houdini invited a bunch of friendly McGill students to visit him backstage following a performance. One was J. Gordon Whitehead, who opted to test Houdini's legendary trick of being able to withstand any punch to the solar plexus. He walloped the master of escape before Houdini had time to flex his muscles in preparation. As a result Houdini suffered internal injuries that graduated into deadly peritonitis, and died nine days later in Detroit. Some have suggested that Whitehead, a divinity student who later became a full priest, intended to kill Houdini, whose popularization of mysticism was considered a threat to the church. One biographer argued that Whitehead could not have been responsible for Houdini's death, as medical experts have pointed out that such a blow might have caused damage, but not the injury that killed Houdini. So Houdini might have been suffering from appendicitis before he reached Montreal. One hopes we're off the hook for this one.

Secret Ghost Stories

• Skeptics might be swayed if they actually saw the calèche wagon on St. Paul in Old Montreal that beckons you in and then disappears when you try to climb aboard. If that doesn't convince them of the existence of local ghostly apparitions, there's always the French soldier known to hang around antique shops in Old Montreal, or the soldiers around the Old Fort on Ile St. Helene who make marching sounds after midnight. Here are the best-told, real-deal ghost stories of the city.

• A headless man with a dazzling candle hangs out at the Le Royer condos at St. Paul and St. Sulpice in Old Montreal. The condo development should have known better than to build on the site of the original Hôtel Dieu hospital that burned down in 1695. Unlike quiet-type ghosts, this one makes way too much noise — walking with heavy shoes and rolling an empty bottle. The phenomena were described by 17th-century patients and hospital staffers who, naturally, reported them to the authorities. Perhaps to shore up the value of their haunted properties, current residents seldom admit to having seen or heard the spirits.

• Mary Gallagher was a successful prostitute whose good looks and charm drove her best friend, Susan Kennedy, to the heights of jealousy. So on June 26, 1879, Susan chopped off Mary's head and popped it into a bucket, a drunken deed that would cost her 16 years in prison. The headless Mary now visits every seven years on the date of her death — at the southeast corner of Murray and William (pictured) — in search of her head, an event that often attracts dozens of spectators. Her next visit will be in 2005.

An Empty House

Nothing will get West End jaws wagging faster than a debate over the future of the empty Cinema V. Opened as the Empress Theatre in 1927, the venue located on Sherbrooke facing NDG Park sported gold and ancient-style Egyptian motifs, but residents were outraged when its new owner sought to turn it into a strip club in 1963. Local puritans in the NDG Community Council tried blocking its application for a liquor license, while veteran bar owner Ma Keller and others described it as a community resource. Her opinion was shared by schoolboys known to group outside the club, hoping to get a peek at showgirls cooling off on the fire escape. The dancers would earn $4 a day and — if you believe the gossip — would occasionally accompany patrons to the adjoining hotel. The building eventually became a repertory cinema and, briefly, a first-run theatre until it was shut down for good. For several years do-gooders have been fighting an uphill battle for funding to restore the building for community use.

Cross at the Corner

The red wooden cross at the northwest corner of René Lévesque and Guy was planted by Grey Nuns to commemorate the execution of a certain Jean Baptiste Goyer dit Belisle, who killed and robbed a wealthy friend and the victim's wife. For his crimes, Belisle was sentenced to death by "torture ordinary and extraordinary." The cross, which is intended to warn us against committing similar nasty deeds, has been a local landmark since 1752.

Mayor Camilien Houde, singer Marie Bolduc, poet Emile Nelligan, and politician L.H. Lafontaine are all at rest there right now, as is psycho criminal Richard Blass. Thomas Darcy-McGee is inside a stone hut with a black metal door. Robert Bourassa is right below a pair of 15x4-foot cement rectangles elegantly bending into each other. Likewise are aptly-named, non-famous souls like Bury and Shallow. Maurice Richard and Jean Drapeau are near the front on a gentle slope. But the Notre Dame des Neiges cemetery, an attractive boneyard with 43 kilometers of pathways and 800,000 graves, hasn't always been such a sleepy place. In its earliest days, medical students would routinely sneak in and dig up corpses for research. In 1975, its underpaid gravediggers went on strike and left 20 unburied corpses in the sun. In '86 management locked the same workers out for wanting to work shirtless. In '88 body parts were exposed for all to see when a new section was dug. Nowadays bodies are buried for 99 years and then removed unless a descendent can be found to pay the meter. And lastly, some historians have suggested that the ancient Iroquois village of Hochelaga wasn't, as many assume, on a downtown site between McGill and Ben's restaurant, but rather where this cemetery now lies. The nearby Protestant Mount Royal Cemetery is the burial ground of famous local names like Redpath, Roddick, McCord, Morenz, and Richler.

• The spirit of a peddler murdered in the 1850s around where Westmount High School now stands spent years of his afterlife terrorizing the residents of the area with the sounds of rattling chains and mysterious bright lights. One scaredy-cat resident took refuge in a nearby home, where a sceptical neighbour teased him for being fearful. The sceptic accepted a challenge to spend a night in the house, and ended up trembling on the floor. The ghost took off in the 1890s, but don't bet against its return.

• Like Casper, the Rev. Edmund Wood is a friendly ghost who likes to hang around the church he founded, the red-roofed St. John the Evangelist Anglican Church (at President Kennedy and St. Urbain). Its current Anglican administrators report that Wood's ghost doesn't really do anything funny or scary, preferring to hang around all the same. Wood's contribution to church design durng his lifetime was to install chairs instead of pews, because important people had developed the habit of renting out the benches — a sort of old-fashioned version of luxury skyboxes in sports stadiums.

Island for a Song

Photo: John David Gravenor

• Back before killing your husband resulted in a movie deal in which Farrah Fawcett plays your life story, ~~Marie-Josephe Corriveau's reward for~~ killing her husband in 1763 was to be judged a witch. The Quebec City woman was hanged and her body was hoisted in an iron cage and left to rot at a public crossroads. The Chateau Ramezay had the good sense to bring the cage to Montreal and put it on display in their museum in Old Montreal. Now that building, facing City Hall, is the new jumping-off point for the ghost of *la Corriveau* to scare the bejeepers out of the town every Halloween.

• White figures jumping around the basement and on the roof, as well as unexplained screams and moans: it's been a real source of curiosity on Pine between Peel and McTavish. The source of the terrifying spectre is the tortured soul of Simon McTavish, a well-heeled fur dealer who died in 1804 while building mansions on the site. They were completed soon after, but then demolished in 1861.

Nun's Island, now a fabulous 29 million-square-foot swank suburban area, was sold by the Catholic church for just $5,000 cash in 1956. In those days the island just south of Point St. Charles was used as a summerhouse for vacationing nuns, who would communicate with nuns onshore by blowing out codes on a horn. The island soil was considered unsuitable for construction and occasional buyers would default on ownership after witnessing massive sheets of spring ice tearing down the St. Lawrence River over the deforested land. One day, Colin Gravenor, a threadbare writer for the shock tabloid *Midnight*, made a million-dollar bid for the land, a deal that entailed $10,000 down and $100,000 payment 90 days later. When he showed up with just $5,000 the nuns' notary signed away the land anyway, confident that the island would revert back to the church for nonpayment by the time the next major payment was due. Gravenor then initiated a letter-writing campaign in which he assumed dozens of names, all of whom urged government officials to build a bridge to the south shore spanning Nun's Island. To his delight, Prime Minister Louis St. Laurent announced the construction of the Champlain Bridge, complete with on- and off-ramps to the island. Gravenor sold the island to developers Juda Gewurz and Joe Remer for $2 million.

Photo: John David Gravenor

When Mayor Jean Drapeau first became His Worship, the western — i.e., English — side of downtown was attracting big projects like the Queen Elizabeth Hotel. But in the east, meanwhile, the big project was the subsidized housing project called Les Habitations Jeanne Mance. Drapeau didn't like the plan one bit, and conducted a vicious campaign to block the provincially backed project. At the end of his first mandate, the crime-fighting mayor learned that his opposition to the public housing project wasn't shared by the voters. Sarto Fournier, possibly benefitting from a good deal of ballot-stuffing, dealt Drapeau his only-ever electoral defeat and soon the wrecking was at work on 400 homes between St. Dominique, Drolet, Ontario, and Ste. Catherine (one resident, a self-styled Ukranian herbalist named Constantin Spodunik, required some convincing to leave). Fournier became a one-term upstart as Drapeau returned to office in 1960 and the public-housing project remains a permanent fixture on the cityscape.

INSTANT ANTIQUE

When it was built in the '80s, Bernard Lamarre wasn't entirely happy with his company's 25-storey headquarters at Peel and René Lévesque. The portly Lavalin Construction CEO was particularly displeased that that the shiny copper façade wasn't green like the oxidized copper roofs of neighbouring buildings, including the nearby Windsor Hotel. When informed that it would take a year or two for the elements to turn his brown building the same shade of mellow green, Lamarre reportedly shouted to an underling, "Oxydez-moi ça!" A special, $500,000 treatment instantly made the copper green. Lavalin later suffered major financial troubles and merged with competitor SNC.

Photo: John David Gravenor

Cured to Death

Don't panic the next time you're enjoying an afternoon sprawled on the grounds of Dorchester Square (a.k.a. Dominion Square) and Place du Canada on Peel now that you have been informed that there are dead bodies beneath you. Until 1870 the green space was known as the St. Antoine cemetery (indeed, Cathdrale Street was known as Cemetery Street back then). For a while it became known as the Cholera Cemetery, as workers swiftly buried anybody they thought might have the disease. Their job was complicated by the morphine cures administered to cholera victims that often made them look dead when they actually weren't. In one case, a young Miss Hervieux was buried quickly, still wearing her dress jewelry. Her family wanted the jewels back and had her coffin reopened. When it was brought to the surface, they found that she had pushed one arm through the opening of the coffin lid before succumbing. She had been buried alive. In 1832, a presumed cholera fatality named Bill Collins awoke while awaiting burial, and strolled down St. Antoine street in his death shroud, causing a police officer to faint with shock. Collins recovered fully.

FENCING CHAMPIONS

Long before the notion of the gated community was invented, the Town of Mount Royal quietly put a fence along their Acadie Boulevard boundary with Park Extension, Montreal's poorest and most ethnically diverse neighbourhood. They explained the fence was meant to "protect children and pedestrians from the fast traffic along Acadie" – although during the same period TMR security squads would eject any Park Ex kids caught playing or meandering on their upscale turf. In 1970, Montreal negotiated to have the barrier removed. In a planned attack that year, 300 students tried to demolish the barrier, which even TMR Mayor Reg Dawson vowed to have removed. Instead of getting rid of it, TMR reinforced it and it stands to this day, a symbolic Maginot Line against the invading poor.

Out in the Cold

The fieldstone building with the slanted roof at Decelles and Fendall in Côte des Neiges is not simply the oldest building in the area. It's also a cautionary tale about evil bureaucratic bungling. Fendall House, named after the family that once owned great chunks of the neighbourhood, belonged to Gertrude Fendall, the last of her clan. In 1990, at age 90, she fell ill, was put under provincial curatorship, and sent to live in an old age home. Once Fendall was gone, government administrators emptied Fendall House and removed all of its contents. According to Fendall's assistant Yvan Chaput, an illiterate raised in an insane asylum as part of the Duplessis Orphan scam, the pencil pushers removed a will pledging the home to him after Fendall's death. The government administrators then proceeded to neglect the historic home: pipes froze and exploded and the floors and walls were damaged by water. The abandoned home has been deteriorating ever since.

The Old Con-and-Brag

For a few years in the 1950s anybody passing the modern, curved building across from the seminary on Sherbrooke and Fort streets would wonder about the fancy British sports cars parked out in front. They belonged to the sales team assembled by one of the city's greatest-ever stock swindlers. From his headquarters in that building, an alcoholic, visionary, one-armed diabetic mystic, Stafford Harriman, defrauded American investors with phony investment schemes. Described by many to have an eerie, mystic-like presence, Harriman would seduce investment analysts with salted mines by day, and get roaring drunk and spend huge wads of cash by night. Harriman even had the temerity to explain his techniques in a story published in the January 1952 edition of the *Saturday Evening Post* called "How to Sell Phony Stocks To American Suckers." He remained a free man, before retiring to a life of meditation.

Photo: John David Gravenor

A Boring Urge

Photo: John David Gravenor

In June 1944, Damase Handfield had a feeling about his plot of land at the corner of Fort and Sherbrooke Streets. His intuition told him there was some Texas tea deep below. So, at considerable cost, he dug an oil well right there on the elegant street – even though experts and 200 other failed Montreal wildcatters told him that the only geyser he'd be likely to hit would be of the aquatic variety. The prehistoric volcanic action that shaped the island makes it unlikely that any oil lies below our land's surface. No oil, ultimately, was struck.

Mme Côme Cherrier ceded her land at Rachel and the Main to the city in 1870, under the condition it forever remain a public market. Her descendants reminded the city of this when they knocked the market down in 1966. They received $92,000 to calm their troubled hearts.

Long ago, the Décarie family donated a chunk of their great west-end farm to make way for the street that later became the Décarie Expressway. But the deal was made on the condition that the land revert back to them if the streetcar lines were ever removed. It took them a while to realize that the streetcars were no longer buzzing, but by 1978, descendants sued to get their land back. The judge sided with them, but offered no compensation.

Descendants of Horatio Admiral Nelson (nephew of the great naval hero) donated land at Drummond and René Lévesque to the city in 1864 under the condition that things like a bus terminal never be built there. So what did the Desmarais Power Corp. built there? You guessed it: a bus station. In 1960, descendants did some loud barking and, soon after, the terminus was moved to its current site on Berri.

It's widely believed that Percy Walters was a dog lover of yore who donated to the public the picturesque park on Penfield that bears his name on the condition that dogs forever be free to roam the grounds. The fine print of his gift actually stipulates that the park forever remain there for children, although playground equipment is oddly forbidden.

Fielding Avenue in NDG remained a verdant oasis in the midst of the suburban housing jungle because its fine print committed it to forever remaining a "common," a condition crafty draftsmen got around by building a pathway through it.

Developers have anxiously eyed such sites as the Dow Planetarium or Place Pasteur (the square at the Berri Metro) for development. No go, though. The Dow brewmeisters ceded the former on the condition that the land serve the public. Joseph Papineau did the same when he donated the square at Berri.

A Not-So-Tall Tale

If you want to see the old midgets museum on Rachel St. these days, you'll be required to strip naked, walk around in a towel, and possibly observe a lot of men getting to know each other in a real hurry. Let's start from the top: Phillipe Nicol, the seventh son of a seventh son, stood under four feet tall, and left town to become a star raconteur with the Barnum and Bailey Circus. Nicol returned to Montreal in 1913 and was unsuccessful in negotiations to have a special small house built for him in Lafontaine Park, so he and his miniature wife settled nearby at 961 Rachel East. They soon had a son, Phillipe Jr. But as we've seen in countless cases of midget princes raised in novelty museums, the 3'8" Phillipe Jr. grew up all wrong. He became an easily spotted menace who threatened local merchants with a toy gun, beat his mom, and, sadly, tried to hang himself in the bathroom of a nearby tavern. The Midgets' Palace finally closed in 1990, amid charges that a tall person cooked the books and ran off with their little fridges and tiny couches. In its current incarnation as a gay bathhouse it's no longer a place where smallness is particularly celebrated.

In Fine Form

Photo: John David Gravenor

It's often said that Paul Lancz's *Tenderness*, a statue at the northwest corner of Peel and Sherbrooke, is an important local landmark. And indeed Lancz never seems to tire of saying it. On his website, Lancz describes his white marble statue of mother and child as "impregnable as the Rock of Gibraltar," and humbly compares his creation to Copenhagen's famous mermaid. Those who share his lofty view of the work can buy a 32-centimeter version of it for $350 on his website.

Photo: John David Gravenor

St. Joseph's Oratory on Queen Mary near Côte des Neiges is the house that Brother André Bessette built – or, to be more precise, was built in honour of the Catholic miracle man whose gentle heart was pickled in a jar after it stopped beating in 1937. Although some naysayers claim that Andy's faith healing was ineffective and only left them one pair of crutches poorer, believers attested so much to his miraculous powers that he was canonized somewhere along the line – which means he's just one step below saint. This copper-topped building was long the second biggest dome outside of St. Peter's in Rome and indeed its bells were originally slated to grace the Eiffel Tower. The oratory remains a spot where you can witness practices that might seem bizarre to the uninitiated: sick pilgrims still climb the many stairs – on their knees – to seek the power of God and get a peek at Brother André's heart in a jar. The heart is less visible these days, being locked in a vault behind a metal grate since it was kidnapped for a $50,000 ransom in March 1973. It was returned, apparently with ransom unpaid (that's their story anyway), in December 1974.

Projects That Never Quite Left the Drawing Board

Concert Hall, 1952

God knows why, but for 50 years it's been considered an urgent priority to build a concert hall for government-subsidized classical music. One hall was proposed for the north side of Mount Royal in 1952. In the mid-'80s a proposal would have plopped a $100-million monstrosity blocking the north side of the intersection of Ste. Catherine and McGill College. Mayor Drapeau then moved the theoretical construct to the square across from the Berri Metro station, and in 1986, Mayor Doré announced a 1,200-seat concert hall called "l'Etoile" on the east side of the Main near Prince Arthur. More recently, the provincial government announced a new fiddleshack for the corner of Bleury and Ste. Catherine – that will cost taxpayers a mere $250 million.

The Tower, 1956-1987

Mayor Drapeau long lamented our city's lack of a landmark tower. First he conspired with Guardian Trust to build a 1,050-foot-high tubular steel structure. Then, in '64, he negotiated to get the Eiffel Tower temporarily moved here and even considered building a knock-off of the Paris landmark. He finally decided on a 1,066-foot tower (the height symbolizing the year of a French military victory over the English) that would represent God, light, and progress. At $28 million, God could wait as city bigwig Lucien Saulnier deemed it too costly. Dissatisfied with the tower on the Olympic Stadium in the late '80s, Drapeau proposed replacing the cross on the mountain with another 10 times its size.

Downtown Drive-in Theatre, 1957

Our Tourist and Convention Bureau recommended that the reservoir at Pine and McTavish be covered and turned into a parking lot and a "tiered, cement amphitheater" — in other words, a drive-in movie theatre.

The Impact of Place Ville Marie

Montreal's original glass-and-steel skyscraper revolutionized the city when it was completed in 1961. Here's why:

Practically overnight, the financial district moved uptown from its traditional base on St. James (since renamed St. Jacques) in Old Montreal. The same phenomenon had already occurred in retail, starting in 1891, when Morgan's department store moved from the same street to its current location opposite Phillips Square, where it is now called The Bay.

The city was criticized for shelling out $7.5 million to widen roads, but was soon raking in an annual $5 million from Place Ville Marie in taxes. That was enough to encourage the mayor to embark on the construction of the Metro.

French Quebec nationalist groups worried that architect I.M. Pei's cruciform tower would be given an English name — as the Queen Elizabeth Hotel had a few years earlier. Politicians at the highest levels twisted arms to make sure it bore a name traditionally associated with the city.

Although frequently described as the city's tallest building, PVM is one of five that rise to about 200 meters, including the IBM-Marathon tower, CIBC, Stock Market Tower and 1000 la Gauchetière.

Its trademark four-way beacon remains one of the city's best-loved features, but for a lesser-known thrill, ask security guards to show you the bullet holes embedded in the pillars of the food court, remnants of a showdown cops had with an armed robber in 1997.

some unforgettable fires

April 1849: An anti-French mob burned down the pre-Confederation Parliament building near Place Royale. So authorities moved the capital of a united Canada out of town, finally settling on a whistle-stop village called Ottawa.

June 13, 1910: A 30,000-gallon water tank fell through the roof of the Montreal Herald building on Victoria Square, starting a fire that killed 32.

February 14, 1918: Thirty-one orphans died at the Grey Nuns' fourth-floor orphanage at Guy and René Lévesque. The orphanage was soon closed but to this day some of the nuns (there are fewer than 300 rapidly aging nuns who live in a fenced-off place where 800 once lived) believe that pictures of the order's founder, Jeanne Mance, wards off fire.

March 2-3, 1922: City Hall on Nôtre Dame Street East went up in flames. The glare in the night sky was so vivid that it attracted people from all parts of town.

January 9, 1927: 78 children died in a stampede after a minor fire broke out at the Laurier Palace cinema (1683 Ste. Catherine East). For 40 years after, unaccompanied children under 16 were banned from Montreal movie houses.

January 21, 1975: Richard Blass shot the manager of the Gargantua Bar (1369 Beaubien East; now defunct) through the heart. He then rounded up the dozen witnesses into a storeroom at the back of the bar, where they died in a fire that Blass set and encouraged by pouring booze on the flames.

September 11, 1972: The Wagon Wheel upstairs from the Bluebird Café went up in flames. 37 patrons died after three young drunks who were refused admission set fire to the stairs in revenge. Exits had been locked shut and, despite the questions of fire inspectors, the city ponied up just $1,000 to $3,000 to compensate families for their loved ones who perished. The Popular parking lot now sits on the site on the west side of Union.

Geodesic Shopping Mall, 1958

Developers unveiled a mock up of *Montreal's Shoppersville* — a Buckminister Fuller-designed, aluminum-domed 65-store mall intended for the corner of Côte des Neiges and Barclay. The mall, which could have been our only architectural example of neo-flyingsaucerism, would have offered shuttle buses, play areas, and a free auditorium. But those goodies weren't enough to seduce locals into okaying a rezoning for the project.

Museum at PDA, 1964

The Montreal Museum of Fine Arts, a fixture on Sherbrooke since 1860, was supposed to get its own building on the plaza of Place des Arts, which effectively would have robbed the city of what we're told is an excellent place to check out lounging boys and babes.

Tube-Shaped Tower, 1965

Ed Reichman planned a 36-storey, $15-million cylindrical tower at Sherbrooke and City Councillors. One of the main would-be tenants, the now defunct Montreal Amateur Athletic Association, planned to relocate from their historic digs on Peel but backed out of the new project when a member furiously opposed the move. The club stayed put, the skyscraper was never built, and the well-intentioned MAAA member got tossed out of the club.

Windsor Wreckage, July 1970

The CPR announced that it would demolish Windsor Station for "one of the largest building projects in the world." The $250-million project was to include a 60-storey tower by the designers of New York's World Trade Center. While unveiling the plan, Canadian Pacific Railway President Duff Roblin subliminally prophesized delays that would last approximately forever. "The trouble about announcing a plan of this sort," he said, "is that everybody expects you to begin yesterday."

Church Mall, 1975

The Grey Nuns at Guy and René Lévesque planned to sell their convent to Swiss developers Valorinvest, who promised to gut much of the historic building for a $138-million complex involving a 44 storey office tower, a 540-room hotel and eight-storey apartment complex. After months of dithering, the province nixed the scheme.

October 26, 1986: Nobody died when the top seven floors of the 15-storey Alexis Nihon office tower went up in flames, even though it was lacking adequate smoke detectors, water pressure, and security guards with the right keys to activate fire alarms.

May 25, 1987: Wilhelmina Tiemersma, a disturbed, 38-year-old transsexual and volunteer organist at the Unitarian Church on Sherbrooke near Guy, thought it an excellent idea to light the place on fire. Edward Maxwell's 1906 architectural masterpiece was burnt to the ground, its foundations being the only thing left at the site. Three firefighters died trying to extinguish the blaze.

June 9, 1998: At the Accueil Bonneau hostel for the homeless, a workman was boring a hole through a meter-thick stone wall when his drill accidentally ruptured a gas pipe. Three people were killed and the building destroyed.

our very own two-fisted rialto: a story of the Main

"People live there and love it; people die there, and dying, love it. Sons follow fathers in the small and large businesses, heritages handed down; nothing can wean the inheritors from the Main's magnificent pull."
– *Montreal Standard*, June 13, 1931

Here's a quick chronology of the St. Lawrence (known to many as St. Laurent) Boulevard strip that defines the city:

1620: Skilled masons create a sophisticated tunnel complex near St. Paul to store arrows and ammunition useful against feared Indian attacks. Construction workers uncovered the shelter in March 1942.

1658: The Main becomes the dividing line between Jacques Archambault's farm and the estate of Lambert Closse. A stream ran south from de Maisonneuve.

1682: Jeanne Le Ber, a young woman from a wealthy family, gives everything up to slum it on the Main at the Congrégation Notre Dame, where she surrenders her fortune for a life of silence, hair shirts, and self-flagellation. She is buried at the order's Mother House on Westmount Avenue.

1695: Notre Dame de la Pitié is built and becomes a hangout for particularly pious nuns. It is torn down in 1911 so the Main can be extended south to the river.

1896: The first projected film shown in Canada screens at a location near what is now Viger Street.

1905: The Main becomes the division between east and west address designations.

1925: The city's first-ever nightclub murder takes place at the Dreamland Cabaret (corner of Ontario, now long gone) on July 22, when Joe Mauro shoots the busboy after nobody takes his holdup warning seriously.

1928: Serving only beer and champagne, the strip's first big nightclub, Frolics, opens in an old fur warehouse at 1417 St. Lawrence, just south of Ontario. Frolics and its 15-piece orchestra folded in 1934.

Floating Convention Centre, 1976

Mayor Drapeau proposed that the city should buy the *France* ocean liner for $50 million and turn the retired French ship into a floating convention centre, hotel, and casino. Not only could he not get anybody to front him the money, but the ship couldn't even come here, her mast too tall to pass under the Quebec City bridge.

The Floralies, 1980

When he was still a flunky for Drapeau, soon-to-be-mayor Pierre Bourque devised an annual flower festival on the site of the Expo 67 World's Fair. The Floralies, possibly the most boring festival in the city's history, failed to attract half the projected four million visitors and was shelved after its only summer.

Bell Canada Skyscraper, 1985

Bell Canada Enterprises planned a skyscraping HQ that would take over and destroy much of the stately block bounded by Crescent, Sherbrooke, Mountain, and de Maisonneuve.

Exponova Amusement Park, July 1994

Mayor Doré announced a $300-million plan to turn the LaRonde amusement park into a year-round theme attraction called Exponova. The rides were to be replaced with 10 pavilions that would stay open even in winter. When questioned

about the appeal of hanging around outside on minus-25-degree winter days, would-be developer Cameron Charlebois acknowledged, "It's pretty chilly, but that's part of its allure." That same year, Mayor Doré announced a $12-million Dinosaurium at the former Quebec Pavilion of Expo 67. Mechanical dinosaurs would sort of move around, according to organizer Barry Sendel, who was granted a free seven-year lease on the land until it was discovered that he was a convicted fraud artist who had been sued 165 times.

Skyscraper Hotel, 1999

The city okayed a 24-storey, $1,500-a-night hotel on the grounds of the old Unitarian Church. When Heritage Montreal attacked the plan, pointing out that it exceeded height regulations, its Turkish developer, Mustafa Tatlici, kept shortening the proposed hotel. It eventually reached zero feet.

1934: A newspaper article describes the effect of the Depression on the lower Main: "Stilled is the bark of rifles in shooting galleries; the impact of lead no longer wakens echoes from tin battleships, silver ducks. Human picture galleries who once flexed their muscles, thus making dormant snakes and dragons spring to life are but nostalgic memories. Not one tattooing establishment flaunts its shingle along this once two-fisted rialto."

1942: Students chant "a bas les Juifs!" (which means, "Down with the Jews!") and smash store windows in an anti-war rally.

1950: After being the target of gunfire at the Café Rodeo on the lower Main, two employees of the nearby Café Canasta – Pat Létourneau and Vic Pollard (whose wife had been robbed and beaten weeks before) – denounce the Main's protection rackets.

1957: Responsibility for a 15-foot-tall mountain of sand near Sauvé was hotly debated at city council after a young boy was buried in the pile, only to be saved at the last minute by a passerby.

1957: Ex-mental patient Fernand Rainville, 31, becomes the Mad Sniper of the Main when he shoots three people from a window of the Alto rooming houses on the corner of Ste. Catherine. A policeman jumped him before he had time to kill himself. His three targets recovered from their injuries.

1959: Mayor Drapeau tears down the St. Lawrence Market, at the northeast corner of Dorchester (now René Lévesque). He then tries to resell it for $620,000. There were no takers and the land sat barren until the St. Jean Baptiste Society built a student dorm there in 2002.

1961: J.J. Paverne, a welfare-court judge, urges Mayor Drapeau to ban kids under 16 from the lower Main, which was dubbed "the city's most hardened artery." The judge was concerned about kids taking drugs, specifically "goofballs."

1961: Future Supreme Court boss Antonio Lamer exposes a racket in which Main tough-guys get a cut of your paycheque. In return the mobsters promised a) not to beat you up, b) to beat up your boss up if he tried to fire you, and c) force somebody else to hire you if you wanted to change jobs.

1961: A study recommending that cars only be allowed to go south on the Main is ignored for 11 years, before the two-way boulevard becomes northbound-only.

1962: Werner Prillwitz, 52, visiting the Main for his first time from New Jersey, has his private parts blown off by a bomb in the bathroom of Café Canasta on the lower Main.

1964: Fabien Biondi retires from his spot on the lower Main where he had shined shoes since 1896. He managed to raise 18 kids on 35-cent shines.

1971: Road repairs are so extensive that businesses suffer and kids flirt with danger. Nat Krupat of Feldman Provisions claimed that "the kids used to play in a hole at least 10 feet deep."

1980: The Montreal Pool Room, long famous for its steamé hot dogs, covers up its pool tables for good. They haven't been used since, except for occasional rentals to movie productions, and the owner has refused offers of $6,000 for their purchase.

1983: A 23-year-old tries to torch 3847 (where the Old Europe Deli is now), flubs his fire, and becomes the Human Torch, running around in flames. The building sustains $100,000 in damages.

1983: A 23-year-old customer, angry because staff move his bicycle outside where it gets stolen, torches the crowded Midway Bar (1219), killing three.

1985: When a fire burns down ten buildings in a section of Chinatown on the east side of the Main near la Gauchetière, Mayor Drapeau tries to prevent the merchants from rebuilding their shops, pointing to a bylaw passed months earlier making future construction residential. The Mayor backs down after local businessman Kenneth Cheung threatens to follow him and give him bad press during the mayor's tour of Asia.

1992: For several years, cops had been looking the other way as prostitutes troll the porno peep-show booths. That ended when Jay Arrington, a pimp from Buffalo, is killed in a fistfight inside one of the establishments.

1990: The Just for Laughs Festival receives $22 million in government grants for a comedy museum in a former brewery just south of Sherbrooke in 1990. Within months, it is seriously in the red. But it's still there.

Some Notable Homes

• Jean Charest, the former Progressive Conservative leader who came home to lead the Quebec Liberal Party, moved into a 4,000-square-foot residence on Victoria Avenue in Westmount. His home, evaluated at a half million smackers, was built in 1909.

• Former PQ Premier Jacques Parizeau lives on Robert in Outremont. The guy who quit after saying Quebec was denied independence by "money and the ethnic vote" kicks off his shoes in a 1911 home that spans 3,200 square feet, and is evaluated at $335,000. His electricity bill runs to about $1,600 a year.

• Former Prime Minister Brian Mulroney lives on Forden Crescent, just east of Murray Park in Westmount. The 1950 home sits on a 15,000-square-foot lot, and is evaluated at $1.95 million. He pays $5,100 to heat the home by gas. From '76 to '81 he lived on top of the hill at 68 Belvedere Road; thanks to tax laws his government passed, the profits he made on its sale were tax free.

• Former Prime Minister Pierre Trudeau lived at 1420 Pine Avenue West, at the corner of Cedar, in a home built on a 7,196-square-foot lot in 1931. The place is evaluated at $538,000 and is an official heritage site. After Trudeau's death, government officials asked to turn it into a museum, but his son, Sacha, who can often be seen zooming around the area on his bike, nixed the offer.

• Nobel Prize-winning author Saul Bellow started his life at 130 8th Avenue in Lachine, before his parents hauled tail to 1092 St. Dominique Street, where he lived until age nine. Then it was on to Chicago.

• Zbigniew Brzezinski, known for his role as U.S. President Jimmy Carter's top security advisor, spent his formative years in the comfort of 60 St. Sulpice Road in Westmount.

• Two-time Quebec premier Robert Bourassa grew up in a relatively low-rent Plateau home at 4837 Parthenais.

• Mordecai Richler's famous literary views of the city were formed at his childhood digs, a second-storey flat at 5257 St. Urbain.

• Lorne "Gump" Worsley, everybody's favourite Montreal-born mask-rejecting goaltending grump, lives on Bonair in Beloeil.

2002: A madman jumps on the roof of a building that adjoins the oddball Karls shoe store at Rachel and burns the landmark down. Coincidentally, owner Ludwig Karls was locked in a longstanding dispute with the fire department, who considered his shoe-strewn building unsafe, and it had been forced to close a long time earlier. Before it burns down, authorities are on the verge of shutting it down again. Karls, said the firemen, seemed to be in no great hurry to save his building. He's suing.

Funny Names

• In a pique over the merging of his town into the recently-formed megacity, Côte St. Luc Mayor Robert Libman rewarded outgoing city councillors by attaching their names to parks in the area. Although not famous for doing anything particularly exceptional – some of the councillors had only served briefly and were elected by acclamation – the half-dozen honourees, who now work in jobs such as school teachers, press flaks, and librarians, accepted the honours. One snag, though: Quebec's Toponomy Commission refused to recognize the instant place names because, with very few exceptions, a person must be dead for one year before having a geographical entity named after him.

• Nelson and Winnie Mandela Park was unveiled under much fanfare in the '80s, but soon city officials were sheepishly erasing Winnie's name from the signs after her image was tarnished by her shocking abuses of power.

• You might wonder why there is no "Zotique" in the Catholic dictionary of saints. It's because the saints of Montreal's streets are actually not saints at all. Somewhere along the line it became fashionable to name geographic locations by combining the former landowner's name with the word "saint."

• In a controversial plan, megacity administrators will eventually switch street names that are duplicated on the newly-merged island municipality. They're desperate to find names for local women and ethnic minorities, so if you can think of any, just give City Hall a shout. You can check *toponomie.gouv.qc.ca* to see if your suggestion has already been used.

What's there to say about the Olympic Stadium that you don't already know? Billion-dollar cost overruns, falling concrete, and a roof that fit like a toque on a donkey isn't news. But the Olympic Village, well, there's a story we just can't resist.

When it came time to figure out where 6,500 athletes would lay their weary heads during the two-week Summer Games in 1976, a provincial government minister suggested they be housed on cruise ships docked in the harbour. But Mayor Jean Drapeau, never one to duff around the links, chose instead to zap a 36-hole municipal golf course near the Botanical Gardens. A number of his councillors broke with him over the issue, and 66,000 people signed a petition demanding that he reconsider. No developer would bid on the project, so Drapeau signed a sweetheart deal at the last minute with construction magnate Joseph Zappia.

The Mayor and Zappia had first crossed swords – but probably just toy ones – in 1970, when Zappia's hastily assembled Montreal Party ran against the incumbent mayor … sort of. Oddly, Zappia's 15 candidates never said a bad word about Drapeau, instead attacking a third party as a bunch of separatists.

Next thing you know, Zappia had *carte blanche* on a deal that rewarded him for every buck the building went over budget. Construction of the 19-storey, 932-unit building (more than 300 of the units are small bachelor apartments) was a slapdash effort. Union workers – led by the infamous André "Dédé" Désjardins (who later became a loan shark and got murdered in a north-end restaurant) – knew the government needed the project finished. So the bricklayers, plumbers, and other card-carrying construction men took advantage of a natural opportunity to go wild on the government tab.

What was planned to be a $33-million project eventually clocked in at $100 million. After the embarrassingly over-budget Olympics were over, the province expropriated the complex from the developers, and, in September 1980, Zappia fled to Saudi Arabia. He eventually faced criminal charges but was acquitted – luckily two key witnesses had died by the time he went to trial. In 1998, Toronto's Metro Capital Group bought the twin piles for $62.5 million, and planned to build 2,100 more units on land behind the village.

Nowadays, the place is a residential complex full of

• The greatest hockey player ever born, Mario Lemieux (hey, it's our book), grew up at the corner of Allard and Jogues in Ville Emard. He's known to chat up the neighbours during frequent visits to his parents, who still inhabit the tidy little duplex on a friendly, tree-lined street west of Monk, Ville Emard's enigmatic main drag.

• Ahmed Ressam, the Algerian-born Montrealer who planned to bomb Los Angeles International Airport, lived at 1240 Fort and concocted his conspiracy in aparment 40, 6585 Park Avenue.

• Maurice "Rocket" Richard lived in a 5-bedroom home on a 9,000-foot of waterfront property at the Southwest corner of Péloquin and Stanley Park (a street name that will soon be changed in his honour) on the Back River (or Rivière des Prairies) in Ahuntsic. When Richard died in May 2000 a real-estate agent tried to cash in on the Rocket's fame by asking an unrealistic $650,000. The home ultimately fetched $400,000.

• When he wasn't living in a jail cell for encouraging French Canadians to resist the World War II draft, Mayor Camilien Houde lived at 4256 St. Hubert. Nearer to his death in 1958, the jovial and charismatic former mayor preferred living in his office on the sixth floor of the Mount Royal Hotel.

old timers, and features a driving range, minigolf course, and Olympic-sized pool. Architecturally, the French-inspired building was criticized for its outdoor approaches that were unsuited to cold and snowy climes. Still, few have complained, although one resident, the father of a recent mayor, is said to have jumped off a balcony to his death a few years back.

Lego on the St. Lawrence

Photo: John David Gravenor

The 158 concrete cubes that make up the apartment structure on the St. Lawrence known as Habitat have incited strong words over the years.

Before architect Moshe Safdie completed his structure in time for the Montreal World's Fair of 1967, Paul Trepanier, the architect-mayor of Granby, called it an "insane plan." *Washington Post* fine arts critic Blake Gopnik described it as "the last great expression of naïve modernism." Architect Joe Baker said, "All Habitat proves is that you can build a garden in the sky for 10 times what it costs to build one on the ground." The *New York Times* called Safdie's book about his baby, "the greatest collection of ideas since the wheel."

In '92, a team of Japanese architecture analysts scoured the planet for unusual buildings and declared this their favourite residential complex. In 1986, residents bought their units for $50,000 a piece; the same units can now fetch up to $700,000. The modular stack of concrete boxes was initially intended to be seven, 25-storey pyramids, but the feds weren't willing to spring that much cash. After completion, Safdie made some noise about building many more like it. He never did. Although he moved to Boston long ago, Safdie – who was a mere tadpole of 25 when he designed the thing – still owns the penthouse unit.

Transportation

Montreal island was inadvertently settled after European canoodlers came ashore to scratch their portaging heads over the dilemma posed by the Lachine Rapids (do we try to jump 'em, go past 'em by land, or load up the musket and shoot some beaver right here?). Ever since, stupendous and just plain stupid transportation solutions have been devised for the city.

English Place Names

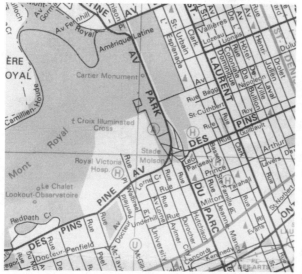

By invoking English-Montreal culture, one can call local names pretty much anything one likes. Boulevard René Lévesque remains Dorchester to many Anglos. St. Jacques is still widely known as St. James. Nobody speaking English ever called du Parc anything other than Park Avenue and if you call des Pins anything but Pine Avenue, you're not talking English. De L'Eglise is Church, while Anglos recognize St. Laurent less as the street than the sprawling northwest borough; St. Lawrence is still the trendy boho hangout also known as The Main. Be warned, local Anglos will look at you like a pitiful hick if you get caught calling Ste. Catherine "Ste. Catharines." Although many opt, quite reasonably, to mostly use the official French names, Anglos can earn respectful nods from other Anglos by invoking obscure historical names, like Common Street (De La Commune), Tannery Hill (the hill south of The Glen, where Ste. Catherine meets Lansdowne), or Crawford Park (a part of Verdun). As for hard-to-say French words? Longueuil can be safely pronounced as "Long-Gail" and Jean Talon you can call "Gene Tallin." In fact you can call any place whatever you want; chances are you'll have to tell the taxi driver how to get there anyway.

Wrong on Reds

Other than Manhattan, Quebec is the only place on the continent that doesn't allow right turns on red lights. The provincial government launched a few pilot projects to give the green light to turning on reds, but a petty scandal ensued, with accusations that outgoing Transport Minister Guy Chevrette fudged the numbers to make right-turns look safer than they were. Regardless, it's widely believed Montreal would remain exempted from a province-wide policy – something to do with reckless motorists and pedestrians who routinely ignore crosswalk signals.

We Love Photo Radar, They Say With a Straight Face

Quebec was the first to install photo radar in 1970 and soon after became the first to un-install it. Seems that spouses would become curious when tickets came in the mail proving that their mates had been some place they shouldn't, leading to quick-tempered fights over marital infidelity. The provincial government reiterated plans to relaunch a photo-radar project, citing the unlikely story that most people want it returned.

Cars on Ice

Ever wonder when the city's first traffic jam took place? Neither did we, but here's what our army of researchers learned. When Norwegian skating queen Sonja Henie arrived at the old Forum with her travelin' Hollywood Ice Review in 1938, motorists brought their Fords, Packards, and Oldsmobiles to a screeching halt for the city's first such uncelebrated event.

Get a License

Back in the day, driving without a license was considered a devil-may-care activity practiced by only the most virile of the carefree class. Nowadays, be warned: get caught driving without a license and it's a $404 fine, $200 for towing fees, and $8-13 a day for storing your impounded vehicle.

FIRST CAR

In 1898, city councillor, real-estate dealer, and blatant showoff Ucal H. Dandurand showed up in town with a steam-powered Waltham Flying Kettle.

Photo: John David Gravenor

FIRST TRAFFIC LIGHT

On Craig (now St. Antoine) where the Palais de Congres now stands. In 1932 it was implanted to let drivers know that the streetcar was coming out of the now-demolished terminus.

A DEADLY SPORT

Montrealers are known to take their jaywalking very seriously. In recent years, cars have been killing between 25 to 40 pedestrians every year on the island, and seriously injuring 140-220 more, many being elderly or very young. Ambulance services report to tending around 30 pedestrian victims a day.

Crosswalks

Unlike in other places where the very presence of a foot on a crosswalk is enough to make cars stop for pedestrians, Montreal drivers zoom through crosswalks as if aiming to mow crossers down. Although Councillor Jeremy Searle was charged with the task of fixing this problem, one would be well advised against placing too much faith in crosswalks. Other than a well-lit crosswalk on Côte des Neiges near Côte Ste. Catherine, trusting that cars will stop at crosswalks remains an invitation to vehicular impact. Even cops ignore 'em: one cruiser driving 100 km/h (60 mph) down Sherbrooke in 1990 killed a student crosswalk-user named Paul McKinnon outside of Loyola High School. Particularly dangerous crosswalks include the one at the entrance to the George Vanier tunnel under the Ville Marie Expressway, the one on Peel south of Ste. Catherine, and the one on Sherbrooke near Harvard.

Jaywalking Corners

Université de Montréal academic Jean-Pierre Thouez produced a study in 2001 asserting that, on average, 29 percent of pedestrians stop at red lights in Montreal. The remaining 71 percent were, we suggest, liars. Meanwhile, he discovered that in Toronto, 56 percent obediently wait for the green. It's widely believed that no pedestrian in history has ever waited for a green light at Ste. Catherine near Drummond or Stanley, but Thouez is the scientist and these are his findings on some of the city's most frequently jaywalked intersections.

Ste. Catherine at Papineau Ave.
Just 25 percent of pedestrians wait for the green at that corner. As a result, five people get hit here every year.

St. Denis St. at Mount Royal Ave.
Only 27 percent wait. Ambulances are ever-ready.

University St. at René Lévesque
Only 29 percent resist the lure of the godlike sport of gambling one's only life against speeding motor vehicles at this crossing.

AVOIDING TICKETS

Although reasonably tolerant of speeders, highway and street cops will sometimes bag you during rush hours for speeding or crossing solid lines (i.e., cutting someone off). Here are a few of the many spots where the fuzz have been known to congregate more often than not.

The Bonaventure Expressway

St. Jacques West around Oxford

LaSalle Boulevard

De la Verendrye in Ville Emard/LaSalle

The Québécois Car

Canada could have become a car-manufacturing nation had only somebody backed Henri-Émile Bourassa, a Montreal genius who built a car in 1899 – four years before Henry Ford came out with his first model. Bourassa's two-seat buggy was pushed by a two-cylinder horizontal engine and equipped with parts made by a local guy named John Millen. His first passenger was Trefflé Berthiaume, founder of *La Presse*. Together they drove down the city's only paved street, Dorchester Boulevard (now René Lévesque), and filled up at the city's only gas station at Ste. Catherine and St. Denis.

Bourassa had previously worked with a young Henry Ford in Detroit and was good friends with Louis Chevrolet, who spent a month at Bourassa's Montcalm home in 1900. When Chevrolet departed, he begged Bourassa to join him in Detroit, but Bourassa, perhaps lacking the confidence to work in English, opted to stay here. While those others went on to greatness, Bourassa ended up using his talents at a wartime munitions factory. He was called out of his 1938 retirement to help develop weapons for the World War II effort.

Make the Cosmodome Your Home

Walk through a space shuttle! Check out a moon rock and hack around with the interactive educational space thingies! Stay for a weekend camp and experience simulated lunar gravity, space movement, and space disorientation! The camp is easily found, just look for a rocket tower on the west side of highway 15 in Laval. Daily admission ranges to $12.
450/978-3600

Serving Your Goth Needs

For all your funeral car needs, Michel Cyr offers a fleet of eight hearses. His models vary from 1936 to '79 to match every one of your dark moods, and are available in any colour that starts with a "b" and ends with a "k."
514/961-8306

Manning the Shaft

There are about 10,000 elevators in this city. Last time we checked, these were the places you could still find manually-operated lifts.

Canada Trust building at 275 St. Jacques Street West. Operated by elevator Queen Rita Robidoux, who has seen the ups and downs of elevator driving for 44 years.

1435 Bleury Street, near Ste. Catherine Street West. Seventy-one-year-old Haitian native Louis Deluscar pilots this baby.

Royal Bank Building at 360 St. Jacques Street West. Two of 'em stand in this magnificent tower built in the 1920s.

Scenic Routes

Gouin

On the north end of the island, near the Back River.

Lakeshore Boulevard

Along the southwestern rim of the island.

Camilien Houde Boulevard

Over the top of the mountain.

LaSalle Boulevard

From Verdun to Lachine, alongside the thundering rapids.

The Right to Stand on the Left

Unlike residents of many cities, Montrealers don't automatically stand to the right when they get on an escalator. This habit forces those in a hurry to cajole, deke, and split the defense in order to get ahead. In April 2002, however, NDG tech writer Darryl Levine started a grassroots campaign to change all that by petitioning Metro authorities to post signs instructing people to adopt the civilized stand-on-the-right/pass-on-the-left custom popular elsewhere. But his campaign didn't roll along as he'd like: transit bigwigs lamely cited operating manufacturers' suggestions that nobody should walk on any escalator. Those opposed to the stand-right, walk-left proposal were surprisingly vocal in support of their stationary ways. One even wrote to a newspaper saying that he had no use of his right arm so he couldn't stand right even if he wanted to. Authorities officially refused to adopt the custom.

The Meaning of Plates

As you surely know, or probably claim to, it was a long-ago Parti Québécois government that changed the slogan on Quebec license plates from "La belle province" to "Je me souviens," which translates to "I remember." Whereas many people interpreted the words to mean that we should remember how the British inconveniently overwhelmed the French on the Plains of Abraham in 1760, the slogan was actually lifted from a poem written by provincial beaureaucrat Eugene Taché in 1883. The full text of the quote reads, "Je me souviens que né sous le lys, je fleuris sous la rose." ("I remember that I was born under the *fleur de lys*, but I blossomed under the rose.") Far from igniting anti-English sentiment as supposed, the words were meant to remind Quebecers that they owed their existence to France (as represented by the lily, or "lys"), but that the rose (England) provided the democratic system and industrial infrastructure to ensure their prosperity.

Next time you see a lonely-lookin' old timer, why not brighten up his or her day and ask about a favourite recollection or two of our city's streetcars? On second thought, we'll save you the trouble by telling you about it here instead. From 1861, at least 20 types of trams rolled through our city streets until, sadly, they were removed in 1959 at the cost of $62 million. The trolley to Cartierville was tall and orange with yellow rattan seats, green blinds, a huge coal stove, and straw on the floor to keep feet warm. Special trams served as paddy wagons, others as funeral cars; the Sherbrooke trolley blew by the empty fields of NDG, while the streetcar down Claremont would come to a screeching halt at Sherbrooke so the driver could point out his friend's grocery store on the southeast corner. Riders joked that the trams were like bananas, because they were green and yellow and came in bunches. But the city's thousand golden galleons helped transport up to 300 million riders a year in the 1950s, considered the blessed era of public transit before big oil companies persuaded city nabobs to remove them. The city started regretting the removal of the streetcars when oil prices skyrocketed in the '70s. As a nod to our city's plentiful supply of electricity and subway-building know-how, there are plans to resuscitate the streetcars. The Rocket that rode down Park Ave. from 1890 could one day be rolling again, while the Metropolitan Transport Agency is also promising a light rail line atop the Champlain Ice Bridge.

LANDING DOWN ON LANSDOWNE

Nasty ice-coated streetcar tracks plagued the city on the morning of December 21, 1942. Halfway down Lansdowne south of The Boulevard, a streetcar driver picked up two children. Soon after, his trolley began to slide out of control, down the steep hill. It flew off the rails at a sharp right-hand turn on to Westmount Avenue, crashing into a post on the corner. A 16-year-old girl died, making her the only passenger fatality in our streetcar era that lasted almost 100 years. The accident, coincidentally, occurred at the exact spot at the southwest corner of Lansdowne and Westmount Avenue where Sergeant-Major Walter Leja, a Canadian army engineer, was seriously injured on May 17, 1963, while defusing one of 14 terrorist bombs placed by the separatist FLQ.

Antique Motorless Ferry

Photo: John David Gravenor

ATLANTIC CROSSING

The Empress of Canada left Pier 8 for its last Atlantic crossing in November 1972, but you haven't missed the boat on ocean travel. It's still possible to satisfy your complete retro travel cravings by sailing to Europe without the Love Boat kitsch. One British company offers you the chance to cross the Atlantic on a cargo ship. A 10-day journey from Montreal to Thamesport, Kent, England or vice-versa will cost you in the neighbourhood of two thousand smackers one-way. Check out cruisepeople.co.uk. Add a thousand and you could book a similar trip on the luxurious QE2. Our network of informants suggests that last-minute deals sometimes go for half price.

The small, green ferry boat that crosses Rivière des Prairies where it meets Lake of Two Mountains has transported cars, bikes, pedestrians, and passengers between Laval and Ile Bizard for eight months a year since the link was opened by Vital Bigras in 1903. By using the force of the eastward current and metal cables for guidance, the flat-bottomed boat doesn't require electricity or gas. The clever contraption remains in the hands of Bigras's descendants and can cross the river in three minutes. One unfortunate mishap occurred in June 2001 when two speedboats tried to outrace the ferry, resulting in two people drowning and two others suffering multiple fractures. Ferry fans can also check out the tug-pulled Hudson-Oka ferry, operated by the Leger family for 90 years before a recent sale, or the cheapest game in town, the 50-cent ferry from the Lachine harbour to René Lévesque Park, a peninsula in Lac St. Louis dolled up with 43 sculptures.

Drive It Again, Sam

Metro users are protected from famously rude ticket takers by a thick pane of glass. Thankfully, our bus drivers have a much better reputation, and include the likes of singing driver Jacques Roy, who patrols the 165 on the Côte des Neiges-Guy route. When about 30 passengers complained of his unorthodox ways in 2000, Roy outmanoeuvred his critics by circulating a petition in support of his vocal stylings. Among the city's other well-loved bus drivers is Christian Lachance, who commands the 80 down Park Ave., distributing candy and balloons to young riders and placing flags on his bus to observe national holidays throughout the world.

Chivalry on the Road

Most people are barely aware that Montreal women get special privileges on city buses. In a progressive policy adopted in 1997, drivers will let a woman travelling solo in the evening disembark at any destination between stops from October to April.

Free Rides

Another little-known fact about our buses is that in recent years the unionized drivers, citing potential physical hazards, have refused to confront non-payers. Surveys have confirmed that an attempt to hop on a bus without paying will basically net you a free ride.

Braking for Babes (and Boys)

A tacit speed limit of about 12 km/h (7.5 miles per hour) rules these glamourjams where hipster-wannabe motorists ogle the ubiquitous pedestrian babes and boys:

Crescent between de Maisonneuve and Ste. Catherine

The Main between Sherbrooke and Pine

Ste. Catherine from Guy to the Jacques Cartier Bridge

St. Denis from Ontario to de Maisonneuve

Photo: John David Gravenor

Subways only showed up in this burgh in the late '60s, but there had been repeated attempts to build one here.

A $100-million subway system was proposed in 1912. By 1914, a smaller, $20-million, four-line subway replaced that plan. In 1917, a $25-million, three-line version linking Place d'Armes to NDG in the west, and Mile End in the north, was the next proposal. In 1929, a $25-million, three-line subway was pitched and, later that year, souped up with a few more stops, raising its price to $65 million. In 1939, the city demanded powers to construct "underground streets." In '43, lobbyists argued that a subway could double property values, quell unemployment, and ready us for our overcrowded future. The municipal Executive Committee and City Council heartily approved a $100-million plan. But the bubbly stayed corked, as the project was voted against for lack of cash. In 1947, French engineers promised to build a subway inside four years, but they never called, they never wrote. (Although, given what French architect Roger Taillibert did to Olympic Stadium, maybe this was a good thing.) In 1959, plans for a tubeway with now-familiar routes up Décarie, Ste. Catherine, and St. Denis, as well as a line up Iberville, was tabled and soon shelved. After the Metro lines were finally in place, an official recommendation in 1973 suggested they also be used to haul freight.

SPRING HAS SPRUNG

Local inventor Gregory Lekhtman has been identified as the ex-boyfriend of ex-Prime Minister Kim Campbell and a big *Six Million Dollar Man* fan. (But then, who wasn't? A Steve Austin fan, that is, not a Campbell boyfriend.) In fact, it was TV bionics that inspired Lekhtman to invent a form of transport that triples your running speed while putting far less pressure on your joints. In 1985, he patented his "Exerlopers" — half-moons of a bouncy metal alloy that attach to shoe soles. An improved model can be ordered on the web for $170 U.S. They enable high-flying running that gets you springing at a pace three times faster than what you can usually clock. There's only one thing that might slow you down while exerloping around town, he said. "People stop you and ask lots of questions. This is the only drawback." We'll pass.

The Snowpranos

Just a few years back, five of the big private snow-clearing players got together to fix prices for clearing our local highways. That forced the minister of transport to pay 40 percent more than would normally be expected. The scam ended when the trust was busted and fined a million bucks. The same operators were free, however, to bid on new snow-clearing contracts.

There's No Business Like Snow Business

Until the early '50s much of the city's snow-clearing strategy relied on freelancers hauling pillboxes, which were simply boxes on skis. Anybody willing to do a bit of shovelling could score a gig with the city, which would pay them to clear designated areas. Shovellers filled their boxes with snow and then pushed them to the nearest drain. Later, the city deployed snow-clearing trucks on the streets that simply threw the snow onto front yards and lawns – a practice that continued until 1962. Westmount and Outremont bought stationary snow melters in 1960, a concept that piqued the interest of Montreal's city fathers. Amid the snow-melting hype, Montreal even tried out a truck that could simultaneously melt snow as it inched along the street, but nixed that concept. Soon, seven built-in snow melters were dug throughout the city, the first being near the intersection of St. Gregoire and Mentana. In September, 1972, the Vallée brothers Robert, 12, and Richard, 11, of 5175 Chambord ventured to the 15-foot metal melting bowl in Mentana Park, where they were allegedly pushed in by three of their friends. Depending on whose story you believed, either some other kids ignited garbage and threw it in after them or else the Vallée boys started fooling around by lighting pieces of styrofoam on their own. In any case, ka-boom! went the melter; a gas leak in the machine caused an explosion. The boys suffered third-degree burns and the melters were removed in 1977, when the city realized they were paying $1.15 per ton to melt snow rather than the pennies it takes to dump it into or near the river. There was yet more talk of using giant microwave snow-melters in 1983, but that was deemed too flaky.

PARKING

Signs that regulate parking in Montreal may be incomprehensible, but try telling that to a judge after you get slammed with a $42 ticket. Be particularly wary of tow zones where rush-hour removals will cost you $143. De Maisonneuve and Côte des Neiges north of Sherbrooke are well-known tow zones. And during the winter, don't ignore the snow-clearance tow-truck fleets. The pain of one ticket has been enough to persuade Montrealers to participate in the immensely popular sport of ticket contestation. City courts are jammed for months by entertaining motorists attempting to change judges' minds.

Shortcuts

We don't recommend you barrel down sleepy alleyways just to cut a few seconds off your commute ... but if we don't, somebody else might, so consider these routes at your own risk.

When Décarie and its service road are busy, try Decelles — one block east (at least until as far north as Paré).

Take the old Laurentien Blvd. (Marcel Laurin Blvd.) rather than the 15 north from the Metropolitan (the largely elevated part of Autoroute 40) when it's busy.

Take the Bonaventure highway ramp to the Champlain Bridge rather than accessing it from the Décarie Expressway.

La Gauchetiere speeds you from Chinatown to Peel St.

William St. gets you out of Old Montreal. (If you're headed for the westbound entrance to Autoroute 20, turn right on Eleanor just before de la Montagne to avoid a traffic light.)

When heading north to Laval, consider a route north on Marcel Laurin, rather than taking the Metropolitan.

Traffic Jams

It might be smarter to note the few places in the city not subject to traffic jams, but that would force us to leave the page blank. Traffic has become a daily purgatory for motorists loitering on our island's 137 kilometers of highways. The network has experienced a doubling of traffic since 1970, while only seeing 14 kilometers of new highways built on the island since then. Here, selected randomly from a wide-brimmed fedora, are some of the routes voted Most Likely to See You Grind to a Halt.

The Jacques Cartier, Victoria, or Champlain bridges are usually hell, as 440,000 cars cross them daily to and from the South Shore, along with the Mercier Bridge and Lafontaine Tunnel. (472,000 cross northern links to and from Laval every day.) Recent talk at the Nicolet commission of adding another bridge to the south shore has quickly dissipated in the mist.

Park Ave. Southbound traffic is regularly hamstrung, as buses share a single lane with cars, trucks, and cyclists. Try not to breathe if carbon monoxide doesn't agree with you.

Autoroute 40 is often a virtual parking lot, particularly between the disjointed sections of Autoroute 15.

The Boulevard in swanky Westmount has staggered lights that will turn red for you every time. Keep a cool head to avoid road rage tinged with class resentment.

Same thing goes for Fleet Road in Hampstead, where you'll be rewarded with a stop sign every 30 paces.

Rack 'n' Roll to Terrebonne

After years of guerrilla tactics in the '80s, our bike activists finally gained the right to take their cycles on the Metro. Now bikers can also carry them on the bus. Unfortunately, we're only talking about 28 buses that go to Terrebonne and back, but it's an attractive place full of bike paths for those who like that sort of thing.

Boating Cops All Dash, No Splash

Hey sailor, here's what to know about dealing with the dozen law enforcement boats that roam our waters on behalf of federal, provincial, and municipal forces. They have the right to board your boat and check for infractions like no oars, not enough life jackets, no bail bucket – that sort of thing. The absence of one of these items will cost you a $252 fine, but the good news is that not many tickets are actually given out. Extrapolating from stats of a recent year, you have a 99.9 percent chance of not getting ticketed when a provincial watercop pulls you over. Of the 5,000 they searched in a recent year, only five got tickets.

Chopper Stoppers

In September 1997, our island cops announced that they'd start patrolling us from above, thanks to a helicopter leased for $600 an hour. Within minutes in the air, the critics were loud and furious and demanded the noisy, invasive chopper be taken down. The eggbeater saw little of our skies after that and by February 2001 it had been ditched from our city cops' plans.

SEPTEMBER 11 (1968)

September 11 was a famous hijacking date in these parts long before the World Trade Center attacks. And it has been such, ever since Charles Beasely of Dallas chose that very date in 1968 to commandeer a plane headed for Toronto and order the crew to, "Take me to Havana." They flew him to our very own Dorval International Airport instead. As a reward for pulling Canada's first hijacking, Beasley was given a six-year, all-expenses-paid trip to the steel-bar hotel.

Curtis and Lisa Sliwa tossed on their berets in 1982 and came up from the Big Apple to launch a local version of the Guardian Angels to help defend locals against real or imagined Metro predators. But their Montreal chapter morphed into a polite, low-testosterone shadow of the American vigilantes as "Les Anges Gardiens" preferred calling authorities rather than personally confront Metro menaces. So the Sliwas started a second "genuine chapter" in '84 but an instructor in the new wing was arrested for gross indecency and the Angels got in more hot water when they poked their noses into the middle of an undercover drug transaction in the Fairview Centre mall. The band tried to kick-start – again – their crime-fighting crusade in '89, but that effort was forgotten minutes after the press conference.

NO SKY-CROSSING HERE

No architectural proposal raises as much indignation as the thoroughly practical air bridges (so elegantly called "passerelles" in French). Long reviled by Mayor Drapeau (although he was ready to make an exception for the ill-fated concert hall on McGill College), city planners and heritage types make the sign of the cross at the very mention of this much-reviled thingy that links buildings above ground to spare pedestrians the horrors of weathering the elements. Two lonely semi-exceptions are the uncovered footbridge linking Place du Canada to the Château Champlain and another inside the Palais des Congrès spanning Viger. In 2002, the ETS engineering school proposed a skyway to link their campus to a new one across Notre Dame near Peel. The plan sparked outrage, even though an industrial-style bridge had linked the two sides just a few years before.

Airport Taxi Wars

The privilege of ferrying passengers to Dorval Airport was once so intense that it led to riots and even a death. In October 1970, the politically-well-connected Murray Hill Limousine Service owned the monopoly on lifts to the airport. That didn't go over well with the independent cabbies who bombed the Murray Hill garage during the FLQ-terrorism era, resulting in a melee that left one guard dead. A taxi to the airport will set you back about $30 from downtown, so we recommend the $11 shuttle from the Berri bus terminus. There's one every 20 minutes from 7am to 11pm.

A Flock of Vigilantes

Seven taxi drivers were killed on the job between 1987-2002, according to the Montreal Taxi Bureau. When in grave danger, cabbies sometimes call out to other hacks by barking "Code 13" into their radios, a signal for other cabbies to a come to their aid. The distress signals are heard rarely, though, as the Taxi Bureau yanked one driver's cabbie license after he cried wolf.

Sick-Horse City

Photo: John David Gravenor

In the 1870s, city transport was greatly compromised by "epizootic influenza." In other words, the horses caught the flu and didn't feel much like jogging round in front of their "Jehus." (That was the local name for a horse-taxi driver; it came from Jehu, an Israeli king known for his prowess on the chariot.)

Transport Curiosities

Somewhere in the dusty files of the unenforced bylaws of the city of Montreal lies a rule threatening to toss motorists in prison for six months — or slap 'em with a $40 fine — if they commit a "breach of common consideration" by splashing pedestrians.

A gang of four crafty criminals was caught in December 1946 with more than a few counterfeit tramway tickets. The phony tix were worth $66,000 in free rides.

According to the Quebec Hydro Electric Commission, 3,640 Montreal street lamps were smashed in 1946. The utility blamed young people.

In July 1946, Mayor Camilien Houde proposed a plan that would subsidize landowners to create parking lots downtown.

A small airport was built near downtown Montreal in the early '70s. The short-take-off-and-landing strip was open for two years near the foot of the Victoria Bridge. It was slated to reopen in 1985, but nearby residents thought otherwise.

When Montreal cops were first equipped with breathalyzer machines in 1971 they reported a huge increase in hit-and-runs, averaging a reported 1,300 such events every day.

In 1991, a leading Montreal road-building company wanted to place a bid on a $20-million contract to build roads at the sprawling James Bay hydroelectric development. Their tender was tossed out rather untenderly, however, because somebody at the company wrote the wrong name on the cheque required to participate in the bidding process.

Our beloved parking meters date back to 1946, and were installed over the cries of the Royal Automobile Club, which feared the practice would discourage the progress of car travel.

Twisted Taxi Gets Record After All

On November 5, 1999, cabbie king Joseph Vaillancourt was just 214 kilometers shy of breaking a world record when his black '63 Plymouth Fury was hit by a truck blasting through a red light at Marie Anne and St. Urbain. More than his car was crushed. The hopes of the 74-year-old who started on the streets in 1947 were also destroyed as his odometer halted at 2,594,955 kilometers – just one day's work short of the record. Being insured for just $4,000, he wasn't able to get the Fury repaired. Then a local actor, Michel Barrette, bought the car and offered to pay the $20,000 repair tab to get the old Fury back on the road. It wouldn't be necessary: a university math professor later informed Vaillancourt that his conversion of miles to kilometers was faulty, and that he had already beaten a record set by California-based Alan Klein's '63 Volks Beetle by a good 15,000 km.

Cabs Galore

Photo: John David Gravenor

With 4,500 hardworking cabbies roaming city streets (down from 6,000 a few years before) with $80,000 taxi permits to finance, you can scratch your ear and – voilà! – a fare-hungry hack pulling up next to you.

It's time for you to really start getting to know the story behind the pumps that have been fuelling the city since the dawn of the automobile, so consider this your primer. For much of the city's recent history, the island was swamped with gas stations, as city officials would take bribes in return for granting operating licenses. Indeed, by 1933, the island offered its mere 63,000 cars a choice of 900 stations to choose from, a total that remained stable for several decades. In 1955, gas pumps were exempted from a closing law that insisted most businesses remain closed on Sundays. In 1958, the rules were finally applied to gas stations run by non-owners, but many stations flaunted the law with the public's support. Massive gas-station strikes crippled the province in 1965. When self-serve gas stations were introduced in 1975, Yves Magnan warned that they were "underground bombs in the heart of residential sectors," figuring that smokers would accidentally blow the places up. In 1980, City Hall tried to outlaw the combined gas station-corner store so common today. In recent years, many of the island's pumps have closed up, leaving nothing but vacant areas filled with toxic soil that require major clean-up efforts.

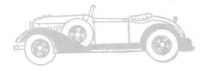

Owners of commercial parking lots are forced to follow strict standards or be fined by the city. Lots must be surrounded by proscribed amounts of shrubbery, parking spots must be of a specific size, and all lots must be paved throughout. When we surveyed the city, not a single parking lot in the downtown area could be found that didn't violate one or more of the rules.

The federal government offered the port to the city of Montreal in 1967. The city turned it down.

The area near Jean Talon and Lajeunesse used to host about 40 used car lots in the early 1950s where you could browse through about 5,000 parked cars.

An epidemic of new dumps for deceased cars tripled the number of old wrecks littering the island between 1960 and 1970. The biggest of these dangerous eyesores was at Papineau and Fleury; another sat at Casgrain and Bellechasse. These car graveyards were eventually chased out through legislation.

Some common transport-related phrases you might hear these days include, "Darn Novabuses," "The Metro will be delayed," or "Transit strike on the horizon." But back in the '40s, the much-rosier transportation catchphrases boasted of us being the "World's Biggest Inland Port," or "World Capital of Aviation." That last phrase might have helped the city attract the United Nations International Civil Aviation Organization (ICAO) and the International Air Transport Association (IATA), as both voted to settle here in 1946 – thanks to a ballot that saw us get 27 votes versus nine for Paris. In 1950, Charter Article 45 set ICAO here permanently but, two years later, members were groaning about our high cost of living, lack of diplomatic tax exemptions, and dearth of legal immunity. Some might have grumbled about the weather, too. In 1954, South American countries led another move to have the organization abandon our city in an exodus initiative that flared anew with French support in 1969. ICAO and IATA were still here the last time we looked.

POLISH AIR RAID ON GRIFFINTOWN

You might insist that Montreal escaped unscathed by air attacks during World War II, but we'd have to remind you about April 25, 1944. At 10:30 that morning, five Polish aviators flying a defective four-motor Liberator from Dorval to an overseas destination crashed into a row of homes on Shannon south of Ottawa Street in Griffintown. Among the eleven dead were James Wells of 230 Shannon, his 20-year-old wife, three-year-old son, and his brother's wife, who lived next door.

the essential bridges

What better way to enter the city than to casually show off to your car-mates your knowledge of the span you're crossing? Memorize this page.

Victoria Bridge

Twenty-six of the 3,000 workers who put this bridge together died during the five years it took to get it over the St. Lawrence. The Grand Trunk Railway's bridge was opened with great pomp and ceremony in August, 1860, by the future King Edward VII. Its foundations disturbed the gravesite of 6,000 Irish immigrants who died in the typhus epidemic of 1847-48 (a large stone monument just north of the bridge's entrance now commemorates the burial place). The bridge was considered necessary to access Portland, Maine, the closest port that remained open during the winter months. Often described as the eighth wonder of the world, the Victoria Bridge was originally covered with metal sheets. It was altered to allow for cars in 1898. Driving over its metal-grate surface might freak you out as the whirring sound makes you think you've got a flat tire.

Jacques Cartier Bridge

Photo: John David Gravenor

Opened in May, 1932 as the Montreal Harbour Bridge, a campaign to change its name succeeded two years later. The Montreal end of the bridge lies to the east of the rest of the bridge because the Barsalou Soap Company refused to allow their lands to be expropriated. The blind curve in the bridge because of this decision has caused many deaths, leading to the bend being referred to as Deadman's Curve. Forty one million vehicles cross per year, making it the second busiest bridge in Canada. Tolls were lifted in '62.

The Essential Canal

Photo: John David Gravenor

The real reason Montreal is here? Two words: Lachine Rapids. Too scary, shallow, and fast. So to save their fur-laden boats and quivering souls, in 1689 settlers started digging a canal around this obstacle to navigation. Mohawks expressed their slight displeasure by killing everybody in the area two years later, derailing the plan. After a few more tries a five-foot-deep, nine-mile-long Lachine Canal finally opened on July 7, 1821. Here are some shallow facts about the shallowest of our waterways:

Fridges, stoves, and other assorted junk, including 85 scrap cars were pulled from the canal in the mid-'80s.

Three men walking along the water were savagely beaten in 1999 by lowerland youth. The teens said they believed the men to be gay.

In 1962, '71, and '83 hundreds of concerned citizens signed petitions to build a fence along its banks. That's because illegal swimmers have a nasty tendency to drown in the sludge-like waters. Indeed, the '62 petition claimed that 45 people drowned in the prior 26 years. The federal Transport Ministry and the Seaway Authority agreed to fence it off in '62. They never did.

In 1958, the mayors of the former island municipalities of Westmount, Dorval, and TMR got together with the popular city councillor for Point St. Charles, Frank Hanley, and agreed to drain it, pave it, and build a two-tier highway on the canal with a Metro line alongside. Hanley toured the Point in an open-air bus and held a dance to raise cash for a legal battle to implement the scheme.

Workers were incensed when officials opted to have a tunnel dug under the canal at Wellington Street using machines rather than employ humans to do the shoveling.

The St. Lawrence Seaway, built along the South Shore, rendered the Lachine Canal obsolete. It reopened to pleasure craft in the spring of 2002, with an estimated 20,000 truckloads of toxic soil that would have cost $40 million to remove remaining at the bottom.

Champlain Bridge

Photo: John David Gravenor

The newest and longest of the St. Lawrence spans is this six-lane cantilever bridge originally slated to span a narrower crossing at Lachine. But expropriating land in Verdun proved cheaper. Thus, dollars determined its current trajectory to Brossard. The last to give up its tolls, drivers had to drop a quarter into baskets until 1990 on what remains Canada's busiest bridge, with 49 million crossings a year. The well-known bridge engineer P.L. Pratley died a year after he started the project. His son, H.H.L. Pratley, took over the job in 1958. When it opened to motorists in 1962, the bridge was only accessible from far-away Wellington St., a problem solved by the opening of the Bonaventure Expressway in '67. Experts warned of an impending structural disaster and ordered immediate repairs in the late '80s. More repairs were completed in '94.

Mercier Bridge

Photo: John David Gravenor

28 million vehicles cross this short-stuff span yearly. Its tolls were initially 50 cents in 1934, although Mohawk Indians of the nearby Caughnawaga reserve (now called Kanawake) were exempted. In the '60s, the heavy traffic flow gave rise to a second span built alongside. Natives blocked this bridge for 78 days during the 1990 Oka standoff between aboriginal activists on one side, and provincial police and military troops on the other. Not to mention the thousands of commuters caught on one side, or the other.

A 31-year-old fell asleep on the railway tracks in Roxboro, half a mile from the Gouin level crossing one September evening in 1992. As he snoozed, one of the guy's legs lay draped over the tracks. We'll spare you the rest of the unfortunate details, but it's safe to say he won't be entering any field goal kicking contests.

The Roxboro level crossing at Gouin and 5th Ave. has seen its share of nasty surprises for those unaware of oncoming trains. In 1987, a girl was killed while walking with a friend. In '89 a trucker was struck and went to the big truck stop in the sky. And in 1991, a 43-year-old driver was decisively slammed by a freight train at the crossing. The miserly community finally sprung $15,000 to put up a gate in 1992.

At the Pierrefonds level crossing at Sunnybrooke and Gouin, two 11-year-old kids thought it would make a smashing prank to raise the lowered gate. Sadly, it was. A car carrying five teens didn't see an oncoming train. Twenty percent – i.e., one – survived.

At St. Ambroise and St. Henri on a Saturday evening in July 1992, a 38-year-old man attempted to hop a CN train. He slipped, was dragged 15 feet and decapitated.

In the early '80s, the Gouin crossing by the Roxboro train station featured a level crossing with lights but no barrier. Ignoring the waiting cars, a young female driver pulled out to pass, oblivious to the oncoming train. Stationary motorists watched in horror and helplessly sounded their horn in an effort to stop her. Misinterpreting their intentions, the woman flashed her middle finger. It was the last thing she ever did.

BULLET TRAIN, ANYTIME NOW

Montreal has a longtime fetish to build a high-speed train to serve the Windsor-Quebec City corridor and New York City. A bullet-like train has been promised since a proposed $2.1-billion Big Apple route and $2-billion Montreal-Toronto service were announced in the early 1980s. One of the little-known train lines that never happened was supposed to service Mirabel Airport. The concept would have entailed building a station where handsome greystone homes stand on the west side of Jeanne Mance, south of Sherbrooke. This supertrain would have zoomed to the airport via a tunnel. Like a long-promised highway to the ill-conceived airport, the train plan wisely never came to pass, and now the airport has stopped serving passengers.

SHIPPING DISASTER ON THE HORIZON

A worrying fact about shipping on the St. Lawrence: in the event of a major oil spill, our very survival would be threatened. Despite this, Canadian inspectors drop in on just one in four ships sailing down the St. Lawrence. Five billion tons of freight gets carried past our friendly island each year. Half the ships are at least 15 years old, the same percentage that exhibit major problems. About 50 shipping accidents occur in Canadian waters in a typical year.

METRO SUICIDES

According to our local ambulance service, at an average of about once a week, somebody jumps in front of a Metro train, closing the service for approximately 45 minutes each time. Only about half of the suicide attempts end in death, mainly because trains slow down by the time they reach the platform.

NDG Pedestrians vs. CPR

Pedestrians can cross railway tracks without official permission in many parts of Montreal, but not so in the NDG district. Since late 2000, the Canadian Pacific Railway (CPR) has aggressively repaired all the handy, man-made holes in the adjoining fence and has started writing out $136 tickets to pedestrian shortcut-seekers trying to get from Upper Lachine to de Maisonneuve. Since the traditional holes in the railway fences have all been plugged, people living south of the NDG tracks have been encircled like Manstein in Stalingrad. All north-south pedestrians are forced to "walk the gauntlet" through a urine-soaked, graffiti-stained, garbage-strewn, and claustrophobic Melrose tunnel. The CPR has scoffed at requests to allow a pedestrian level crossing on their right-of-way, calling such a proposal dangerous. This despite the fact that no train casualties of illicit crossers are known to have occurred on this stretch of track since its opening in the 1880s.

Beat a Trail to the Rail Museum

From William Van Horne's booze-and-poker-fuelled stewardship to our gloriously extinct streetcars, Montreal's contribution to the country's rail heritage is celebrated at the Canadian Railway Museum at Delson St. Constant, about 15 miles southwest of Montreal. Pop in to see the Montreal Tramway's open-top observation cars that once shuttled tourists on a 10-mile loop around the mountain from downtown at a semi-extortionate 25 cents (tickets were stamped at 6.25 cents each). Also, poke your head in to see our first Canadian-built locomotive, which was forged at the CPR shops in 1886. And get a gander at Van Horne's legendary, private railway car, complete with an ornate interior that includes flashy, carved mahogany details. It was built in 1883 at the cost of $25,000 – more than a little pile of dough in those days.
122A St. Pierre, St. Constant

Côte St. Luc's traffic xenophobia

The Côte St. Luc district has long enjoyed tossing a stick in the spokes of those trying to get around. Here are a few of the episodes.

1963: City council approves the connection of Cavendish Boulevard to nearby Highway 40 to ease transportation woes. A citizen complains, launches a lawsuit, and blocks the project, forcing millions of drivers and even CSL residents to drive great distances around the neighbourhood. In recent years, suggestions that Cavendish be hooked up to Highway 40 at its north end inspired geriatric residents to swear they'll lay down in front of traffic rather than let it happen.

1966: Residents of the then-municipality complain that their houses shake and their homes' foundations are being jeopardized by the 161 bus that passes in front of their homes. The ornately-named Warnock-Hershey Report dispelled their farfetched complaints.

1970: According to former Montreal City Councillor Sam Boskey, Côte St. Luc was offered a Metro station in their municipality. They turned it down.

1974-84: As well as trying to ban car washes and For Sale signs in car windows, CSL banned all non-residents from driving down Emerson Road. Innumerable unwitting drivers that failed to see the tiny sign were slapped with tickets for driving down the street during these years.

2002: Borough officials vowed to no longer allow the popular Tour de l'Ile mass-cycling event from taking over any of its streets for one day a year. They claim the display unduly inconveniences residents.

THE RELUCTANT ROAD

Camilien Houde, Montreal's most charismatic and bombastic mayor of old, once declared: "A road over the mountain? Over my dead body!" So sure enough, he died and was buried on the edge of the mountain. Then Mayor Jean Drapeau built a road over the mountain and named it after Houde.

DRILLING TO DRUMMOND

In the late '50s the city had a notion to extend what's now de Maisonneuve, but a large residential building called Drummond Court sat smack dab in the middle of their route. Solution? The city bought the building and built a tunnel through the main floor of the structure for a cool $3.2 million. So go have a look — er, it's a bit late now to see this oddball landmark. After 40 years, the city finally demolished the bizarre thoroughfare in 2001.

Photo: John David Gravenor

Tow to Tango

There was a day when drivers could get away with parking for free on private lots after hours. But in recent years, lots have made deals with towing companies to remove your car if you don't buy a ticket from a machine and place it on your dash. The lot gets a couple of bucks in the deal and the towing company makes the approximately $100 it demands to get your car back. Drivers can beat the system if they follow a few rules, but first some context.

In 1987, the towing folks messed with the wrong guy when they removed hotshot lawyer Reeven Pearl's new Benzo from a lot near Phillips Square, then hauled it to the north end and demanded immediate payment for its return. Pearl went to court against the practice and 1991 he won a $7-million classification decision against the towing company for extortion. The tow-artists declared bankruptcy and regrouped under a slightly modified name with comparable practices.

Here's the info you need to know if your car is towed after hours for not having a ticket on its dash: 1) you are not legally required to pay immediately for the return of your car, and 2) you don't have to sign anything. Call the police right away if the towing company insists on immediate payment or the signing of documents. Once you have your car, the towing company will send you a $100 invoice with the name of a collection agency they claim will get on you if you don't pay up. But don't rush to your chequebook. Insiders say it's a bluff as the towing companies won't likely pursue you for the payment.

Photo: John David Gravenor

In the 1950s a clamour grew into a din (or did the din grow into a clamour?) to have a north-south highway linking Authoroute 20 to Autoroute 40. Several plans resulted: first, urban planners argued for an artery on Côte des Neiges Road. City officials announced that the hilly street would be widened to 200 feet to accommodate major flows of traffic. That idea was replaced by a potential architectural Armageddon that would have seen St. Denis widened for traffic, with an elevated route south of Sherbrooke and an underground section for some distance north of Sherbrooke.

In 1959, planners proposed transforming St. Lawrence into the north-south autoroute, with a six-lane freeway stretching eight miles. It was intended to permit motorists to peel from one end of the island to the other in under 10 minutes. By 1961 they were planning to drill a $288-million tunnel through Mount Royal from Victoria Square to the Metropolitan Expressway. It would have joined a separate, east-west tunnel linking the intersection of Park and Rachel to Décarie.

Planners next considered making Cavendish the north-south route, but it was considered too far west. So they settled on Décarie, a cruising strip lined with big-box restaurants named Piazza Tomasso, Pumpernicks, Miss Snowdon, and Miss Montreal. Some objected to the $43 million project that would demolish 1,000 homes. City bigwig Lucien Saulnier disliked it, scoffing that it would "allow drivers to get from Upper Lachine to the Met (Autoroute 40) in four minutes rather than eight." The car lobby, which included Décarie-area auto dealer Harold Cummings, jumped in to support the plan over other alternatives like building a Metro line down the street. Countless homes were demolished and city landmarks, such as the marble-and-mahogany Royal Bank building at Queen Mary and the tranquil Orphans Park, disappeared as the costly digging cracked the foundations of hundreds of homes along the route. After

Unrealized Highway Hype

The local Roman Catholic clergy lobbied for a magnificent east-west boulevard sprouting from the Monument National near St. Lawrence and Dorchester (now René Lévesque) boulevards in 1903.

The Royal Automobile Club, peeved that cars travelled on average of only six miles an hour downtown, demanded elevated roads. For starters, they wanted them from the Victoria Bridge to Dorchester, from Atwater to the Jacques Cartier Bridge, above all CNR train tracks and on both sides of Mount Royal.

completion, the Décarie Expressway surpassed noise and pollution norms, and the traffic trench cut an open scar through the neighbourhood. Various proposals to cover it have come and gone over the years and all measure of merchants watched helplessly as the strip gradually died.

In the 1950s, planners threatened a road through Laurier Park and a tunnel under the Victoria Bridge.

In the '80s, Mayor Doré and the province agreed to turn the Metropolitain into a two-level highway by adding a tunnel below the existing autoroute.

In 1988, the province promised bus lanes across the Champlain Ice Bridge, and a $2-billion beltway of highways around the island. The plan was revived in later years.

Venice on the St. Lawrence

Had city authorities left well enough alone, we would be living like Venetians, punting around hundreds of little streams and rivers throughout the island. Many of the detailed records of our forsaken waterways were destroyed when the Parliament building burned in 1849, but here are some long-gone streams that have since been killed off by man.

A 20-mile river flowed south from Little St. Peter's River at Mount Royal's Beaver Lake, through Côte des Neiges, Westmount, and Lachine, before doubling back to NDG, into Lac aux Loutres, a small lake now gone from the trainyards of St. Henri, before eventually emptying into the St. Lawrence near Nun's Island.

The Torrent of Outremont went down Côte Ste. Catherine, Outremont Avenue, into St. Viateur Park, then down Park Avenue before hustling on to Lafontaine Park.

The Lafontaine Torrent came down behind Hôtel Dieu hospital to St. Louis Square, which once contained the city's reservoir.

The St. Martin River meandered along present-day St. Antoine St. before heading south where it emptied at Pointe à Callières next to Place Royale in Old Montreal.

Other lost rivers include: Rock Creek, a 10-mile waterway in the east end, and Migon Creek, which flowed through the north-end St. Michel district.

There's a frequently-repeated French Canadian epigram mouthed
in moments when one's spirit to persevere begins to flag: "Lâche pas
la patate!" ("Don't drop the potato!") Indeed, throughout Quebec you'll
often see the proverbial tater held high as athletes and competitors do
their best in sports ranging from polo to petancle. Scope the naked truth
of this chapter and fondle our thorny underbelly of leisure activities
ranging from beach volleyball and hair golf to nudism.

Inches From History

Montrealers are mighty proud of the role their city played
in Jackie Robinson's migration to the big leagues. Brooklyn
Dodgers president Branch Rickey started Robinson at his
team's minor-league affiliate, the Montreal Royals, in 1946.
Later, he called Robinson up to the majors as the first African-
American player to break the colour barrier. But few people
realize that when he came to Montreal, Robinson wasn't
alone. Two other players, both pitchers and both black, were
also given contracts at the same time. But Roy Partlow and
Johnny Wright, didn't make the final cut and were sent
downriver to play for the Three Rivers Royals. A mid-sized city
with a black population of zero, the town adored them: not least because their talent
helped the team win that year's Canadian-American League pennant. Wright became the
second black player to be signed by the Brooklyn Dodgers. And both
were teammates once before on the
1943 Homestead Grays, champs
of the first Negro World Series.

If you thought polo was just a T-shirt logo, you haven't seen the sport played at Hudson/Sainte Marthe. Polo is alive and well here, just minutes off Montreal Island. At one time an influential force in cross-border polo, the Montreal polo club toured and competed in Ontario and New York state since early in the 20th century. But then came the Wars, the Depression, and a shift from country to city living. Before long, the "Sport of Kings" as it was played here was abandoned.

But that sorry situation started to change when Fred Choate's employer, the Bank of America, transferred him from Boston to their Montreal offices in 1980. A polo enthusiast, Choate brought his ponies with him but was disappointed to learn Montreal's polo club was out of business. Undaunted, he set out to recruit potential players, most from the Hudson area. A half-dozen riders soon took to an improvised polo ground, and the game has been growing ever since.

Today the **Montreal Polo Club** has 20 active members and grounds equal to 50 football fields in size – enough to host more than 100 polo ponies in any tournament. Local veterinarian Dr Gilbert Hallé lives full-time on site and works as the chief groundskeeper, too. Visiting players from throughout North America and the Caribbean have described the Montreal Polo Club's grounds as the best facilities in Eastern North America.

The annual Polo Classic is the most popular event, with top international competition, entertainment, and food. Admission is free, except for the occasional charity match. Games are played four times a week, weather permitting.

From Montreal, take Autoroute 40 West towards Ottawa. Get off at Exit 17 and turn left on Route 201 (Montée Lavigne). Continue about 3.4 km (2 miles) and turn right on Chemin Park St. Henri. Watch for the signs. *450/458-0719; polo.ca*

Light & Shadow

They didn't run on gas or petroleum. The first street lamps in North America burned whale oil. Installed here in 1815, they didn't give off much light, and were known to leak oil on pedestrians. Lamps burning an impure gas were introduced in 1838. They were brighter but burned with a hiss and froze in cold weather, needing occasional thawing with menthylated spirits.

Lamplighters climbed their ladders, turned valves, and sparked the gas with their glowing tapers. Electric streetlights ended their jobs in the 1880s.

Illuminating landmarks is popular because it's pretty. But like a bottled blonde, the practice has dark roots. The man credited with inventing lighting architecture was Albert Speer, a friend of Adolf Hitler and a Nazi minister of armaments. You can print a map of the city's lighting tour off the web. *ville.montreal.qc.ca/ vieux/planlum/eng/circuia.htm*

Boule's Paradise

With more than 20,000 enthusiasts in this province alone, pétanque may be the biggest little sport you've never heard of. Sort of a cross between bocci and curling, pétanque is played one-on-one or between two teams. The object is to toss your boule (a grapefruit-sized ball) near the target-ball, or "coche," while keeping your opponent's boule at bay.

There are three kinds of throws: the high lob, the half lob, and the rolling throw. The boule is thrown underhand with the palm of your hand facing down instead of up. It feels funny at first.

In Montreal, the **VIP Pétanque** club hosts an international tournament every summer at Lafontaine Park, complete with a dinner and awards ceremony. It has been the site of tournaments since 1956. Club coordinates, rules, and other information can be had on the Pétanque America website. *petanque.org*

Here are some brilliant night spots in Old Montreal:

Place Jacques Cartier, the Bonsecour Market and City Hall

Place d'Armes, particularly the art deco Aldred Building facing the southeast corner

The old Customs House on Place Royale

The lofts and businesses on St. Paul between St. Pierre and McGill streets

De la Commune Street facing the Old Port.

Photo: John David Gravenor

Former NFL running-back Tshimanga "Tim" Biakabutuka learned how to play football while living and studying in Montreal. As his way of saying thanks, he returns every year to teach local kids what he knows – for free.

Born in Kinshasa, Zaire (now Congo), the multilingual, six-foot veteran of the Carolina Panthers stages two football camps; one of them at Vanier College, his old *alma mater* in Ville St. Laurent. He spends his daylong sessions giving workshops about all aspects of the game and directing non-contact drills. Held every spring, you can find out more by calling the college's sports department (514/744-7126).

Meanwhile, Trevor Williams beat all odds and became good enough at basketball to earn a spot on the 1996 Canadian Olympic team. Now he's giving back to poor kids who share his early dreams by holding basketball camps for underprivileged youth, an effort that has attracted teaching visits from the likes of Tod McCollough and Steve Nash.
514/932-4340; twasba.com

The New Gladiators

What do Peter Worrell, Georges Laracque, and Donald Brashear – the toughest, scariest figures in NHL hockey – have in common? All three are Quebecers and all three are black. Coincidence? Perhaps. However, reports have shown that black Quebecers are often denied their fair share of the economic pie. It's an established fact that playing tough is one way to escape poverty and dead-end conditions.

CHAMP SCHOOL

For more than 40 years, Lindsay Place High School has been giving its students a sporting chance – and a chance to make it in sports. With more than one-third of the 1,150 students playing on the school's 25 teams (they're all called the Eagles), the Pointe Claire school has produced a disproportionate number of big-league athletes.

These superjock grads include seven-foot-one-inch Chicago Bull Bill Wennington, NHL defenseman Mark Hardy, and NFL football players Bill Hitchcock (Seattle Seahawks) and Ian Beckles (Philadelphia Eagles).

TALL TALES

Pascal Fleury wanted to be a hockey player when he was growing up in Montreal. Problem was, the son of 6-foot-plus Haitian immigrants would have to have awfully strong knees. On skates, the 7'1" Fleury would tower over all other competition, leaving him vulnerable for low-bridge attacks. So he played basketball instead. After a stint with the Harlem Globetrotters, the 32-year-old found himself shooting hoops in Nantes, France.

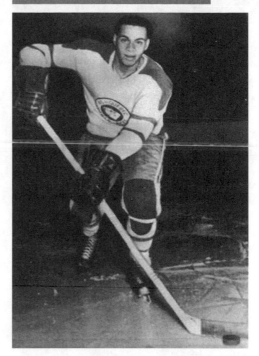

URBAN VOYAGEURS

There's little to stop you from launching your canoe into the raging Lachine Rapids, although we recommend staying in the gentler waters close to shore. Experienced canoeists prefer the western mouth of the Lachine Canal. Drive up with your canoe and just plunk it into the ancient waterway. When you paddle out into the St. Lawrence, the current will grab your boat, sending you downstream fast. Pretty soon is a good time to climb back ashore, cross the peninsula to try it all over again. Then head for liquid refreshments at one of the canal-side terraces.

Closer to downtown, you can rent slower-moving paddleboats and other water craft at the Lachine Canal boat concession south of the Atwater Market. Just cross the footbridge from the south end of the market.

Question: What athlete made history in Montreal as the first black player to appear in the big leagues? If you said Jackie Robinson, you're wrong. Robinson may have broken baseball's colour barrier, but he did it in Brooklyn (after he was called up from the minor-league Montreal Royals). And while hockey never instituted a ban against black players, they were never represented on the NHL ice until January 18, 1953. On that night at the Montreal Forum, a visiting member of the Boston Bruins named Willie O'Ree made hockey history. A New Brunswick native whose career would be shortened by an eye injury, O'Ree didn't score in his side's 3-0 victory that night.

Coincidentally, O'Ree met Jackie Robinson years before that night. When O'Ree was 14, his baseball team won a trip to Brooklyn to see the Dodgers play. As part of the trip, O'Ree was introduced to some players, including Robinson. "One day, I'll play in the NHL," the boy told his idol. Knowing a thing or two about longshots, Robinson just smiled. Today, O'Ree writes a Q&A column for the NHL's website at *nhl.com*.

Photo: John David Gravenor

on the beach

When the going gets hot, the hot get going – to the beach, that is. Okay, it isn't Maui; it's not even Blackpool. But we don't lack for water, sand, lifeguards, and hot weather from early June to late August.

Bois de l'Ile Bizard

To get there from downtown, take Autoroute 40 West and exit at St. Jean Boulevard North, continuing to Pierrefonds Boulevard. Turn left, continue to Jean Bizard Boulevard, and make a right across the bridge. Turn left at the first traffic light at Cherrier. Continue until De l'Eglise and turn right. Drive to Bord du Lac Road and turn right to get to the park. *514/280-PARC*

Cap St. Jacques

This beach in a nature park has a leafy location where Lake of Two Mountains empties into the Rivière des Prairies in Pierrefonds. It's about a 25-minute drive from downtown. Take Autoroute 40 West, exit at Ste. Marie Road, and turn left on to Anse-a-l'Orme Road. Turn right and continue to the end. Turn right on Senneville Road (Gouin Blvd). Continue for two kilometres to the visitor information centre. Expect to pay $4 for parking and another $4 per adult for beach access. *514/280-PARC*

Ile Notre Dame

Beach nuts can simply walk, bike, or in-line skate to the sands of Jean Drapeau Park. (You can drive too.) Located on a man-made lake in the middle of the Formula One racetrack, this beach is artificial, but who cares? The water's filtered! Start out from the Old Port end of the Lachine Canal bike path, follow the signs leading to Cité du Havre (a peninsula opposite the Old Port waterfront). You'll pass Habitat 67, a unique housing project that resembles a galaxy of linked concrete boxes. It dates back to the 1967 World's Fair. Now look for the signs marked Ile Notre Dame. Once on the island, follow the next set of signs leading to the beach.

A Paddling We Will Go

Canoeing becomes an extreme sport when springtime comes around as the region's rivers and streams swell with snow melt. By the last two weeks of May, conditions are perfect for white water canoe adventures near the city. Be careful of strong currents and frequent flooding that can swamp parked cars. The annual runoff's finished by about June, when you have to travel farther and brave the new crop of blackflies.

Canoe/kayak rental locations:

L'Aventurier
1610 St. Denis; 514/849-4100

La Cordée Plein Air
2159 Ste. Catherine E.;
514/524-1106

Kayak Sans Frontières
7770 Blvd LaSalle; 514/595-7873

Photo: John David Grovenor

It's best to arrive early on a sunny day, as prime spots get snapped up fast. Besides, you want to get your admission's worth: around $3 for kids and less than $10 for adults. For details on renting sailboards, pedalboats and that sort of thing, phone 514/871-1798. Open every year since 1990, few people know this wasn't the first artificial beach planned for the island. In 1931, an environmentally suspect plan to build a vast "bathing beach" from the island to the South Shore was made public.

If you want to go on a canoe or kayak camping trip but don't have the slightest clue how, call one of these established outdoors-adventure companies:

Boreale Tours
6830 Park Ave.; 514/271-1230

Detour Nature
154 Villeray St.; 514/271-6046

Excursions Seconde Nature
5067 A Marquette St.; 514/528-1910

Hitching Nature's Ride

Late every April for a few decades now, a few thousand thrill-seekers pull on their wet suits and jump into the thundering Richelieu River. The spine-tingling Descente des Rapides is the highlight of the Aquafête de Chambly and marks the launch of the scuba-diving season in Quebec. Wolf's Mouth, as this stretch of the river is known, doesn't quite live up to its ferocious moniker, but wet suit-clad participants are challenged to stay afloat as they're swept downstream for a 15-minute ride, dipping and flying through more than a mile of white water rapids. Some wear knee and elbow pads, but if anybody ever got killed doing it, organizers have been good at keeping it a secret. After the adrenalin rush ends, trucks ferry the snorkelled participants back to the starting point, where much Quebec-style partying has been known to ensue. Admission is not much more than $20, and you don't have to be a scuba diver.
514/252-3100, 450/658-7310, 800/265-3093; bassinenfete.com

A Need to Speed

After Quebec's first Formula One champion, Gilles Villeneuve, was tragically killed in a May 1982 qualifying session, his grieving family left the familiar bustle of their Monaco home to settle in the quiet village of Villars, Switzerland. Registered at the local Beau Soleil school, young Jacques Villeneuve's friends included the son of the African dictator, President Mobutu, and singer Serge Gainsbourg's daughter, Charlotte. He also spent a lot of time on the ski slopes. If you walk into the lobby of a humble ski resort called l'Hotel du Golf, you will see the silver trophy they award to winners of an annual ski race. Now look at the names of past winners and you'll that of see Jacques Villeneuve. Villars is also where Villeneuve met his soon-to-be manager, the Scotsman Craig Pollock, then the school's sports director. Pollock says Villeneuve was a good enough skier to compete in World Cup races. But driving was in the young man's blood. A keen Dungeons and Dragons player, Villeneuve has another hobby besides skiing – he plays the piano. He took lessons in the 1990s, but says he'd never perform in public. He frequently visits relatives in Montreal and looks in on Newtown, the hotel-bar he co-owns on Crescent at de Maisonneuve.

Street Racing

A clandestine summertime sport begins innocuously enough as youth converge every Thursday at the parking lot outside the Orange Julep diner on Décarie near Paré. On a different night the lot outside a coffee shop in the Chomedy district of Laval also plays host to the draggers.

After hanging around comparing wheels and making small-talk about big engines, the lots suddenly empty as drivers frantically reconverge at another secret, predesignated spot that changes from week to week. Police are constantly trying to prevent the meets, but their hands are usually tied. If you want to know more about local car culture, check out this legit website: 514.streetracing.org.

THE OLD PASSPORT SHUFFLE

Pointe Claire tennis great Greg Rusedski didn't get the hometown treatment when he competed at Montreal's 1995 Canadian Open tennis championships. In fact, the crowd of 6,500 booed him even before he started playing. His crime? Earlier that year, the former student of Lower Canada College decided to move to Britain and refer to himself as a British player.

TREADING TROUBLE

West Island native Carolyn Waldo, the golden girl of synchronized swimming who went on to become a CJOH-TV sports broadcaster, wasn't one to shy away from controversy. Waldo, who bagged double gold at the 1988 Olympics, blasted former teammate Sylvie Fréchette for making a comeback at the expense of young up-and-comers. Fréchette, whose father died when she was three and whose boyfriend killed himself a week before her 1992 Olympic Games appearance, was famous for being shafted out of a gold medal in a judging error (she was awarded one after the Games were over) and went on to work for Cirque du Soleil.

Every Canadian of a certain generation knows that the great Canadiens star Maurice "Rocket" Richard always wore the number nine. Or did he?

Storyteller Roch Carrier contributed to the sweater's fame with his story *The Sweater*. It's about a small-town boy whose mother orders him a Canadiens sweater. But the order gets mixed up and he gets a Maple Leafs jersey instead. Forced to play in the hated Toronto colours, the boy is humiliated in front of his friends. In fact, when Carrier was growing up in the 1950s, his whole team wore a number-nine Canadiens sweater, like their hero, Maurice Richard.

But Richard himself didn't always wear that number, as Carrier explains.

"At the beginning of his career, Richard was number fifteen, and one day this very shy, non-talkative man went to see his boss, Frank Selke, and said 'Boss, no more fifteen, I want nine.' 'How come?' Selke asked. 'I want nine because last night I got a daughter … nine pounds … so I want nine!'"

board to run

It's always *High Noon* on The Main, where police match wits with local skateboarders. Until it was largely grassed over in 2002, the unofficial centre of the city's sk8 scene was a tiny park called Place de la Paix, on the east side of St. Lawrence between René Lévesque and Ste. Catherine. Unofficial because it's against the law to skateboard there. Under a 1996 municipal bylaw, skateboarding is banned from all streets, sidewalks, and public areas. Boarders are supposed to go to the skate-park ghettoes, and police aren't shy about enforcing the rules. Consequently, many skaters are always ready to flee or hide their wheels. The expression "Five-O!" serves as a warning whenever the blue-and-white fuzz patrol creeps into view. Other cities have embraced the skateboarder, but not Montreal.

In fact, Montreal created a great indoor skate space in 1997. Called the Tazmahal – or "Taz" – the 70,000-square-foot park on Berri attracted tens of thousands of skateboarders until it was demolished in 2002 amid promises of a new Taz to be built in far-off Rosemont. But even then, half the space at the Taz was reserved for inline skaters.

If the city wonders why skaters prefer streets and school rails and museum plazas (like the one at de Maisonneuve and Bleury), they only had to look at their own outdoor parks, which tend not to be designed by skaters. The most popular of these, at Jarry Park, was described by a veteran skater as "lethal" and "dangerous." Sharp-edged metal sheeting could be seen peeling away from plywood ramps full of dangerous holes. The concrete in the bowls tended to crack and chip. If you visit, make sure to wear long pants, gloves, elbow pads, and a helmet.

One popular skate spot is right by Olympic Stadium. Its vast seas of concrete feature outdoor plazas, rails, stairs, ledges, and even a rare oval full-pipe, which you get to by following the paved ramp behind the stadium that leads to the soccer field and track-and-field area. The pipe is adjacent to the running track, just facing the entrance.

HAIR GOLF

Creators of the world's greatest sports get their due in history, but they're almost all dead. You've got Abner Doubleday of baseball fame, and ex-Montrealer James Naismith, who came up with a game called basketball. And recently, more influential bodies have come onside to describe Montreal as the birthplace of ice hockey. But among the living, The Great Antonio stands alone for his invention of the unique game of hair golf.

No longer content pulling multiple loaded buses and appearing on programs like Johnny Carson's *Tonight Show* as he did in his earlier days, the legendary local strongman took to growing his hair and inventing new sports. The aging behemoth sports seven-foot dreadlocks wrapped in duct tape that drag on the ground whenever he saunters around this town, where everybody knows his name.

The hair doesn't just look cool; it also serves as a functional golf driver, which Antonio uses to slam balls laser-straight down the middle of city streets, and putt on subway platforms and in the parking lot of the Dunkin Donuts on Beaubien west of St. Michel. In 2002, the Great Antonio further revolutionized sport by inventing hair baseball. He'll challenge anyone to a round — or an inning — if you've got the Rapunzel-like locks to take him on.

Some other places to skate:

Ahuntsic Park

10555 rue La Jeunesse, 514/872-0769

Boisbriand Skatepark

Located in the arena on Grande Allée, Boisbriand

Brossard Skatepark

Near the arena on Rome Boulevard

Boucherville Public Skatepark

As good as it gets around Montreal. Take Autoroute 132 East to De Mortagne Blvd. and exit. Turn left, get over to the right-hand lane and turn right on Rivière aux Pins. Turn right again on Du Lac St. Continue about four football fields until you see the park on the right beside the police station.
450/449-8346

Jarry Park Public Skatepark

Metro De Castelneau, close to the Main
285 Faillon W., 514/273-1234

Lachine Skatepark

LaSalle Park, between Victoria and St. Antoine in Lachine

City of Trees

The answer is: Montreal has the largest one in Canada. And the question, Alex, is: What is an arboretum? An arboretum is a nature preserve intended for trees. The Morgan family donated their 245-hectare tree display to McGill University in 1945, complete with Canada's largest aggregation of exotic and native tree species. Twenty distinct collections with more than 150 species reach for the West Island sky, including balsam, fir, pine, spruce, maples, lindens, and birches. One of the best spots of the forest is found at the stand of old-growth maple dating back 200 years. With luck, you can spot dozens of mammal and reptile species, and hundreds of bird varieties in this oasis, which features 15 miles of self-guided interpretation trails and cabins to rest your feet. Try to spot a few feathered friends on the forest management trails, which in the summer are open only to hikers and bird-watchers. Wintering birds remain long after the 20 km of groomed cross-country ski and snowshoe trails are opened for the colder months. Admission is about five bucks for adults, with membership plans available. To get there from downtown, take Autoroute 40 West to Exit 41 and look for the signs. *514/398-7811*

Ghost Spotting

Legend has it that, every night at sundown, restless spirits wander the streets of Old Montreal and lurk along the ancient waterfront. For those adequately brave of constitution and not too deep of pocketbook, there are three spine-chilling activities staged all summer by a company called the Old Montreal Ghost Trail.

The New France Ghost Hunt introduces you to the city's most famous phantoms. You will encounter and hunt ghosts from the French colonial era. Apparations like a Mohawk warrior, a French fur trader and a British officer will all appear before you as if they were made of flesh and blood. (But work with me, Baby: they're dead!)

Montreal's Historical Crime Scene recreates some of the city's most notorious crimes. In just one evening, you get to know some true-to-death evildoers and their unfortunate victims alike, before serving on a jury of peers to decide the

A MOVING ENCOUNTER

We're all pawns in the game of life. Especially the sixteen living chess figures who — along with knights, bishops, kings, and queens — make up the Living Chess game at the Stewart Museum. Staged at the fort on Ste. Helen's Island, these living pieces wear costumes to portray historical characters. A master chess player takes on the public just after the noonday gun. It is one of many summertime events at the fort, in addition to military tattoos, pipe-and-drum concerts, and exhibitions. Dates vary for Living Chess, so check with the museum *(514/861-6701; stewart-museum.org)*. To get to the old fort, take the Metro to Jean Drapeau station, or drive/ride to the island via the Concord or Jacques Cartier bridges.

fate of the infamous miscreant.

Traditional Ghost Walks are conducted by local sorceror-storytellers, who point out and illuminate the secret wonders of the narrow roads and dark alleys of Old Montreal. But be prepared for major spookings by by terrifying ghosts when you least expect it.

Tickets are less than $15 for adults, less still for students and children. For information and reservations, call (514/868-0303) or visit the web (phvm.qc.ca). The ticket office is located in the Bonsecours Pavilion in the Old Port, just south of Place Jacques Cartier.

A COMESTAR IS BORN

We don't know if a Holstein bull is capable of feeling pride, but with more than a million ejaculations to his credit, Comestar Lee deserves to feel that warm glow of accomplishment. Lee was only the second stud in Quebec artificial-insemination history to pass the million mark, and all of that at less than ten years of age. Sired by Hanoverhill Raider, himself the offspring of the legendary Blackstar, Comestar Lee's mother is Comestar Laura Black, an issue of 1995's cow of the year, Comestar Laurie Sheik. His grandpa, Starbuck, was such an accomplished beast that he was cloned in 2000.

The Comestar farm has been in the cattle-breeding business since the mid-'70s. They welcome visitors year-round, and can satisfy all your cattle-sperm needs. Heck they sell embryos, too. The farm is located at 108 A, Route 116, Victoriaville. *819/758-8688; comestar.qc.ca*

Room at the Top

Photo: John David Gravenor

Montreal has no shortage of hilltop vistas to peer out over the horizon but if you're in the Old Port, the best way to catch a bird's-eye view is to climb the tower of the **Notre Dame de Bonsecours Chapel**. The first stone chapel on this site was built in 1655, thanks to the persuasion of Marguerite Bourgeoys, who consecrated the building to the memory of the Virgin Mary. It burnt down but was rebuilt by 1771 and became known as the Sailors' Church, in part for its position overlooking the port, and for the fact that sailors have donated miniature wooden ships. Some of these can still be seen hanging from the chapel's rafters. The basement contains the Marguerite Bourgeoys Museum, a treasure trove of archaeological curiosities.

Now hop to the tower, after paying the $6 museum fee. But first you have to ascend several flights of tightly winding, rustic stairs. The observation tower offers breathtaking 360-degree views, and it's seldom busy. The largest of the angel statues that surround the observation tower was made famous by local poet-songwriter Leonard Cohen as the "lady of the harbour" of his debut hit, "Suzanne." The chapel-museum is located east of Bonsecour Market. *400 St. Paul E.; 514/282-8670; marguerite-bourgeoys.com*

Beating the Clock

In 1968, police officer Steve Olynyk was watching the Habs on TV when his little boy noticed that the game clock kept counting down after the whistle had blown.

"Daddy, Daddy, why is the clock still running?" asked Junior.

"I don't know, but I'll sure find out," said Daddy.

Olynyk was an old-school cop whose father endured persecution during World War I, like other local Ukranians. When he retired from his $17,000-a-year police job in 1975, Olynyk said he'd miss "kicking down doors" the most and was later elected mayor of the South Shore community of Greenfield Park.

Olynyk settled the timekeeper scandal with typical panache. He started an investigation, infiltrated seven hockey games at the Forum, and eventually busted a ring that involved NHL timekeeper André Dandurand, who was cheating the clock with great regularity in a scam to help bookies with their bets. Dandurand was fired and fined $500.

Moon Mining

Montreal has its fair share of swank jewellers catering to the rich and decadent, but to see a really rare rock, check out the $4-million moonstone on permanent display at the **Cosmodome Space Science Centre**. Retrieved by the crew of Apollo XV, the stone dominates an exhibit recounting the history of NASA moon-shots, which also features a real, used spacesuit. Donated to the museum by NASA in 1994, the dull, porous stone measures about two by four inches. Visitors are sometimes mesmerized by its out-of-this-world charms. However, it's strictly look but don't touch. The last time people lined up to see dirt in Montreal was during the Expo 67 world's fair. At that time, NASA was promoting its upcoming moon landing, so the United States pavilion featured an extensive, simulated moonscape. But since there were no handy moonstones in 1967, NASA settled for volcanic rocks and red dust shipped in from Arizona.

2150 Autoroute des Laurentides; 450/978-3600; cosmodome.org

GLAM TIME

If you don't follow the Formula One racing circuit, you might miss out on the free entertainment that's available the week before the annual race at Gilles Villeneuve Circuit.

The bizarre social experiment sees rich young millionaires and Eurotrash socialites invade the city to jam streets at the beginning of every June. Outdoor venues traditionally include Crescent Street, which is closed off for a few days to feature rows of classic sports cars, wheel-changing competitions, and other fast car-related stuff. Companies like BMW, Ferrari, and Mercedes routinely showcase their next-generation automobiles, while F1 drivers and celebrity race fans like Jim Carrey, Kiefer Sutherland, Jack Nicholson, and Edward Norton hang out at places like Buona Notte, which bags up to $200,000 in that one week. To those indifferent to the thrill of burning rubber, the Main offers outdoor fashion shows, acrobatic performances, and giant-screen spectacles. It's a car-friendly event, but good luck finding a parking space. For the complete schedule, visit online at *grandprix.ca*.

Montreal – Home of Football

A sports item in *The Gazette* of May 15, 1874 suggests that Montreal played a key role in the evolution of North American football. The newspaper reported that Harvard University invited the McGill University football team to play a match at Cambridge, Massachusetts. The problem was that both teams played different versions of the game. Harvard played a form of soccer with a round ball, while McGill played "rugger," or rugby, using an oval-shaped ball. To equal the advantage, it was decided that two games would be played: one according to the rules of soccer, the other by rugby rules. Football was never the same again.

LOST ON THE WATERFRONT

Next time somebody tells you to get lost, tell 'em you need ten bucks. Located near the clock tower at the east end of the Old Port, the Maze in Shed 16 is open from May through September. Featuring obstacles, traps, and play zones, the maze is redesigned with various themes throughout each season. Admission ranges from $10-$11.
*514/499-0099;
labyrintheduhangar16.com*

Geographical Head Start

The only time Jack Todd's "Monday Morning Quarterback" column was actually written on a Monday morning occurred on February 2, 1998. On that date, *The Gazette* sports columnist filed his odds-and-ends article during the Winter Olympic Games in Nagano, Japan – 14 times zones ahead of Montreal.

Date With Destiny

Olympic breast-stroke specialist Victor Davis was the proud holder of a world-record-setting gold medal when he came to Montreal to regain his form in 1989. On November 13, 1990, the frequently hotheaded 25-year-old visited the Brasserie Bellevue in Ste. Anne's with his girlfriend. Following her into a bathroom for a heart-to-heart talk, his last-ever conversation was described as candid, urgent, and expressive. As he stepped out of the nightclub on to the Ste. Anne's strip a few minutes later, he was confronted by a set of youths who expressed their dislike of his face by running him over with their car. Davis died two days later from brain injuries.

Although professional sports teams politely hold tryouts for locals, few if any ever make it. But in 1970, a local promoter rented an east-end loft space and held a no-kidding cattle call for roller derby players.

The entrepreneur was the legendary, old-time PR man, Norman Olson. He started out in biz as a smart-aleck kid with a gossip column, gathering info by sidling up to gangsters and mouthing his trademark line: "So who do you hate?" Olson went on to a career in publicity, where he'd hold stunts involving tightrope walkers crossing high above Ste. Catherine. He had an aspiring poster girl "donate" her body to the McGill science department and had midgets in sandwich boards walk around downtown to promote products. But roller derby would be his highest-profile gig.

Resembling a bloodless version of the game depicted in the sci-fi flick *Rollerball*, the indoor sport was played on a prefabricated track that could be taken on the road. The athletes wore old-fashioned four-wheeled roller skates. By the late '60s, an aggressive version of the sport was a hit on American television. That's when it showed up in Montreal with Norman Olson's Canadian All Stars, which was broadcast on French-language TV's *Match sur Roulottes*.

At 24 hours a day, Olson's auditions lasted several days. Thousands came out hoping for a crack at sports stardom. Not many made the cut, but those who did played alongside Skinny Minny Miller, a black woman from Philadelphia who gained icon status here for serving savage straight arms to those brave enough to try passing. Eventually, the game fizzled out because it got too expensive to haul the track from city to city.

IT'S RAINING HASH

Montreal sports journalist Michael Farber, who now writes for *Sports Illustrated*, once described the outspoken Expos pitcher Bill Lee as "a cross between Albert Einstein and Robin Williams."

Lee, who was known as "the Spaceman" for his stories of sprinkling marijuana on breakfast cereal, made an appearance in the "Comedy of Sports" lineup at the 1991 Just For Laughs comedy festival. True to form, he was ready with a good stoner's tale:

"The first game I was pitching at Olympic Stadium was a 2-1 game against the Cubs, and these young fans kept running down to the dugout whenever I came off the mound and were throwing tin foil at me," Lee told a packed house at the old Club Soda back when it was still on Park Avenue. "The two things I hate are litter and Astroturf, so I picked up the tin foil. When I got to the clubhouse, I found out I had 21 grams of hash."

LOOK! UP IN THE SKY! IT'S A RICH GUY

Let's face it. Sometimes you're just not in the mood for making nice. You feel less like Jekyll, more like Hyde. You're mad as hell and want to shoot up the place like Rambo on diet pills.

Well, now you can. In just one session, **Bigfoot Paintball** will train you to be a crack helicopter soldier and then take you up in a specially-designed chopper to assault ground troops from the sky. Rat-tat-tat!

And at about $2,400 an hour plus tax, it's a steal — if you have an expense account (most bookings are made by corporations). If that's too steep for you, there are 25 fields for a ground-based battle among shacks, a fort, and a lake scattered with two dozen linked islands — for about $40.

Centre Récréatif Bigfoot Inc., St. Alphonse Rodriguez; 450/883-0000; bigfoot-paintball.com

It's hard to beat the Mont Tremblant International Youth Hostel for a cheap vacation — winter or summer. With rates of about $20 for a bed in a dormitory or $30 for a private room, you get a central village location with a view of a lake and mountains. Not to mention easy access to the Petit Train du Nord bike path and the No. 2 ski resort in Eastern North America. And right next door is the province's largest protected area, Parc du Mont Tremblant.

If you want to try cycling the vast trail networks, the hostel's Bicycle Package clocks in at about double the basic dorm rate, and includes a set of well-tuned wheels. During the winter, your basic Ski Package chops the cost of hitting the slopes. A shuttle bus to the lifts is part of the deal.

Culturally, the village outpunches its weight with galleries, festivals, performances, as well as a surprising range of shopping, services, cafés, restaurants, and dance clubs.

In the winter, you can ski, snowshoe, and snowmobile along groomed trails, as avid capitalists happily rent out any needed equipment. In the summer, the area is suited to cycling, horseback riding, fishing, swimming, canoeing, windsurfing, pedal boating, racquet sports, and hiking — particularly along the banks of the Rivière du Diable, a heartbreakingly beautiful place to be, especially when the leaves change colour.

The hostel is located at 2213 Chemin Principal, Mont Tremblant village. For less than forty bucks, a Hostelling International membership card is worth considering. Ask when you reserve by phone at 819/425-6008, or e-mail at info@hostellingtremblant.com. *hostellingtremblant.com*

Pedal Pushers

Photo: John David Gravenor

With more than 660 km (400 miles) of designated city paths, Montreal has been called the best bicycle city in the world. From lawyers to thieves, athletes to slobs – everybody loves the ample lanes on streets like Rachel and Brébeuf. And you can get to most city attractions and parks by bike. Some even ride through the snowiest depths of winter. You can ride to a ferry and visit the Boucherville Islands, cross Parc Jean Drapeau and head for vast stretches of the St. Lawrence Seaway via the ice bridge to the South Shore and take a spin around the F1 track. Or head up to suburban Laval, with its brand-new network of paths, many with quiet, riverside views and detours to the lower Laurentian mountains. **La Maison des Cyclistes** (514/521-8356, 800/567-8356; *velo.qc.ca*) can help get you started.

Anti-Bike Backlash

For one spring Sunday every year since 1985 cyclists have taken over 50 kilometers of local streets for the **Tour de l'Ile**. About 30,000 riders pay about $20 to join in the fundraising that helps Vélo Québec promote bike riding. But in recent years many motorists have bitterly complained of being inconvenienced by the event. Meanwhile, increasing numbers of big name politicians have sided with agitator Murray Levine's longstanding campaign to boycott the event until it agrees also to become a bike-a-thon to raise money for other charities.

POWER PEDALS

While electric cars may still be the fad of the future, two-wheeled versions are already catching on. More than two million electric bicycles are sold around the world every year. Quebec has not one but two manufacturers of power-assisted bicycles. The Mikado Volta is made by Procycle of Saint Georges and retails for about $1,800. Another company in Saint Georges, Groupe Procycle, makes the Elektron II (about $1,000) and the deluxe Volta ($1,800). All three are driven by an electric motor mounted on the rear hub.

HONEY OF A RIDE

After you've had enough of its beach, Oka Park is your starting point to embark on La Vagabonde bicycle trail, which winds through rural maple stands and honey farms, all the way to Saint Eustache about 50 km (30 miles) away. For more information, contact Oka Park (450/479-8365, 888/PARC OKA). You can also call the La Vagabond trail office (450/491-4444).

The Inside Volley

In 1973, legendary local lefty Robert "Bicycle Bob" Silverman helped establish the outdoor volleyball courts on a blip of greenery on Park Avenue, south of Duluth Street. It's easy to find the courts as they're backed by the spray-tagged, 19th-century walls of the Hôtel Dieu hospital to the east. The seven courts open at noon and close at twilight from mid-May to September and welcome anybody who just shows up and is willing to part with $2 to play all day. The courts buzz with activity as highly-competitive, beach-style players jockey for courts with the less-competent, more community-oriented six-on-sixers. Silverman says that proof of the benefits of the sport go beyond just fitness and fun: he reports that seven marriages got their starts on the courts, while only two fights have occurred in their long history.

Kayak King

Ilya Klvana, a McGill student from Côte des Neiges had never kayaked long distances when he built a cedar-strip kayak and popped it in the fast-running waters of British Columbia in May, 1999. Six-and-a-half months and 9,500 kilometers of paddling and painful portaging later, Klvana, packing a 200-year-old guidebook, finished his trip in chilly l'Anse-aux-Meadows, Newfoundland to become the first and only person ever to kayak Canada from west to east.

DIAMONDS AREN'T FOREVER

Not long ago, some recreation apparatchik down at City Hall decided to figure what kind of playing fields Montrealers wanted most. They found that 8,000 people had signed up for soccer — roughly the same number as played baseball. But city parks were lopsided in favour of baseball players, as 185 of them were equipped with baseball diamonds, while there were only 99 soccer pitches. So in a reverse build-it-and-they-will-come move, the city set about transforming 35 baseball areas into soccer fields, where young kids can perfect the essentials of the sport, like writhing in pain while faking an injury. Among the parks that made the switch are Oxford Park, Mackenzie King Park, Macdonald Park, parc St. Benoit, parc St. Donat, and parc St. Michel.

a place to bare their own

Toronto has its Hanlan's Point, Vancouver its Wreck Beach, but Montreal, in spite of its self-proclaimed libertarian bent, has no recognized, organized nude beach. So you'll have to settle on something a little less recognized and organized.

Head up to the beach at Oka Provincial Park, northwest of Montreal. Once you hit the sand, walk to your left around the point from the main beach until you see nude people enjoying the sun, a bracing zephyr tickling their peachfuzz.

Although the cops haven't cracked down on nudists since naked pioneer Gaetan Couture was arrested in his St. Jerome back yard in 1951, the occasional Oka nudist has stepped into hot water for inappropriate behaviour. In 1997, the mayor of Oka, Bernard Patry, bitterly complained about them. But enforcement went nowhere after a small number of tickets resulted in a public outcry.

Oka Park also offers camping and a popular beach for those not ready to strip to the bone. Find it 55 kilometres (33 miles) northwest of Montreal. Take Autoroute 13 or 15 North to Autoroute 640. Head west in the direction of St. Eustache. The road takes you right into the park.

While going bare is conditionally tolerated at a few locations, nudists have long pined for an official beach where they can hang their hats … and jeans and underwear and everything else. Some lobby for a location closer to the city – ideally something like the

beach on Ile Notre Dame. François Audet, president of Quebec's nudist association, says nudists should receive official sanction at least for security reasons.

Meanwhile, nudists have met discreetly every Sunday evening at the downtown YWCA *(corner of Crescent and René Lévesque)* since 1997. Admission is usually under $10.

ROUND THE WORLD AND FLAP AGAIN

Back in '76, the city was fluttering with countless red flags featuring the distinctive logo of the Montreal Olympic Games. They flew on flagpoles, at city hall, and tiny ones flapped from car antennas. But only one of them orbited the earth 286 times. Astronaut Dave Williams, who grew up in the West Island community of Beaconsfield, brought the flag with him during a 1998 NASA Space Shuttle mission. Now living in Texas, where he trains fellow astronauts, Williams told us that the flag's presence symbolized "that, with hard work and perseverance, maybe our dreams can come true." He later donated it to the Canadian Olympic team, which had it pinned up in the athletes lounge at the Sydney games.

Photo: John David Gravenor

To find out more about nudism in Quebec, contact the Quebec Federation of Naturism. *514/252-3014; fqn@fqn.qc.ca*

Some nearby nudist camps:

EASTERN TOWNSHIPS

Centre Vallée Rustique 2000

Come, naked ones, to this mountainside plateau, with a mature forest and walking trails. There's a pool, racquet sports, sauna, convenience store, laundry room, library, bar, and other facilities.
40 chemin des Bouleaux, Frelighsburg; 450/298-5372

LAURENTIANS / LANAUDIERE

Centre Naturiste Oasis

Not far from Montreal sits the Oasis, a family-oriented nudist community where some people live year-round. Sandy trails lead to a sandy beach that leads to a shallow, uh, sandy lake. Activities include a pool, racquet sports, volleyball, softball and special events like a corn roast (mid-August), Mini Halloween and Christmas in July.
7111 chemin Curé Barette #1, LaPlaine; 450/478-1929; centrenaturisteoasis.qc.ca

Domaine de l'Éden

Known for its Body Painting Festival, this resort 30 minutes north of the city offers watersports, mini golf, a corn roast (mid-August), and other events. Camping facilities include restaurant, community centre, whirlpool bath, and bar.
63 St. Stanislas, St. Lin Laurentides; 450/439-6012; domaineeden.qc.ca

MONTÉRÉGIE REGION

Centre Naturiste La Pommerie

This ecological-oriented nudist area occupies an impressive chunk of rustic nature that includes a vineyard, community garden, stables, and massage therapy centre, three pools, racquet sports, archery and a weekly wine tasting.
2914, route 209, St. Antoine Abbé, near the American border; 450/826-4723; pommerie.com

EVER LEAP A SHEEP?

Instead of explaining the cultural differences in Quebec, locals often say, "Vive la difference." There are so many unique traditions here like, say, jumping sheep. Really. For three seasons of the year, locals and visitors alike meet at the waterfront to jump over sheep.

But before you get the wrong idea — the "sheep" in this case is just French for whitecaps — *les moutons*. And the St. Lawrence River has an endless supply of those. So for about $40, you climb aboard Jack Kowalski's custom whitewater boat for a tour of the voracious Lachine Rapids. The company suits you up in waterproof gear, except when it's really hot. On those days you can wear your bathing suit under your life jacket. Saute Moutons is located by the Clock Tower in the Old Port.
514/284-9607; jet-boatingmontreal.com

Okay, Rock, Pull Over

Bob Martin of Montreal, an immigrant from Scotland, combined his love for curling with his knack for math and physics and – presto! – the mild-mannered accountant invented the Speed Trap, a $500 device that uses two boxes and a laser beam to measure the speed of curling stones "immediately, accurate, and easily." About half the national curling teams at the Salt Lake City Olympics had access to the units. The coaches say they're great, and scientists use them for ice-related research. There's more on Martin's website. *rockscience.qc.ca*

No Bigness Like Show Bigness

ANDRE THE GIANT

He portrayed a friendly giant in Rob Reiner's *The Princess Bride* and played the sasquatch on *The Six Million Dollar Man*. But the late André the Giant started his climb to fame right here in Montreal.

Born in France in 1946, André Rousimoff developed a condition known as giantism. He weighed more than 500 pounds at the time of his death in 1993. (His likeness became a popular underground image for snowboard and "sk8ing" enthusiasts.)

As one of the biggest stars of the (formerly named) Worldwide Wrestling Federation he had a perfect record until some high-profile losses to Hulk Hogan in the 1980s.

While he was fighting here – as Jean Ferré – in the early 1970s, locals used to see André driving around the city in a car that was missing the front driver's seat. Too tall for a normal car, he operated it from the back seat.

Curling Rinks

CENTRAL

Montreal West Curling Club
17 Ainslie Rd., Montreal W.;
514/486-5831

Outremont Curling Club
1325 Saint Viateur W.,
Outremont; 514/271-2310;
geocities.com/curlingoutremont

Royal Montreal Curling Club
1850 de Maisonneuve W., Montreal;
514/935-3411

Town of Mt. Royal
Curling Club
5 Montgomery Ave., Town of Mount
Royal; 514/733-7153

SOUTH SHORE

Mont-Bruno Curling Club
1390 Goyer, Saint Bruno; 450/653-
6913; curlingmontbruno.com

Otterburn Legion Curling Club
318 Connaught St., Otterburn Park;
450/467-0881

Saint-Lambert Curling Club
660 Oak St., Saint Lambert;
450/672-6990

Photo: John David Gravenor

WEST ISLAND

Baie-d'Urfé Curling Club

*20599 Lakeshore Rd., Baie d'Urfé;
514/457-5900; bdcc.n3.net*

Glenmore Curling Club

*120 Glenmore Rd., Dollard des
Ormeaux; 514/684-6350;
GlenmoreCurling.com*

Lachine Curling Club

*4105 Fort Rolland, Lachine;
514/637-9521; lachinecurling.com*

Pointe-Claire Curling Club

*250 Lanthier Ave., Pointe Claire;
514/695-4324;
pointeclairecurling.com/home.html*

**Sainte Anne-de-Bellevue
Curling Club**

*11 Tunstall Ave., Senneville;
514/457-5505*

One of the oddest parks in the city is the sculpture garden on the south side of René Lévesque, between Fort and St. Marc. The largest of the unusual sculptures looks like an unfinished version of the museum across the street, with sprawling foundations but no roof.

Not too many people visit this park; fewer know its name: **Esplanade Ernest Cormier** (pictured). Cormier was a Montreal architect and engineer whose prestigious designs include the main complex of Université de Montréal and his own celebrated home at the intersection of Pine and Cedar, which former Prime Minister Pierre Trudeau eventually bought and in which he died in 2000. Never crowded, this odd park with a mini-orchard is a nice secret spot to escape the hustle of Ste. Catherine Street a few steps to the north.

Speaking of local architects, here's another quirky spot. **The Macauslan Brewery and Terrace**, which serves refreshments on the Lachine Canal bike path, occupies the former site of the Maxwell Brothers' wood-finishing factory. Among the city's most successful architects, Thomas and W.S. Maxwell built some of our earlier great buildings, including the Montreal Museum of Fine Arts at the northwest corner of Sherbrooke and Crescent.

One of the finest surviving examples of the Maxwell brothers' wood interiors can be seen in the theatre of the former High School of Montreal (now the F.A.C.E. alternative school), on University between Sherbrooke and Milton. Actor Christopher Plummer (pictured), who grew up in Montreal, was among the budding thespians who trod those Maxwell boards.

Als Move in Mysterious Ways

If it wasn't for a certain Irish supergroup, the Alouettes would likely have been a distant CFL memory by now. In 1997, the Als were drawing near-empty houses at Olympic Stadium, their venue far east of downtown. Indeed, attendance woes at the Big O had contributed to the team's bankruptcy once before in the 1980s. (The team would resurface temporarily as the Concorde). But in '97, the reformed Als found themselves in the playoffs, earning them the right to play a home game against the B.C. Lions. One problem: Olympic Stadium was booked that day for a concert by Bono (pictured) and U2. The team came up with a plan to quickly upgrade their old downtown home, Percival Molson Stadium, and play the game there. The aging facility, which was named after an old-time Molson from the early 20th century – not the successful one by the same name who tragically shot himself in the early '60s – had been home to the team during its glory decades before. Although run-down, the mountaintop stadium with a view of the city skyline proved magic for the team, and it soon become their permanent home. Now Als games are routinely sold out and they have returned to prosperity. Thanks, Bono.

NEW WORLD RINKS

We see it again and again: Prairie upstarts curl on the world stage and win time after time. How soon they forget that Canada's curling roots were put down right here in Montreal. In fact, North America's very first curling association – the Montreal Curling Club – was established to meet demand in 1807. Now known as the Royal Montreal Curling Club, it was the first sporting club of any kind on the continent. During the late 18th and early 19th centuries, the game was chiefly played by Scottish immigrants on the frozen surface of the St. Lawrence River. Because of a constant shortage of imported granite stones, the first "stones" they used were forged from iron reclaimed from cannon balls. Some players preferred iron rocks well into the 20th century. Today, the game is mainly played indoors with standard stones and it has enjoyed a revival among young players. Check out Curling Quebec to know more.
888/292-2875; curling-quebec.qc.ca

Overhaul of Fame

Photo: John David Gravenor

BACKSTAGE FROM THE HABS

A tour of the **Bell Centre** is actually an educational, behind-the-scenes peek at a high-tech entertainment production facility. And Canadiens fans will enjoy it, too. You get to see multi-functional amphitheatre, home of the Canadiens hockey club, and site of major rock shows. You'll visit the Canadiens' Hall of Fame, television studios, a press conference room, luxury lounge, press gallery, artists' and corporate luxury suites, and the Habs' dressing room (during the off-season only). The tour costs less than $10 and lasts 1 hour 15 minutes. English tours run Monday through Sunday at 11:15am and 2:45pm. *at the foot of Stanley at 1260 La Gauchetière West; 514/925-5656, 800/363-3723*

For 75 seasons, before it was transformed into a gaudy entertainment palace in 2001, the Canadiens called the **Forum** their NHL home. The building, which was originally intended for the NHL's Montreal Maroons, replaced a rollerskating rink called The Forum. Since its construction in 1924 – in less than six months at a cost of $1.2 million – the Forum underwent many mutations. The first big renovation came in 1949, when a second-floor section was added to the original structure. But the hockey temple still looked pretty much unchanged when the Beatles played there on September 8, 1964.

After the Montreal world's fair came and went, the Forum's owners decided it was time to upgrade the building. So in 1968, they tore it apart, installing thousands of seats, ten corporate suites, and at last removed view-obstructing structural columns. Escalators on the south side of the building were illuminated to look like gigantic, crossed hockey sticks. The damage? A cool $9.5 million and by the time it was finished, not a single brick from the original arena remained – nothing but the original ice-refrigeration system and furnace.

Since 2001, the building has been home to the **Pepsi Forum Entertainment Centre**, featuring the 4,300-seat AMC movie megaplex, climbing walls, interactive games, restaurants, and an outdoor Walk of Fame saluting Canadiens stars (including Maurice "Rocket" Richard) and their 24 Stanley Cup victories. *2313 Ste. Catherine St. at the corner of Atwater; Atwater Metro; 514/93-FORUM; forum-pepsi.com*

pardon me boy,
is that the li'l train of the north?

Photo: John David Gravenor

It was the little train that couldn't. And cyclists are thankful it failed.

Most people don't remember the little railway line that ran through the rolling Laurentian hills. Known as the "P'tit Train du Nord" ("Li'l Train of the North"), the Canadian Pacific Railways line was shut down in 1989 after nearly 100 years of service.

As the "ski train," it was a favourite among the wooden-ski set who rode from downtown Montreal to the early downhill centres of the Laurentians.

After the train was gone, locals didn't know what to do with the old right-of-way. After the tracks were pulled up, a group of citizens set out to establish the longest "linear park" in North America at some 250 km (120 miles).

Stretching from St. Jérôme to Mont Laurier, cyclists and hikers use the trail in the warm months, while cross-country skiers and snowmobile freaks use it in the winter. The park wends alongside and through woods, agricultural landscapes, valleys, rivers, and lakes. Rest areas are set up along the way, and information panels provide details on local history and landmarks. Services include bike and ski rental, picnic and rest areas, restaurants, camping facilities, and free parking. Free guidebooks are available at tourism centres.

To reach the foot of the trail from Montreal, take Autoroute 15 North to St. Jérôme. Follow the signs to the free parking at the old station on rue de la Gare. There is even a shuttle service that brings you to a distant point from which you can cycle back to your car. *800/561-6673, 514/990-5625; laurentides.com*

OTHER TRAILS

Grandes Fourches

In the Eastern Townships, the 125 km (75 mile) route links the communities of Rock Forest, North Hatley, Lennoxville, and Sherbrooke. *800/561-8331, 450/297-0654; sders.com/tourisme*

For everything you wanted to know about cycling in Montreal, don't be shy to try one these resources:

Lachine Canal Bike Path
514/732-7303; poledesrapides.com

La Maison des cyclistes
at the corner of Rachel and Brébeuf streets; 514/521-8356, 800/567-8356; velo.qc.ca

Montréal Infotourist Centre
800/363-7777;
tourisme-montreal.org

Office du tourisme de Laval
450/682-5522, 800/463-3765;
tourismelaval.qc.ca

Piste des berges
514/732-7303

Société d'animation de la Promenade Bellerive
514/493-1967

MONTREAL CITY DRIVING RULES

Visitors who think Montreal is full of crazy drivers just don't get it: motorists on this island play by their own rules. A list of these tongue-in-cheek rules, complete with nuggets of wisdom, has been circulating on the Internet. Here's a sample:

Don't look pedestrians in the eye — that's a sure sign of driver weakness. Pretend they're not there and floor it.

Never use your direction signals. No self-respecting Montreal driver would surrender the power of surprise. The signals are just there for decoration.

Make way for the rusty clunker. You've got more payments at stake.

Just because you're swerving radically doesn't mean you're drunk. Even the cops know you're just avoiding the ubiquitous potholes.

Always pass on the right, unless the other driver gives you no other choice.

Always drive pedal to the metal, especially when it snows. If you slide off the road, somebody will turn up with a shovel.

Parc du Corridor Aérobique

Winding through all sorts of terrain — wilderness, lakes, rivers, and streams — this "aerobic corridor park" stretches over more than 33 kilometres (20 miles) along the old Canadian National railway bed. It passes through four municipalities and forms a loop with the larger P'tit Train du Nord trail. Open to cyclists and hikers three seasons of the year, it's left to skis and snowmobiles in winter. Admission and parking are free. Pamphlets are available through tourism offices. *800/561-6673; laurentides.com*

Park de la Rivière du Nord

Twenty-five scenic kilometres (15 miles) separated into easy and hard stretches. Wilson Falls is a great place to picnic. From Montreal take Autoroute 15 North to Exit 45 and follow signs. *1051 Blvd. International, Rural Route 2, Saint Jérôme*

Mont-Orford Provincial Park

A ski centre in the winter, this scenic park near the town of Magog has 50 km (30 miles) of trails for expert to novice riders with lots of rocks and, sometimes, mud. From Montreal, take Autoroute 10 east to the Mont Orford exit. About 90 minutes by car. *sepaq.com/en/index.html*

Mont-Tremblant Provincial Park

This is Quebec's first and largest provincial park. Seven bike trails criss-cross 58 km (35 miles) of lakes, rivers, and mountains. Open from early May until the first snowfall. La Diable trail, a family riverside favourite, is a 9 km (5 mile) round-trip, or about two hours. La Pimbina is more challenging, 26 km (15 miles) for die-hard cyclists. L'Assomption and La Cachée offer views on lakes and waterfalls. To get to La Diable entry point from Montreal, take Autoroute 15 North. (After Sainte Agathe, the 15 merges with Route 117.) Get off Route 117 at Saint Faustin Lac Carré, and head for Lac Supérieur. *800/665-6527; sepaq.com/en/index.html*

Ski Bromont

Offers more than 100 km (60 miles) of trails accessible by chairlift. Serious rides for hardcore downhillers. Located 45 minutes east of Montreal via Autoroute 10. Exit Bromont. Rental, lodging available. *866/BRO-MONT; skibromont.com/ang/velo*

Ski Mont Tremblant

Pay-to-use trail network with quad charilift to the summit. Great après-ski scene at the European-style village at the foot of the mountain. From Montreal, take Autoroute 15 North to Sainte Agathe. After Sainte Agathe, the 15 merges with Route 117. Continue on the 117 North past Saint Jovite. Two km (1.2 miles) after Saint Jovite, at the light, turn right on Montée Ryan (second Ultramar gas station on the left). Follow indications for Tremblant (about 10 km/6 miles). *866/836-3030; tremblant.com*

Lost Flora of Montreal

Four centuries have been hard on Montreal's natural habitat. Forests have been felled, rivers buried, meadows and thickets shoved aside for housing. Many plants and herbs disappeared from the landscape but they're not forgotten by McGill University, which has a world-class collection of specimens at the Macdonald College Campus. A key component of this collection of more than 130,000 specimens is made up of plants gathered by a young physician in the early 19th century. Andrew Holmes collected more than 500 specimens from pristine locations that have long since been transformed by civilization – bogs, trails, the St. Pierre River, Papineau's Wood. Many of the species he collected have disappeared entirely from the island. Before Holmes died in 1860, he donated his collection to McGill, which maintains it as part of the McGill University Herbarium, which operates an active program of research and exchange.
Room MS2-032, Macdonald-Stewart Building, 2111 Lakeshore Rd. Ste. Anne de Bellevue; 514/398-7851 ext. 7864; collections.ic.gc.ca/holmes

In Search of Strikes & Spares

Weathering the decline of the east end is an unself-consciously retro bowling alley on Aylwin Street, **Salle de Quilles Aylwin.** The tiny, immaculate, two-level, dozen-lane facility has been there "for over fifty years," according to the woman tending the steel grill at the snack bar. She says that dozens of bowlers scored 300s that year. We're sceptical. *1411 Aylwin; 514/521-7136*

SOME MORE BOWLING ALLEYS

Au Drome
16 alleys of duck-pin bowling.
5650 Iberville St. near Mount Royal; 514/521-7651

Boulevard Lanes
54 ten-pin and 18 duck-pin lanes. Open 24 hours two days a week (summer); four days the rest of the year.
4400 Jean Talon E. at Pie IX; 514/729-2829

Le Forum
Featuring 24 duck-pin lanes. In the heart of the Plateau Mont Royal at 920 St. Zotique E., (near St. Hubert) *274-0797.*

Paré Lanes

30 ten-pin lanes, arcade and billiard games, bumper bowling, restaurant, satellite TV, bar. Cosmos Bowling on weekends features sound-effects, music and high-tech lighting — the lanes and balls glow under black light. Special rates.

5250 Paré, 514/731 9626

Photo: John David Gravenor

Rose Bowl Lanes

This gem from the Golden Age of bowling offers 72 lanes, half ten-pin and half duck-pin. Open 24 hours a day, year-round.

6510 St. Jacques St. at Cavendish Blvd., 514/482-7200

Salon de Quilles International

26 computerized lanes with touchscreens. Pretty long hours.

6590 Park Ave. at the corner of Beaubien, 514/276-7222

A Track By Any Other Name Would Still Smell

The old Blue Bonnets raceway was born way back in 1840, on a far-off location near the steep hill that links Ville St. Pierre to Montreal West. The track was named after a nearby pub that was run by a local Scotsman.

In 1953, thoroughbred owners deserted the track, by this time moved to its present location just west of the Décarie Expressway, rather than run their horses at night under the newfangled lights. It has remained strictly harness racing ever since.

Blue Bonnets was renamed La Piste Ville Marie in 1966 but everybody just ignored that. So more recently they dubbed it again as **Le Hippodrome**.

But a parcel of land like that is bound to get developers' fingers twitching. In 1947, there was a plan to convert the track into 1,100 apartments for war vets. In 1973, businessman Robert Campeau announced plans for a $10-million, mixed-use site with a mall, offices, and apartments where the parking lot is now. (There are now quite a few stores on the western half, anchored by factory outlets for retailers like Roots, Pier 1, and even a Walmart.)

Recently, city councillor Marvin Rotrand tried to get the racing action shipped off to the suburbs — sticky beer floors and all — so the city can jam 10,000 new residents on the site.

Money is still the place's lifeblood. In order to keep the track running, governments have lost more cash on the site than have all the dyslexic handicappers in the world. And it's all to protect the 10,000 jobs of Quebec's horse-racing industry.

Dining

MERCI! Grâce à vous on célébre notre
70 ieme anniversaire

THANKS! To all our customers...you made it possible!

Photo: John David Gravenor

Maria Francesca LoDico is the former restaurant critic and food columnist for *Hour*. Most recently, her food and travel writing has appeared in *enRoute* and *Saturday Post*. A collection of her sensuous and mouth-watering food essays will be published next year. She is currently developing a television show about food and ethnicity and writing a memoir about growing up in Sicily.

Maria Francesca LoDico's ultimate insider guide

I was born hungry.
— Julia Child

Yes, Virginia, there once was a world without restaurants. The word itself comes from the French *restaurer*, to restore. In the early 18th century, chocolate and red meat were thought of as "restaurants" capable of restoring lost strength. That was before modern eateries, when housewives bought bread, roast mutton, and fritters at inns, taverns, markets, and bakeries. The first restaurant came into being in 1765 when a Parisian bouillon-seller named Boulanger opened for business. He placed a sign on his door that beckoned in Latin, "Come unto me, all you whose stomachs are aching, and I will restore you." And the rest is culinary history.

Montrealers have always taken Boulanger's message to heart. We are a culture that is obsessed with food and we *love* dining out. Montreal is, after all, a world-renowned gastronomic capital with a multitude of restaurants, shops, and markets to support its vibrant food culture. Once, Montreal was thought of as Canada's only gastronomic destination. Today, some argue, we've been bumped off our lofty perch by Toronto and upstart Vancouver. Still, Montreal is a food lovers' paradise on so many levels. Bakeries produce buttery croissants and crunchy baguettes, markets feature Quebec's regional bounty, delis serve artery-clogging smoked meat, *casse-croûtes* dish out steamies, cafés kick-start our mornings with deluxe java fixes, *fromageries*, *charcuteries*, *boucheries*, chocolatiers: Montreal's got all of that and more.

The French restaurant has the oldest historical roots in Montreal and many venerable institutions are part of the very fabric of the city. So French cuisine has not fallen out of favour here as it has elsewhere. However, a dining scene long dominated by several variations on the French theme has given way to a more complex brew of ethnic restaurants. Further spicing things up is a brat pack of young cooks lead by Fred Morin, Jean-François Vachon, and Martin Picard. We even have a cuisine to call our own. The celebrated Toqué, L'eau à la Bouche, and La Chronique are at the forefront of the homegrown "*nouvelle* Quebec cuisine," a reinterpretation of French "*cuisine du tirroir*" (traditional farmhouse cooking) based on the use of regional, seasonal produce and the development of dishes inflected with Quebec's particular cultural influences. *Nouvelle*

Quebec cuisine has made stars out of notable chefs Normand Laprise, Anne Desjardins, and Marc de Canck.

What follows is a selective list to help you navigate Montreal's tremendous dining scene. This guide is by no means comprehensive and I encourage you to vehemently disagree with my suggestions and modify them according to your own experience and palette. I love nothing better than a debate about food because eating is intensely personal. "Taste is an intimate sense. We can't taste things at a distance," says Diane Ackerman in *A Natural History of the Senses*. When a meal lets you down, it breaks your heart because, as Boulanger figured out hundreds of years ago, we turn to food for sustenance and comfort and, in his famous words, to be restored.

So on with some restorative advice! *Bon appétit!*

The Problem With Menus

Usually, "missspeellings" and "gramertacal" mistakes are a sign of sloppiness. But in Montreal, "toasts," "nutmegs," and "fishes" are often the sign of idiosyncratic translation. Also, an "entrée" is often an appetizer, not to be confused for a main dish.

Semantics, Semantics

Do not identify yourself as a gourmet when you might in fact be a glutton or a greedyguts. From the *Larousse Gastronomique*: "There is a hierarchy which starts at the bottom with the *goinfre* (greedyguts), progresses to the *goulu* (glutton), then the *gourmand*, the *friand* (epicure), and the *gourmet*, and finally the *gastronome*. In 1835, the Académie Française made the word *gastronomie* official: it therefore rapidly gained currency despite being rather pedantic and unwieldy." Got that?

UN HOTCHICKEN

Laurier Barbecue is rumoured to have invented the type of hot chicken sandwich we like best: with barbecue sauce and peas on top. *381 Laurier W., 514/273-3671*

what Montrealers talk about when they talk about food

"We suffer from too much choice. Sometimes Sandra [his wife] and me spend an hour just trying to decide where to go. She'll say to me, 'Where do you wanna eat.' And I'll say, 'I don't know. Where do *you* wanna go?' And she'll say '*I* don't know. *You* decide.' We're so spoiled.

We go to Florida for vacation and easily spend $100 on bad pizza and salad. That's crazy. So every day I just have a big, cheap breakfast, like at Denny's. But we suffer because it's not Montreal. Nah, there's no place like home."
– Stefano Guerra, owner and manager of Café Via Crescent

"Montreal was from the beginning cross-cultural. The city has that history, a strong influence coming in from other places. And, it's a culture that likes to go out. And, we have long winters, which means the thing you want most is comfort in food. So we developed high standards, one of the best standards of international cuisine in North America."
– Pierre-Emmanuel Moyse, a Montreal lawyer who hails from France and likes very stinky cheeses

the quintessential Montreal

NOUVELLE QUÉBEC CUISINE

Toqué!

Normand Laprise has been hailed a culinary genius, our very best and most innovative chef at the forefront of nouvelle Québec cuisine. Toqué's seasonal ingredient-based menu is a fusion of various confluences. Signature dishes: salmon tartare, salads of greens and herbs produced by organic farmer Pierre-André Daignault, foie gras Toqué, venison from the famed Boileau farm, Quebec lamb. Casual service with a friendly and informative staff in a funky setting.
3842 St. Denis, 514/499-2084

THE FRENCH RESTAURANT

French cuisine falls into several categories. *Haute cuisine* goes back to Louis XIV and his infamous 12-hour feasts at Versailles during the 19th century. This traditional or classical French food features the very rich and elaborate dishes described by Escoffier.

Cuisine bourgeoise is the French homecooking served at most bistros or brasseries and featured in Julia Child's *Mastering the Art of French Cooking*.

Nouvelle cuisine only dates back to the 1970s. It goes against the richness and elaborateness of haute cuisine and is in favour of fresh ingredients and natural flavours.

Chez La Mère Michel

Owner Micheline Delbuguet is the doyenne of Montreal's French dining scene. Her Belle Époque townhouse evokes the past as does an *haute cuisine* menu right out of the *Larousse Gastronomique*. Buttery sauces rule supreme as do *coquilles* St. Jacques, *coq au vin*, and elegant desserts like Grand Marnier soufflé.
1209 Guy, 514/934-0473

BEST MARKET CUISINE

La Chronique

Marc de Canck is renowned for his exceptional use of the freshest market ingredients. His fish, seafood, and sweetbreads are a triumph as is the crème brulée trio — chocolate, coffee, and lemongrass/star anise. With a wine list to match.
99 Laurier W., 514/271-3095

The **Jean Talon Market** *(7075 Casgrain, 514/277-1588)* is Montreal's shining glory of fresh produce and regional specialties like maple syrup and apple cider. Honourable mention goes to **Capitol** *(158 Place du Marché du Nord, 514/661-9306)* for meat, game, poultry, deli meats, Italian provisions, and gourmet take-out, **Fromagerie Hamel** *(220 Jean Talon E., 514/272-1161)* for local and imported cheese and **Un, Deux, Trois** *(7010 Casgrain, 514/803-3673)* for sublime, orgiastic truffles with flavours like lavender and port/blue cheese. Worth checking out are the nearby **Anatol Spices** *(6822 St. Laurent, 514/276-0107)* where everything is sold by the gram and Italian foodstuff at **Milano** *(6862 St. Laurent, 514/273-8558)*.

Le Paris

40 years of haute cuisine at its most traditional: cod brandade, headcheese vinaigrette, eggs mayonnaise, tripe à la mode.
1812 St. Catherine W., 514/937-4898

Les Cheênets

Renowned for its 50,000 bottles of wine, glittery dining room, and waiters in tuxedos. Michel Gillet's menu stars frog's legs, Dover sole *meunière*, and crêpes Suzette.
2075 Bishop, 514/844-1842

THE BISTRO

No city (other than Paris, that is) does a bistro quite like Montreal. **L'Express** couldn't exist anywhere else. It's a little bit of Paris in Montreal, this city's bistro *par excellence*, the epitome of chic with its checkered floors, zinc bar, and mirrors. Welcoming jars of home-preserved *cornichons*, Dijon mustard, and baguette hint at the great bistro favourites to come: *pot au feu*, braised veal cheeks, steak-*frites* — the fries are served with mayonnaise. Cap off your meal with *crème caramel* and an *allongé*. *Et quelle surprise*, L'Express is relatively inexpensive given chef Joel Chapoulie's fabulous food. Montreal at its dining essence. *3927 St. Denis, 514/845-5333*
Au Bistro Gourmet *(2100 St. Mathieu, 514/846-1553)* offers the fanciest of experiences while **Au Petit Extra** *(1690 Ontario E., 514/527-5552)* offers one of the most romantic gilt-framed rooms. The 26-seat **Le Bistingo** *(1199 Van Horne, 514/270-6162)* is the coziest. All serve hearty standards like cassoulet, duck confit, and bavette. **Fouquet's** *(2180 de la Montagne, 514/284-2132)* falls in the great tradition of the elegant Parisian brasserie with shining takes on *cuisine bourgeoise*. **La Gaudriole** (825 Laurier E., 514/276-1580) is unpretentious and chef Marc Vezina proffers the highest of gourmet pleasures at bargain prices.

Photo: John David Gravenor

It's bring-your-own-booze, silly. The BYOB resto is such a phenomenon in Montreal and Prince Arthur (between St. Laurent and Carré St. Louis) and Duluth (east of St. Laurent) are BYOB central. Unfortunately, these restaurant meccas are dominated by Greek feeding troughs. For a decent BYOB experience, drop by an **SAQ**, the Quebec wine, spirits, and beer commission *(3565 St. Laurent, 514/842-1660 and other locations)*, and dine at *brochetterie* **Le Jardin de Panos** *(521 Duluth E., 514/521-4206)*. Of the few French bistros nestled here, **La Colombe's** *(554 Duluth E., 514/849-8844) table d'hôte* is the most promising.

For a terrific BYOB outing, try **Le P'tit Plateau** *(330 Marie Anne E., 514/282-6342)*, a corner-street bistro with a tin pressed ceiling and toqued cooks facing the room in an open kitchen. Sample menu: kidney stew, rabbit terrine, grilled onglet with blue cheese and pine nuts.

S M O K E D   M E A T

Schwartz's Montreal Hebrew Delicatessen

When referring to "the legendary Montreal smoked meat," we're talking about Schwartz's dry-cured beef brisket prepared in the original smoker used by Reuben Schwartz himself in 1930. Hesitate when asked "lean, medium, fat?" and the waiter decides for you. Schwartz's slices it oh so

Photo: John David Gravenor

BEST PLACE TO CELEBRATE YOUR THESIS DEFENSE – IF YOUR ADVISOR IS FOOTING THE BILL

Le Caveau

Housed in quaint Victorian building. French *cuisine bourgeoise* boasts traditional dishes like escargot, rack of lamb, and sweetbreads. Patronized by profs from nearby McGill and Concordia. Conversations sometimes recall a hilarious spoof in *The Onion* of today's critical practices about a Harvard student "unable to restrain his reflexive impulse to deconstruct": "I just wanted to order some food from Burrito Bandito. Next thing I know, I'm analyzing the menu's content as a text, or 'text,' subjecting it to a rigorous critical reevaluation informed by Derrida, De Man, etc. derived from the cultural signifiers evoked by the menu, or 'menu.' Man, I've got to finish my dissertation before I end up in a rubber room." *2063 Victoria (downtown), 514/844-1624*

BEST RESTAURANT TO GO TO AFTER PLAYING HOCKEY

Momesso Café

Named after owner and former hockey player Sergio Momesso. You're here for the espresso and sausage subs hot off the grill.

5562 Upper Lachine Road, 514/484-0005

BEST PLACE TO GO DURING A BLIZZARD AND WHAT TO ORDER

Café Santropol

The snow is coming down fast, it's -45 with the windshield factor, and you're ... accchoooo, sniffle, sniffle. Getting stranded at Santropol is just like being at home. Share a humungous sandwich and a pot of tea. In summer, Santropol boasts Montreal's Eden of garden terraces.

3990 St. Urbain, 514/842-3110

Photo: John David Gravenor

thin and layers great heapings on rye. Best with a Mrs Whyte's pickle, Cott's Black Cherry Coke, and french fries. The char-grilled steak comes with a side dish of liver and a frankfurter. I'm serious.
3895 St. Laurent, 514/842-4813

THE MAIN A.K.A. ST. LAWRENCE

Around St. Laurent just north of Prince Arthur is a life-altering experience of food shops. It's the smells that hit you first, smoked meat and schnitzel and barbecue chicken and roasting coffee beans. **La Vielle Europe** *(3855 St. Laurent, 514/842-5773)* leads the pack for cheese, sausage, and preserves, **Zinman & Fils** *(102 Roy E., 514/843-6652)* for artisanal poultry, fowl, and rabbit, **Hungarian & German Meat Market & Delicatessen** *(3843 St. Laurent, 514/844-6734)* and **Slovenia** *(3653 St. Laurent, 514/842-3558)* for smoked bacons, sausages, dried chabay, and specialty items, and **St. Lawrence Bakery** *(3830 St. Laurent, 514/845-4536)* for challah, marble and black Russian bread, and poppyseed cake.

Photo: John David Gravenor

BAGELS

Fairmount Bagel Factory & St. Viateur Bagel Shop

It's often said that in this bagel-crazy town, debating the merits of the Fairmount "beigel" versus a St. Viateur "bugel" is a serious, even rabbinical question. There's nothing more Montreal than the sight of a worker at either 24-hour shop sliding a 10-foot *shibba* out of a wood-fired brick oven with two dozen crackling-hot bagels. Nope, they're nothing like New York's: they've got a charm all their own and "white" means sesame while "black" means poppyseed.
74 Fairmount W., 514/272-0667; 263 St. Viateur W., 514/276-8044

All About Kosher

The European Jews who settled here in the early 20th century also brought us a few kosher restaurants. **El Morocco** *(3450 Drummond, 514/844-6888)* is popular for family celebrations, hinting at the exotic with its low tables and tent-like ceilings. Sample menu: couscous, tagines, filo roll-ups. **Exodus** *(5395 Queen Mary, 514/483-6610)* also features Moroccan cuisine, **Casalinga** *(5095 Queen Mary, 514/738-5772)* offers Italian fare, and **Pizza Pita** *(5710 Victoria in Côte-des-Neiges, 514/731-7482)* makes a delectable slice.

Our Daily Bread

Expat Montealers lament the difficulty of finding good bread where the ubiquitous Wonderbread rules.

Le Fromentier *(1375 Laurier E., 514/527-3327)* will make you forget all other bread. The artisanal, organic bakery has a selection of about 40 baked goods including pizza, *fougasse*, and *feuillettes* made from traditional and wild grains. Baker Benoit Fradette describes his place as a studio where he practices the philosophical alchemy of yeast and flour.

Première Moisson's crusty baguettes are top-rated. Also renowned for their homemade preserves, take-out, cakes, and pastries. Locations include: Central Station, Jean Talon Market, Atwater Market.

CROISSANTS

Butter-infused, crispy, flaky, golden-brown. The very best at **Pâtisserie Duc de Lorraine** *(5002 Côte-des-Neiges Rd., 514/731-4128)*, **Pâtisserie de Gascogne** *(4825 Sherbrooke St. W., 514/932-3511 and 237 Laurier W., 514/490-0235)*, **Pâtisserie Belge** *(3485 Park, 514/845-1245)*, **Au Bon Croissant** *(2160 St. Mathieu, 514/935-7846)*, and **Pâtisserie Bruxelloise** *(860 Mont-Royal E., 514/523-2751)*.

BEST PLACES TO LET THE FOLKS TAKE YOU (OVER $15/PERSON)

Gibby's

Rustic steakhouse in Old Montreal with several roaring fireplaces. For special celebrations, Gibby's makes a big hoopla with cakes and sparklers. *298 Place d'Youville, 514/282-1837*

Mikado

Just in case the parental unit is squeamish about raw fish, Chef Mikio Owaki offers over 35 cooked Japanese dishes. The folks can wet their feet on sushi and sashimi or simply order teriyaki dishes, marinated grilled meats, and stir-fries. *368 Laurier W., 514/279-4809*

Photo: John David Gravenor

Thailande

Excellent fish and seafood, soupes and noodles in a casual setting. *88 Bernard W., 514/271-6733*

BEST PLACE TO TAKE THE FOLKS (UNDER $15/PERSON)

Amelios

Pizza (choice of whole wheat crust) and pasta in a cozy neighbourhood resto. Non-smoking.

201 Milton, 514/845-8396

Terrasse Lafayette

Greek favourites and pizza at cozy neighbourhood brochetterie with vast terrace.

250 Villeneuve W., 514/288-3915

BEST PLACE TO TAKE GRANDMA

Café de Paris, Ritz Garden

Real silverware, crystal, and china and an old-fashioned tea service. Granny will be tickled pink by the waterfall and baby ducklings in the pond. In winter, brunch or lunch inside. Casual French menu.

Ritz-Carlton Hotel, 1228 Sherbrooke W., 514/842-4212

POUTINE

Say it loud and proud: *"Poutine! La poutine, ça c'est le Québec!* (Poutine! Poutine – now that's Quebec!)" A tower of french fries topped with cheese curds and smothered with hot gravy. Best served in a Styrofoam container. With a *Journal de Montréal*. The city's most celebrated chefs make gourmet versions and it's on the menu at Burger King. Sidle up to the counter at the following and place your order: *"Poutine! La poutine!"* **La Belle Province** *(1216 Peel, 514/878-8020, 481 St. Catherine W., 514/288-1736, and various locations)* and **LaFleur** *(3620 St. Denis, 514/848-1804 and various locations).*

Blue collar joints La Belle Province and LaFleur are also famous for another quintessential Montreal meal: two steamies (hotdogs), fries, and a coke.

DAVID MCMILLAN'S GOURMET POUTINE

Ingredients
1 cup duck gravy
2 large potatoes cut ⅓" x 2½"
Stilton
Fresh chives, finely chopped

Fry potatoes until golden brown. Drain well on paper towels. Stack them into a 4-6" tower with a hollow centre. Fill the centre with Stilton. Top with chives. Pour the sauce over the tower. Serves 2.

Photo: John David Gravenor

Photo: John David Gravenor

Even if you've never been to **Wilensky's Light Lunch**, every Montrealer has through osmosis. This is partly because it was used as a set in the film version of Mordecai Richler's *The Apprenticeship of Duddy Kravitz*. The 70-year-old lunch counter has been everything from a cigar emporium to a barber shop. There's only one thing to order: The Special, a grilled salami and bologna sandwich. Catch it as it comes whizzing down the counter with a cherry coke. *34 Fairmount W., 514/271-0247*

Other food memories stored in Montreal's collective unconscious: chomping on **Coco Ricco** barbecue chicken sandwiches *(3907 St. Laurent, 514/849-5554)* or **Dic Ann Hamburgers** *(10910 Pie-IX)*; 3am binges at **The Main**; admiring pyramids of fresh fruit at the **Jean Talon Market**; getting on the bus with the singing driver who gives away jellybeans.

You go to **Ben's Delicatessen** *(990 de Maissonneuve W., 514/844-1000)*, a 1908 landmark, to pay homage to a bit of the past. Autographed photos of stars like Raveen and Liberace hark back to Ben's heyday.

Canada's last drive-in is **Orange Julep** *(7700 Décarie, 514/738-7486)*. The Small O (it's 60-ft round and made of orange fibreglass) is as recognizable as the Big O. Named after the frothy orange drinks

Photo: John David Gravenor

served with steamies, burgers, and grilled-cheese sandwiches. Waitresses in minis roller-skate up to your car to take your order. The only problem is that they're only open during the summer.

Montreal Pool Room *(1200 St. Laurent)* is a temple dedicated to the cult of *le steamie* and *pourqwhy pas*? Hotdog and bun are steamed instead of grilled. Located in the red light district since 1912. Pool is no longer played here, so for sport join the hooker and cop making nice while scoffing down steamies topped with relish, cabbage, and onion.

In decor and 'tude, **Spirite Lounge** *(1205 Ontario E.,*

BEST ROMANCE-ON-A-BUDGET (UNDER $20/PERSON)

Coffee/Tea/Me

Photo: John David Gravenor

Coffee, tea, or me dates are popular with Montreal's café culture. The wraparound terrace at **La Croissanterie Figaro** *(5200 Hutchison, 514/278-6567)* is host to a vibrant summer scene while the interior of art deco statues, marble-topped tables, and copper pans oozes warmth on a snowy winter's day. Go skating at the nearby St. Viateur park and warm-up here with *cafés au lait* and *chocolatines*. A second location *(3575 Park, 514/849-4890)* is in the same mall as rep theatre Cinéma du Parc. **La Petite Ardoise** *(222 Laurier W., 514/495-4961)* is a brick-walled café with classic home-made desserts like *tarte tatin* and *crème brulée*.

Olive et Gourmando *(351 St. Paul W., 514/350-1083)* in Old Montreal is simply exquisite. Vahlrona chocolate banana brioche, Belgian chocolate pecan cookies, classic cinnamon buns, olive baguette, foccacia, Cajun chicken/guacamole/mango panini, Illy coffee. Bike-ride down the Lachine Canal and make your way back to Olive et Gourmando.

Brodino *(174 St. Viateur W., 514/271-1844)* is delightful for its solid wooden counter where you can sit close to your date and accidentally bump knees. Italian-style "sangwiches," as my cousin Joey likes to say, hearty soups, kick-ass espresso, and brownies.

Pack up one-of-a-kind sandwiches – roast beef/parmesan/carpaccio, marinated goat cheese/turkey/Stilton sauce – from **La Foumagerie** *(4906 Sherbrooke W., 514/482-4100)* and picnic at Westmount Park or the mountain.

514/522-5353) is the Black and Blue Ball all year round. The flamboyant vegetarian resto is decorated with tin foil, lots of it, and polyester. Once you're seated, you are accosted by a waiter who tells you that there is only one choice, "Okay? And if you don't finish everything, you will be fined $2 which we match and give to charity. You get no dessert." And if you don't finish your dessert, "you are banished from the restaurant forever!" Oh spank me, please!

quintessential Quebec in Montreal

Photo: John David Gravenor

In my favourite review of *Goldmember, salon.com* made a case for the "liberating gusto" of toilet humour. So this dining chapter comes complete with a toilet gag. In high school, the most anticipated lunch special included *fèves au lard* (baked beans with maple syrup) so that those nasty boys could let lose with all manner of flatulence. After lunch, it was phhhhht! and phhhhht! And it's often said that a quintessential Québécois meal wouldn't be complete without *fèves au lard* and a bit of phhhhht!

Authentic Québécois cuisine is hearty indeed, also featuring pea soup, *tourtière* (meat pie), pig's feet, *cretons* (ground pork with lard), *pâté chinois* (shepherd's pie), *ragoût de boulettes* (meatball stew), and *pudding chomeur* (poor man's pudding).

These eateries are located in French neighbourhoods and offer homey renditions. Such sundries as pizzaghetti are not strictly speaking Québécois and can be found in establishments serving *"mets canadien."*

Chez Clo
3199 Ontario E., 514/522-5348

La Binerie Mont-Royal
367 Mont-Royal E., 514/285-9078

Ma-am-m Bolduc!
4351 Delorimier, 514/527-3884

most romantic rooms

Casa Napoli

For the couple with a sense of humour. Enormous replicas of ancient Roman statues adorn this place. Reserve La Grotta – a table for two in a cave – for an absolutely kitschy, but private, Italian affair.
6728 St. Laurent, 514/274-4351

Laloux

For the French kissers. Dubbed "Paris on Pine," the setting couldn't be more gorgeous and you will feel absolutely gorgeous. André Besson's *nouvelle cuisine* is just as sophisticated – *foie gras*, scallop mousse, salmon and caviar potato crêpe. Share Le Grand Dessert, a sampling from the sweet menu. With a wine list to match.
250 Pine E., 514/287-9127

Le Lutétia

For the lush-ious couple. Begin with Happy Hour in the hotel's sumptuous lobby – crystal chandeliers, a fountain, a baby grand. Afterwards, Eric Gonzalez's sumptuous nouvelle cuisine awaits you in Le Lutétia's positively baroque setting of cherub frescoes and upholstered tapestry. A must: pressed duck, the house specialty. Exemplary wine list.
Hôtel de la Montagne, 1430 de la Montagne, 514/288-5656

Maiko Sushi

For the geisha in you. Subdued blue and salmon décor with a ceremonial kimono adorning one wall. A series of interlocking dining rooms plus one tatami room and a sushi bar. Fine tempura and Japanese specialties. Draft sake and Japanese beer.
387 Bernard Ave. W., 514/490-1225

BEST FIRST DATE RESTOS

Pushap

Saturday night ritual begins with dinner at Pushap followed by disco bowling, glitter ball and all, at **Paré Lanes** *(5250 Paré, 514/731-9626)*. Pushap specializes in homestyle vegetarian Punjabi food and sweets sold by the pound.
5195 Paré, 514/737-4527

Bangkok

Don't let Bangkok's location in a downtown mall fool you. Somphop Vichenker prepares cheap but exemplary pad thai, green curry chicken, barbecue duck with coconut milk. After your meal, shoot pool or go bowling (with balls that glow in the dark) at **Sharx**, on the main floor of Le Foubourg.
2nd Floor, 1616 St. Catherine W., 514/282-5757

BEST MOVIE DATE RESTO

Star of India

After catching a movie at a downtown megaplex, share scrumptious butter chicken, spicy madras curries, and tandoor specialties.
1806 St. Catherine W., 514/932-8330

BEST PLACE FOR EXCHANGING FLUIDS ... SO TO SPEAK

FonduMentale

In a century-old house with original woodwork. Classic fondues – Swiss cheese, Chinese, wild game, chocolate. The first to lose the dunk picks up the tab. In the middle of the meal, have a *"coup de milieu"* (a shot of Kirsch). Afterwards, kiss your date.
4325 St. Denis, 514/499-1446

BEST RESTOS FOR INTRODUCING YOUR NEW MATE TO FAMILY AND FRIENDS

Think of tapas (Spanish & Portuguese) and mezze (Mediterranean & Middle Eastern) as a kind of nibbling to accompany copious amounts of alcohol – wine, sherry, and sangria with tapas and ouzo with mezze. Typical dishes: dolma, Spanish omelet, broad beans, tripe, spicy snails. Sure to be the next big thang.

Feast on mezze at **Rumi** *(5198 Hutchison, 514/490-1999)* and **Ouzéri** *(4690 St. Denis, 514/845-1336)*; tapas at **Casa Tapas** *(266 Rachel E., 514/848-1063)* and **Tasca** *(172 Duluth Ave. E., 514/987-1530)*.

Le Petit Moulinsart

For romantics who don't wanna grow up. Characters from the French comic strip *Tintin* decorate this Belgian bistro. Have your brewski – the lively bar offers some 150 brands – with *moules et frites* (mussels and fries).
139 St. Paul W., 514/843-7432

Ristorante Da Vinci

For the "he's into sports and she's not" couples. This is where the Habs dine after home games. So the guy gets to check out the Canadiens memorabilia. And the girl? She gets to enjoy a cozy dinner with her big guy at the reserved table by the fireplace or the corner one overlooking the garden. On the menu: fresh oysters, risotto, gnocchi. Excellent Italian wine list.
1180 Bishop, 514/874-2001

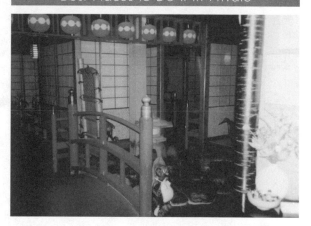

Best Places to Do It in Private

Call around to your favourite places and ask how they can accommodate you for a private affair. In a pinch, inquire about the tatami rooms at sushi emporium **Katsura** *(2170 de la Montagne, 514/849-1172)* or the very kitschy **Tokyo Sukiyaki** *(7355 Mountain Sights, near Jean Talon, 514/737-7245)*. **Prato** *(3891 St. Laurent, 514/285-1616)* makes terrific thin-crust pizza and pasta and has an entire back section available. **Le Paris Beurre** *(1226 Van Horne, 514/271-7502)* serves up confident cuisine bourgeoise and can accommodate up to 35 people in a private room.

Maeve Haldane, restaurant critic for *Hour*, sums up the appeal of dinner dates: "Eating with someone is a nice way to test the waters. Let's say you're sharing a huge plate of sushi. Is the other person heavy on the wasabi, afraid of the pickled ginger? Will they offer you the last piece of salmon maki? Do they like to watch you eat? After all, to be interested in food is to be interested in life."

Alep *(199 Jean Talon E., 514/270-6396)* is an Armenian-Syrian resto by the Jean-Talon Market. Make a meal of delicious starters such as *mouhamara*, *moussaka* and *sabanegh* or feast on exemplary grilled meats.

Au Messob D'Or *(5690 Monkland Ave., 514/488-8620)* is Montreal's oldest Ethiopian restaurant. Feed your date morsels of *injera*, an enormous flatbread covered with Ethiopian stew. Tear off a piece of the *injera*, roll up some of the stew, and pop it into your date's mouth.

Bombay Mahal *(1001 Jean Talon W., 514/273-3331)* and **Punjabi Palace** *(920 Jean Talon E., 514/495-4075)* offer unadorned Indian homecooking in the heart of a busy south-Asian neighbourhood. Savoury lassis, chana samosas, tandoor dishes, and curries at bargain prices.

Jardin du Cari *(12 St. Viateur W., 514/495-0565)* is a Guyanese/Caribbean resto where you can feast on roti with hot lemon sauce, curries, and patties. Caribbean soft drinks and peanut punch also available.

Pho Bang New York *(970 St. Laurent, 514/954-2032)*: sweating over tonkinese soup in a cramped Chinatown resto is about as good as foreplay gets.

take-out love

Batory Euro-Deli

Pierogis and blintzes, borscht, cabbage rolls — comfort food at its best. Eat in (there are only four tables) or take-out and get to know each other at home.
115 St. Viateur W., 514/948-2161

BEST RESTO IF RELATIONSHIP IS PROGRESSING SATISFACTORILY

Le Passe-Partout

Chef-baker James MacGuire's Passe-Partout is only opened a few days a week, so snag a reservation for a truly unique gourmet dining experience. MacGuire's commitment to light French cuisine with flawless technique is unmatched. Wonderful duck and scallops, spectacular cheese board of raw milk, goat, and blue, fantastic homemade ice creams. Small but thoughtful wine selection.
3857 Décarie, 514/487-7750

Worth Renting a Car For

Two gourmet experiences of the highest caliber are just a bit of a drive out of Montreal. They come with a hefty price-tag: dinner for two approximately $250-$300. But splurge and make an unforgettable weekend of it at these country inns.

Auberge Hatley *(325 Chemin Virgin, North Hatley, 800/336-2451)* offers a gorgeous view of Lac Massawippi and surrounding gardens and hills. Chef Alain Labrie makes excellent use of the herbs and greens from the Auberge's own greenhouse. Inventive modern French cuisine. Great cheese course of local and imported raw-milk beauties. Outstanding cellar. Dinner jackets are required. 1½-hour drive from downtown Montreal.

L'Eau à la Bouche *(3003 St. Adèle Blvd., St. Adèle, 450/229-2991)* has made a star out of Anne Desjardins and her brand of regional market cuisine starring heirloom vegetables. Signature dishes: Wild mushroom sauté, roasted squab, seared scallops, lamb. A wine-lover's paradise.

For something a little closer to home and not so harsh on the wallet, **Le St. Augustin** *(15196 Rue de St. Augustin, St. Augustin de Mirabel, 450/475-8290)* fits the bill. It's about ½ hour north of Montreal and a romantic dinner for two can come in under $150. Sensational market cuisine by chef and owner Jean-Paul Giroux.

Make Your Own Gourmet

On Laurier west of Park you'll find two premiere gourmet shops of local and imported treats. **Anjou Québec** *(1025 Laurier W., 514/272-4065)* specializes in French foodstuffs and **Gourmet Laurier** *(1042 Laurier W., 514/274-5601)* in European.

WHAT TO ORDER AFTER GETTING TO HOME PLATE AND CALLING IN SICK THE NEXT DAY

Order in the city's best take-out from

Le Gourmet Hot and Spicy

(1616 St. Catherine [Foubourg Mall], 514/937-6000 or 7373 Décarie, 514/731-1818). Szechwan menu with unbelievable General Tao chicken, hot pepper beef, hot and sour soup.

Or: order succulent barbecue chicken; tender and juicy with a crisp, golden skin and subtle seasoning. Accompanied by gravy, fries, bread, and coleslaw:

Chalet BBQ

5456 Sherbrooke St. W., 514/489-5554 and 6825 Décarie, 514/739-3226

Côte-St-Luc BBQ

5403 Côte-St-Luc, 514/488-4011 and other locations

St-Hubert

various locations, order 514/385-5555

most exciting new restaurants (under two years old)

Au Pied de Cochon

Enfant terrible Martin Picard has a delicious sense of humour: a cartoon of him waving a frying pan while riding a smiling pig serves as the resto's insignia. ("*Au Pied de Cochon*" refers to pig's feet.) His bistro/brasserie menu is full of hearty dishes dominated by artisanal meat. Dine by the hearth, the inspiring wood-burning oven.
536 Duluth Ave. W., 514/281-1114

Café Via Dante

Tuscan homecooking by a grandma-turned-professional-cook. The robust osso bucco is what beckons because few delights parallel slurping out the gooey marrow. On the eastern border of Little Italy.
251 Dante, 514/270-8446

Chorus

Outstanding nouvelle cuisine in an intimate setting. Thierry Baron's market-based menu sports original takes on classics like salad *Niçoise* with fresh tuna and quail eggs and beer-braised pig's cheeks.
3434 St. Denis, 514/841-8080

Cube

Minimalist modern American cuisine in the chic St. Paul Hotel, winner of the Best of Canada Design Awards. Claude Pelletier offers a very contemporary, pared-down menu, each item bold and innovative. If you're looking for ambitious cuisine, Pelletier is the chef for you.
St. Paul Hotel, 355 McGill St., 514/876-2823

Le Latini

Whether it's romance or business, the best place to talk someone into something is in Le Latini's wine cellar. It's just you, your guest, and a private waiter in a candlelight cantina housing thousands of bottles. The porcini risotto and rapini and fresh clam spaghettini are out of this world as is the tiramisù. Otherwise, Le Latini is *the* place for expense accounts and power business lunches where cigar-chomping is *de rigeur*. And nobody works a room like owner Moreno De Marchi. Work it, baby, work it!
1130 Jeanne Mance, 514/861-3166

BEST RESTO FOR CLOSING AN IMPORTANT DEAL

Moishe's Steak House

Schmoozapalooza for the Jewish business establishment, accountants, and lawyers. A Montreal institution that blends deli touches (kosher pickles, chopped liver, potato latkes) with generous char-broiled steaks of various cuts.
3961 St. Laurent, 514/845-1696

BEST VEGETARIAN

Chu Chai

Gourmet Thai vegan-friendly food. Masterpieces of forgery include fake chicken, shrimp, pork, and duck dishes made from seitan and tofu.
4088 St. Denis, 514/843-4194

Les Délices Bio

Macrobiotic menu with outstanding desserts.
1327A Mont-Royal E., 514/528-8843

Govinda

All-you-can-eat India-inspired buffet.
263 Duluth E., 514/284-5255

Les Vivres

Vegan-friendly and organic in communal setting. Chapatis smothered with "fake" butter. "BLT" with smoked coconut. Excellent.
4434 St. Dominique, 514/842-3479

Wrapps

Vegan cuisine focused on wraps and rolls. Sample fillings: Jamaican curry, soy cheese and basil, aubergines and sun-dried tomatoes.
5124 Sherbrooke W., 514/482-8542

La Bastide

Inventive southwestern French cuisine in a charming resto with billowing curtains and a terrace.
151 Bernard W., 514/271-4934

Nonya

Experience the flavours of Jakarta – *gado gado*, *nasi goreng*, lamb shanks in coconut sauce. Includes a dining section for sitting on the floor.
1228 St. Laurent, 514/875-9998

Restaurant Carmel

Local Canadian spin on invigorating dishes in a lovely room with fireplace and stone walls. Sample menu: caribou shepherd's pie, stout-marinated pork chops, venison osso bucco.
245 Bernard W., 514/276-6222

Savannah

Sail down the Savannah River by savouring Kenneth Buckland's Southern American fare – cheese grits, collard greens, gumbo, chicken-fried steak.
4448 St. Laurent, 514/904-0277

Zen Ya

Psssst. Fantastic and inexpensive sushi and sashimi in a nondescript building just east of Phillips Square. Robbie Dillon, a connoisseur and bonafide goon whose "interests" have led him to sample fare from all over the world, had this to say: "You get into the building, the elevator. It all looks scabby. But then the food! Wow! Ask for Nick. Tell him you know me."
2nd floor, 486 St. Catherine W., 514/904-1363

the theatre of dining

Not to be confused with tepid dinner theatre, the theatre of dining is that perfect combination of great food and great drama. I would argue that every single meal tells a story, as does every recipe.

Globe

Character-driven vehicle starring, well, yes, the stellar food, simple and honest made with local, organic ingredients. Sample menu: lamb stew, slow cooked rabbit, grilled calf liver. Photo: John David Gravenor
Matched by a complex wine list.

But Globe also stars celebrity chef David McMillan, a towering fellow with tattooed forearms and a motor-mouth who can't wait to retire from cooking so he can become a full-time artist. Co-starring sous-chef Fred Morin, so obsessed with food that after working back-breaking shifts at Globe he goes home to make cheese in his bathtub. The VIPs who dine at Globe – it is *the* place at which to see and be seen – round out the supporting cast of beautiful people. Will David ever make lamb stew for Bobby DeNiro's dog again? Will Ben Affleck return to man the bar? Stay tuned....
3455 St. Laurent, 514/284-3823

Le Muscadin

Le Muscadin is all about the art of serving. Tableside, a tuxedoed waiter opens a bottle of wine, from a cellar reputed to hold 10,000 bottles, in an ostentatious decanting ceremony. Another waiter drops two egg yolks into a copper bowl, adds sugar and Marsala, and whisks it all up over a low flame. He pours the zabaglione over strawberries and *voilà*! Dining pageantry at its best.
639 Notre Dame W., 514/842-0588

BEST ROOMS WITH A VIEW

Chez Queux
View of the Old Port and Place Jacques Cartier.
158 St. Paul E., 514/866-5194

Le 737
Perched 737 feet above sea level, 360 degree view of downtown and the river.
46th Floor, 1 Place Ville Marie, 514/397-0737

Tour de Ville
A revolving restaurant with a view of downtown and Old Montreal.
Delta Hotel, 30th Floor, 777 University, 514/879-4777

BEST VIEW AND FOOD

Nuances
High-rolling view from the third-floor Casino restaurant. Glitzy décor and formal dining – dinner jackets are mandatory. Chef Jean-Pierre Curtat's fancy French menu features lobster, pigeon, filet mignon. Frequent guest celebrity chefs. Championship wine list.
1 Avenue du Casino, Ile Notre Dame, 514/392-2746

Queue de Cheval

Murder, betrayal, love. This is the stuff of drama. But meat, gristle, and bone? La Queue de Cheval Steakhouse & Bar has one of the best shows in town. The focal point is the restaurant's enormous charcoal grill under a grand copper chimney. A railing of waist-high clay pots separates the open kitchen (which descends a few steps) from diners as in an ancient Greek theatre. Watch as a fleet of cooks labours over USDA Prime beef age-dried in-house.
1221 René Lévesque, 514/390-0090

in festival city ...

Les Fêtes Gourmandes Internationales

A culinary whirlwind tour of the world – over 500 dishes from several continents – held every August.
Ile Notre Dame, 514/872-6120

Montreal High Lights Festival

Every February, an annual festival of classical music, exhibits and gastronomy. About 30 renowned chefs prepare special tastings and give cooking demonstration. Everyone from Rob Feenie to Charlie Trotter has attended.
montrealhighlights.com

Just Plain Freaky

Every November the Insectarium hosts bug tasting events. Sautéed locusts, wax-worm corn fritters, and chocolate-covered crickets anyone?
4581 Sherbrooke St. E., 514/872-1400

best power lunches

Alexandre
For the bon vivant business type, a Parisian brasserie replete with waitresses in sexy attire.
1454 Peel, 514/288-5105

Beaver Club
One-of-a-kind restaurant for dining with movers and shakers in an old boy's club amid nostalgic reminders of Canada's fur trade history. The food ain't bad either; old world fare such as caviar, roast beef, Cornish hen. Formidable wine list. Every January, members dress up as yesterday's fur barons for a special commemorative dinner.
Queen Elizabeth Hotel, 900 René Lévesque W., 514/861-3511

Chez Delmo
Lunch on oysters, lobster bisque, and grilled halibut at two mammoth bars with judges, bankers, and shipping executives.
211-215 Notre Dame W., 514/849-4061

Le Bourlingueur
Delectable lunchtime *table d'hôte* for under $20 in a whimsical harlequin décor. For the relaxed, non-threatening power lunch.
363 St. Francois Xavier, 514/845-3646

Da Emma
Favoured by cooler-than-thou entrepreneurs and dot.commers. North Italian homecooking stars seafood antipasto, suckling pig, roast lamb. Impressive wine list.
777 de la Commune W., 514/392-1568

Titanic
Soups, salads, and sandwiches in a cantina-style setting popular with Old Montreal's younger entrepreneurs and lawyers.
445 St. Pierre, 514/849-0894

Photo: John David Gravenor

BEST BREAKFAST
Breakfast is about eating in a joint, brunch ain't. The best of the joints, both Montreal institutions:

Cosmos
5843 Sherbrooke W., 514/486-3814

Dusty's
4510 Park, 514/276-8525

BEST DIM SUM
For Chinese brunch in a teahouse, bring a large group of ravenous people to **Asie Moderne** (*1017 St. Laurent, 514/875-8888*) or **Lotté** (*Hôtel Furama, 215 René-Lévesque Blvd., 514/393-3838*) to sample dishes that you grab, literally, from the laden carts rolling by. Menu sampling: potstickers, sesame seed balls, steamed pork buns, mango pudding.

BEST POWER BUSINESS DINNER

Les Halles
Classic French dining in a highbrow restaurant for bigwig politicos and business people.
1450 Crescent, 514/844-2328

BEST BUSINESS DINNERS ON A BUDGET

Le Commensal

For the lefty biz type. High-end vegetarian buffet.
1204 McGill College, 514/871-1480; 1720 St. Denis, 514/845-2627 and other locations

L'Entrecôte Saint-Jean

For the conservative/blue chip business type. Only one thing on the menu: steak-frites served with soup, salad, coffee, and profiteroles.
2022 Peel, 514/281-6492

Reuben's Deli

For the "make-me-a-deal-I-can't-refuse" type. Traditional deli with excellent smoked meat.
892 and 1116 St. Catherine W., 514/844-1605

Soy

For the young entrepreneur. A cornucopia of Asian food (Korean barbecue, Balinese baby squid, steamed dumplings) in a minimalist environment.
3945 St. Denis, 514/499-9399

Taj

For the "conquer or be conquered" type. Chef Sharif Khan's Indian buffet is equally popular with students and profs. Double Diamond beer on tap.
2077 Stanley, 514/845-9015

BEST BRUNCHES

Montrealers love their weekend brunches, long, luxurious affairs of gossip mongering and "morning after" sexual politics. Words in English and French, and umpteen other languages, waft past our ears, mingling into a linguistic brew that is exquisitely *Montréalais*.

BRUNCH WITH A TWIST

Byblos

Middle Eastern brunch punctuated by aromatic touches and special dishes like *boranis* and date omelets.
1499 Laurier E., 514/523-9396

Senzala

Hugest brunch in the city. Original menu: Brazilian flavoured milk drinks, grilled fruit kebabs, and poached eggs on half of an avocado or mango.
177 Bernard W., 514/274-1464

BEST STANDARD BRUNCH

Bagel Etc.
4320 St. Laurent, 514/845-9462

Beauty's
93 Mont Royal W., 514/849-8883

Eggspectations
198 Laurier W., 514/278-6411 and 1313 de Maisonneuve W., 514/842-3447

L'Avenue
922 Mount-Royal E., 514/523-8780

Le Toasteur
950 Roy E., 514/527-8500

best souvlaki

Marathon

This family establishment that has become an institution for its souvlaki. Tender pork or lamb cubes marinated in secret herbs and spices. Tzatziki so garlicky that whoever kisses you will know you ate at Marathon's. You can bus it to Laval, but driving is faster. *824 Curé Labelle (Chomedy, Laval), 450/681-9449*

HONOURABLE MENTION

Marvens Restaurant

880 Ball, 514/277-3625

Souvlaki George

6995 Monkland, 514/482-0040

Villa de Souvlaki

5347 Sherbrooke St. W., 514/489-2039

Non-Standard Supermarkets

Montreal has some impressive Greek and Middle-eastern supermarkets. **Marché Adonis** *(9590 L'Acadie, 514/382-8606)* and **Marché Akhavan** *(5768 Sherbrooke W., 514/485-4744)* have a tremendous selection. Tucked away downtown are two notable places, **Marché AlMizan** *(2167 St. Catherine W., 514/938-4142)* and **Marché Noor** *(1905 St. Catherine W., 514/932-2099)*.

Tip Top

There's no excuse for bad tipping unless the service is abysmal. 15 percent of the bill (before taxes) for standard service, 20 percent for exemplary, and a little more if the bartender takes you home.

BEST RESTAURANTS WITH BARS

Bistro on the Avenue
(50 and over crowd)
1362 Greene Ave., 514/939-6451

Cafeteria
(under 45 crowd)
581 St. Laurent, 514/849-3855

Monkland Tavern
(mixed crowd, great food)
5555 Monkland, 514/486-5768

BEST BARS WITH RESTAURANTS

Mussels and steak sandwiches at **La Cabane** *(3872 St. Laurent, 514/843-7283)*, an East Indian menu at **Scratch Kitchen** in the Copacabana *(3910 St. Laurent, 514/982-0880)*, and tapas at the hipster-trendy **Laika** *(4040 St. Laurent, 514/842-8088)*.

Picasso *(6810 St. Jacques W., 514/484-2832)* delivers breakfast any time of day or night, so it's the favourite *livraison gratuite* restaurant of Westend potheads. **Supermarchés Quatre Frères** *(3701 St. Laurent, 514/844-1874)* is the city's only 24-hour supermarket and among the city's top-three pick up joints. There's nothing like a mound of ripe fruit to get the pheromones all juiced up! **Main St. Lawrence Steak House Delicatessen** *(3864 St. Laurent, 514/843-8126)*, a.k.a. The Main, is a legendary favorite after-after-hours place.

BEST RESTOS FOR PARTIES OF 8

Greek revelry with a bouzouki band Thursdays-Saturdays at **Mythos** *(5318 Park, 514/270-0235)* and family-style platters of roast lamb and calamar at **Panama** *(789 Jean Talon W., 514/276-5223)*, Portuguese grill favorites at **Doval** *(150 Marie Anne E., 514/843-3390)*, Cantonese at **La Maison V.I.P.** *(1077 Clark, 514/861-1943)*, and Peruvian fare at **Pucapuca** *(5400 St. Laurent, 514/272-8029)*.

OTHER NOTABLE AFTERHOURS JOINTS

Arahova Souvlaki

(open until 5:00 a.m. Friday-Saturday)
256 St. Viateur W., 514/274-7828

Euro-Deli

(until 4:00 a.m. Thursday-Saturday)
3619 St. Laurent, 514/843-7853

Resto du Village

(24 hours)
1310 Wolfe St., 514/524-5404

Young and Urban

Join dilettante wiseguys at **Buona Notte** *(3518 St. Laurent, 514/848-0644)* and **Quelli della Notte** *(6834 St. Laurent, 514/271-3929, also has a cigar lounge)* and Grand Prix jet setters at Jacques Villeneuve's **Newtown** *(1476 Crescent, 514/284-6555)*. Go to **Continental** *(4169 St. Denis, 514/845-6842)* for an artsy bistro buzz, **Soto** *(3527 St. Laurent, 514/842-1150 and 500 McGill Ave., 514/864-5115)* or **Ginger** *(15 Pine E., 514/844-2121)* for some sushi savvy, and **Sofia** *(3600 St. Laurent, 514/284-0092)* to satisfy your techno groove.

best restos for taking out-of-towners

La Rapière

Those hankering for the glories of classic French cuisine will fall in love with the fine Rapière. For 30 years, this institution has been serving dishes like home smoked goose breast, foie gras, and an excellent cheese course. Stained-glass windows in an elegant room.
1155 Metcalfe, 514/871-8920

Le Club des Pins

Lovely Provençal setting, as if you've walked into a field of lavender. Jean-François Vachon is one of the city's youngest practitioners of Quebec nouvelle cuisine and he makes the most of local ingredients such as Boileau venison and Quebec organic farmers' produce. (At press time, however, rumour had it that Vachon was leaving for the exciting new restaurant to be opened in 2003 in the Hôtel Godin, a venture of the investors behind Globe and Buona Notte.)
156 Laurier W., 514/272-9484

Apple-Picking

Spend a crisp autumn weekend in September or October apple picking on one of Quebec's many orchards. Buy homemade pies, preserves, juice, and cider. Find a list of apple orchards online at *lapommeduquebec.ca.*

Sugaring Off

For about six weeks between March and April, 100-year-old maple trees are tapped for sap and Quebecers go sugaring off in the Montérégie and Laurentides regions. All-you-can-eat sit-down buffets of the traditional food that pioneer lumberjacks ate in winter. Dinner is often followed by live music, dancing and hayrides. The most famous of the cabanes is **Sucrérie de la Montagne** *(300 St. Georges, Rigaud, 450/451-0340).*

BEST BURGERS

L'Anecdote
1950s style diner with a mushroom sauce burger, grilled cheese, and club to die for.
801 Rachel E., 514/526-7967

La Paryse
Generous burgers on kaiser with a variety of toppings including a special with cream cheese and bacon. Ouch! The chocolate cake is one of the best.
302 Ontario E., 514/842-2040

BEST FRIES

At the Belgian **Frites Alors!** *(5235A Park, 514/948-2219; 1562 Laurier E., 514/524-6336; 433 Rachel, 514/843-2490),* chips are served the old-fashioned way — wrapped in newspaper. Order yours with one of their ten sauces. At **MondoFritz** *(3899 St. Laurent, 514/281-6521),* have them with beer. And the very best: **Patati Patata** *(4177 St. Laurent, 514/844-0216)* makes long and thin curly fries (kind of like linguini) served in a french fry basket. Have them with delicious burgers or filet of sole.

BEST NOODLES

Pho Hoa

6230 Côte-des-Neiges,
514/343-5018

Tampopo

4449 Mentana, 514/526-0001

U & Me

1900 St-Catherine W.,
514/931-0081

Wakamono

1251 Mont-Royal E.,
514/527-2747

Zyng

1748 St-Denis, 514/284-2016

Les Remparts *(Auberge du Vieux Port, 93 de la Commune E., 514/392-1649)* is a candlelit basement restaurant with fortress walls across from the Old Port. Chef Janick Bouchard's contemporary cuisine is simply divine. Linger over dessert in the cognac and cigar lounge. During the Fireworks Festival, dine on the rooftop terrace for a breathtaking view. Well-chosen winelist.

For Mediterranean flavours, delight in chef José Rodriguez's fish and seafood at **La Maîtresse** in the Hôtel Versaille *(1800 Sherbrooke W., 514/939-1212)*. For a more glamourous Mediterranean experience, there's **Terra** in the sumptuous Hôtel Europa *(1240 Drummond, 514/866-8910)*, a stunning all-white dining room. At **Chez Chine** in the Holiday Inn *(99 Viger W., 514/878-9888)* it's Cantonese at its best and at **Zen** in the Omni Hotel *(1050 Sherbrooke W., 514/499-0801)* it's Chinese and Szechwan in a sleek and contemporary atmosphere.

St-Paul Hotel Bar *(355 McGill, 514/380-2222)* has raw power – fish, seafood, sashimi, and carpaccio – in sleek designer digs. The mohitos pack a punch.

best ice cream

Ben & Jerry's
   All-American flavours like chocolate fudge brownie, chocolate chip cookie dough.
   1316 de Maisonneuve W., 514/286-6073

Le Bilboquet
   Special flavours: moka praline, maple syrup, choco-orange, chestnut. Outstanding sorbets.
   1311 Bernard W., 514/276-0414

Ripples
   Vanilla ice cream often cited the city's best. Special flavours: chocolate-raspberry truffle, lychee, guava-grapefruit, green-tea, halvah, chai.
   3880 St. Laurent, 514/842-1697

Roberto
   Italian ices and ice creams like stracciatella, Baci, cassata, hazelnut, pistachio.
   2221 Bélanger, 514/374-9844

best seafood

Delfino

Chef George Georgi serves the freshest fish and seafood grilled, spicy Cajun-style, or sautéed in a Provençal or meunière style. Intimate and romantic.
1231 Lajoie, 514/277-5888

Desjardins

An old-fashioned fish and seafood restaurant: there's a lobster tank on the premises and lobster is served every which way you can – boiled or broiled, cardinal, Newburg.
1175 Mackay, 514/866-9741

Ferreira Café Trattoria

Traditional Portuguese cuisine in a stunning Mediterranean ambiance with tile mosaics against royal blue background. 7-8 catches of the day, grilled squid and sardines, seafood rice, salted cod. Connoisseurs can choose from about 50 varieties of port offered by the glass.
1446 Peel, 514/848-0988

Isakaya

Chef Shige Minagawa does wonders with yellowtail neck, toro, oysters, octopus, and lobster sashimi.
3469 Park, 514/845-8226

Maestro S.V.P.

Montreal's oyster temple with as many as 15 varieties on any given day.
3615 St. Laurent, 514/842-6447

Milos

Among the top restaurants in the city. The Greek resto serves up flawless fish and seafood. Don't miss the Milos special starter – deep-fried paper-thin zucchini, eggplant, and Kasseri cheese. Fabulous modern Mediterranean ambiance with fresh ingredients displayed on ice fronting an open kitchen.
5357 Park, 514/272-3522

BEST EMPANADAS

La Chilenita

4348 Clark, 514/982-9212 and 152 Napoléon, 514/286-6075

Photo: John David Gravenor

Chez José

173 Duluth E., 514/845-0693

Supermarchés Andes Gloria

4387 St. Laurent, 514/848-1078

CHEAP AND CHEERFUL CHINATOWN

Crispy Peking duck, mouth-watering dim sum (7am-3pm daily) and Cantonese classics at **La Maison Kam Fung** (1008 Clark, 514/878-2888). At **Hong Kong** (1023 St. Laurent, 514/861-0251) try the Peking duck, lobster, barbecue pork. Shopping bliss at **Marché Kim Phat** (1057 St. Laurent, 514/874-0129).

best ethnic restaurants at a glance

CARIBBEAN

Caribbean Curry House
6892 Victoria, 514/733-0828

Photo: John David Gravenor

Ma's Place
5889 Sherbrooke W., 514/487-7488

Pick's
5155 de Maisonneuve W., 514/486-1857

ELEGANT CHINESE

Aux Délices de Szechuan
1735 St. Denis, 514/844-5542

Bon Blé Riz
1437 St. Laurent, 514/844-1447

Le Piment Rouge
1170 Peel, 514/866-7816

INDIAN

Ganges
6083 Sherbrooke W., 514/488-8850

Golden Curry House
5210 St. Laurent, 514/270-2561

Mysore
4216 St. Laurent, 514/844-4733

ITALIAN

La Cantina
9090 St. Laurent, 514/382-3618

Lucca
12 Dante, 514/278-6502

Pronto Gastronomia
4894 Sherbrooke W., 514/487-9666

Resto Sans Noms
9700 St. Michel, 514/389-6732

JAPANESE

Sho-Dan
2020 Metcalfe, 514/987-9987

KOREAN

Hwang-Kum House
5908 Sherbooke St. W.,
514/487-1712

Man-na
1421 Bishop,
514/288-1703

Photo: John David Gravenor

LEBANESE

Daou
519 Faillon,
514/276-8310

La Sirène de la Mer
1805 Sauvé E., 514/332-2255

Zawedeh
3407 Peel St., 514/288-4141

BEST OF LITTLE ITALY

Il Mulino
Rustic Italian homecooking.
Recommended: gnocchi, pastas,
guinea hen livers, fish soup. The
tiramisù is the real deal and the
semifreddo is a real treat.
236 St. Zotique E., 514/273-5776

BEST SUSHI

Koji's Treehouse
Tri Du is our supreme master of
Japanese cuisine. Signature dishes:
Hawaiian opa, sashimi oysters,
striped bass tataki, Tri's Deluxe sushi
maki (smoked salmon, cucumber,
black caviar, and Alaskan crab) and
Eye of the Dragon (salmon, squid,
flying fish roe).
4120 St. Catherine W.,
514/932-7873

M E X I C A N

Fandango
3807 St. André, 514/526-7373

P O R T U G U E S E

Restaurant Jano
3883 St. Laurent, 514/849-0646

Rotisserie Portugalia
34 Rachel W., 514/282-1519

BEST THAI

Chao Phraya

Casual but elegant Thai food
with a menu featuring some
150 items. Soups and curries are
outstanding with hints of fresh
lemongrass, coconut, or ginger in
almost every dish.
50 Laurier W., 514/272-5339

T H A I

Red Thai
3550 St. Laurent, 514/289-0998

Thai Grill
5101 St. Laurent, 514/270-5566

T U N I S I A N

Étoile de Tunis
6701 de Chateaubriand Ave., 514/276-5518

BEST VIETNAMESE SUBS

Hoàng Oanh

Bành mi with chicken, pork,
beef, or vegetarian dressed with
pickled carrot, radish, cilantro,
very hot peppers, and spread with
paté or mayo.
1071 St. Laurent, 514/954-0053
and 7178 St. Denis, 514/271-8668

V I E T N A M E S E

Escale à Saigon
107 Laurier W., 514/272-3456

Hoai Huong
5485 Victoria, 514/738-6610

Pho Bac 97
1016 St. Laurent, 514/393-8116

Pho Bang
6135 Côte-des-Neiges, 514/344-9776

Souvenirs D'Indochine
243 Mount-Royal W., 514/848-0336

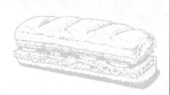

What do you get when you combine a high-rise full of galleries, a rodeo photographer, and stick in a bad-boy sculptor for good measure? Only the most unforgettable chapter on culture anybody could conceivably write about this lemon-shaped island in the stream. Say goodbye to your outsider status and get set to be schooled about the mayor who smashed down miles of art, the million-dollar painting gallery a school board keeps Top Secret, and uncounted other tales from the city so arty that its name, in fact, is an anagram for "lemon art" (or "ran motel" or "ram elton" …). Okay, enough jibber-jabber. Let's get on with it.

The One-Ring Empire

In the mid-'80s, a local street performer had an idea for a new kind of circus. Guy Laliberté, a fire-eating stilt-walker, wanted to shake the dust off the tired circus concept and give it a modern feel. The idea was to nix the animals and have one ring instead of three – so the tent could be erected on small urban clearings. Young performers would entertain audiences and move on, playing before crowds around the world. The performances would stress physical prowess and feature lavish multimedia productions. The training envisaged acrobatic skill mixed with artistic interpretation.

But the first 50 bankers that Laliberté appealed to for funding laughed in his face. So along with some fellow street performers, he turned to the Quebec government, and – voilà! – La Cirque du Soleil was born.

The little group was awarded a cultural grant of $1.5 million to purchase some equipment, much of which they used immediately to drive to an arts fair in California on the promise of top billing but no money up front. By the time they arrived at their destination, they didn't even have enough money for gas to return home – they had put everything they had on the line. But their gamble paid off. Crowds and critics alike adored the Cirque du Soleil.

Less than two decades later, the Cirque has become a major cultural phenomenon, with more than 2,000 employees worldwide. Their costume factory alone has more than 250 employees and their huge headquarters in north Montreal sit near the site of the abandoned Miron limestone quarry.

Today, Laliberté is the Cirque's president and chief executive officer. Now the bankers will fetch him an espresso with the wave of a finger.

Melvin Charney had a dream – to create a corridor of art as part of the Olympic celebrations. Working with a small budget, the artist collaborated with several confreres to create Corridart. For three weeks in July 1976, the mostly visual art exhibition would turn Sherbrooke into a nine km (five mile) linear park from Atwater to Olympic Stadium. One artist, Pierre Ayot, recreated an exact replica of the cross on Mount Royal laid on its side on McGill campus. Another artist depicted a pointing Mickey Mouse hand to represent an Iroquois directing Champlain to Montreal. Local developer David Azrieli, who had earlier demolished the much-loved Van Horne mansion in order to build the faceless office tower at the northeast corner of Stanley and Sherbrooke, objected because the finger seemed to point accusingly at his building. Another Corridart installation featured a looped recording of a voice detailing the cost of the Olympic Games. Just after Corridart went up and the Olympics were about to start, Mayor Drapeau ordered the installations removed.

Three years after Drapeau's infamous act, the mayor bumped into Charney at, appropriately, the Montreal Museum of Fine Arts. "He looked at me, trying to remember who I was," Charney says. "I told him, 'We've met in another corridor of art.'

"Drapeau suddenly turned beet red. His wife, who didn't know who I was, had started talking to me at this point. Drapeau simply grabbed her hand and pulled her away."

The St. Leonard Dictionary

If there's a second Latin Quarter in Montreal, it would be St. Leonard, where you can live, work, and shop in Italian. Montrealers of Italian descent are triply blessed, as most of 'em speak their mother tongue, as well as English, and French. But they also have their own local dialect, as this tongue-in-cheek St. Leonard dictionary from lesjokes.com points out:

Aieee – An exclamation meaning "You can't be serious!"

Alla masse – Much. A variation of the French *en masse*. (At the wedding, there was food alla masse!)

Boh – A reply indicating "I don't know." (Girl: Where did Mommy go? Brother: Boh, how should I know?)

Bod'uh dem – Both of them. (Which one do you want? You want bod'uh dem?)

But – "Except for," when used at the end of a sentence. (It was pouring that time we went camping; we had a nice time but.)

Colour – Flavour. (What colour ice cream you want, grape?)

Embombalate – Confuse, disorient. From the English "discombobulate." (When the soccer ball hit me in the head, I was embombolated.)

Eryting – Everything. (A big plate like dat guy's ... he ate eryting.)

Husher – An usher, specifically at a wedding. (I have to rent a tux pecuz I'm a husher at my cousin's wedding.) See also pecuz.

Mingia (also, meenkia, meezeenga, meeee, maiee, etc.) – Actually male genitalia, although it's come to mean female genitalia because it sounds feminine. From Italian slang. Often used as a swearword, expression of surprise or exclamation.

More by down dere – In that direction. (Lady: S'cuse me...but where's the Bonanza store? Young guy: Aieee ... more by down dere.)

Pecuz – Because. (Mike: What did you do yesterday night? Mary: Na-ting. Mike: Why? Mary: Eh, pecuz my budder, he took off with da car.)

Irono – I don't know. (Joe: I heard you had an accident. Mario: Mingia, Joe, irono what happened but the van hit my car.)

Shkoff – To eat ravenously. (You guys, I'm starving ... let's go shkoff.)

Zaggerate – Exaggerate.

No Nudes is Good Nudes

Although Montreal has an anything-goes kind of image, nudity was still enough to get an artist's show closed down less than two decades ago. On July 28, 1987, police entered the Fokus Gallery on Duluth Street and seized an 8x10 colour photo of a woman's hand holding an erect penis from the window of the Fokus Gallery on Duluth Street. Then they threatened artist Martin Leibowitz with charges under the Criminal Code prohibiting the exhibit of indecent exhibitions. It was the first time in two decades that art had been seized in Montreal, and the police did some more seizing when the *McGill Daily* newspaper tried to reprint the picture for its readers to judge. The bust sent such a chill down local spines that by the next year, eleven drawings of nude figures were yanked off the walls by brass of the Galerie Alliance, a non-profit gallery on Sherbrooke West backed by an insurance company. A boss at the gallery defended the self-censorship by saying Frank Mulvey's eleven realistic drawings of male and female nudes could harm high-school students passing by the gallery.

The Quebec Chainsaw Sculptor

Every artist has a favourite tool. Picasso had his paintbrush, Karsh his camera. And Laurent Godon has his chainsaw.

The native of St. Jovite uses a chainsaw to carve 300-pound blocks of ice into expressive works of art. Godon, who's an interior decorator by trade, has been recognized by the *Guinness Book of World Records* as the world's fastest ice carver. At the Old Port in January of 1992, he earned his second world record and a $3,000 prize for sculpting 60 works in ten hours and forty minutes. It takes about eight minutes for him to complete a sculpture.

Phantom of the Art House

Photo: John David Gravenor

Have you ever wondered where museums keep all the stuff you're not allowed to see? Literature, art, artifacts, furnishings, manuscripts, historical objects – Montreal's most impressive depot is right downtown in the former Dow Stock Cellars at the southeast corner of Peel and Notre Dame Streets.

Once owned by a popular brewery, the towering industrial cathedral now warehouses overflow items from 30 city museums, including the Montreal Museum of Fine Arts and the Canadian Centre for Architecture.

There is so much stuff in the temperature-controlled warehouse that support structures had to be reinforced just to keep the building from falling down, while all surfaces have been treated to minimize dust.

The building's southern half stood derelict many years after the brewery went broke. In 2000, a young British Columbian named Nasim spent six months as the building's lone squatter. For comfort and a place to sleep, he dragged a discarded sofa up nine flights of stairs by himself. Outside a high window, he painted a one-word message – LOVE – that could be read from street level for more than a year. That message was sprayed away by an anonymous graffiti artist in 2001. By then, however, Nasim had moved back out west.

Art on the Outside

The **Montreal Museum of Fine Arts** is as good-looking outside as in. The architect brothers Edward and William Maxwell lovingly piled Vermont marble at a slight angle to highlight its flowing pattern, which was unveiled in 1912. The four columns at the top of the front steps are the largest marble columns in North America, weighing 26 tons each.

Experts at McGill's Redpath Museum usefully point out that each column is equal in weight to seven elephants.

The **Jean-Noël Desmarais Pavilion** across the street is also made of the same marble from near Manchester, Vermont. It was completed in 1991 by architect Moshe Safdie, whose Habitat 67 apartment complex near the casino is so cool that Donald Sutherland was shot dead there in one of his movies.

Photo: John David Gravenor

Venues
For Readings, Book Signings, & Launches

Bibliophile Bookstore
5519 Queen Mary Rd.;
514/486-7369

Beaconsfield Library
303 Beaconsfield Blvd.;
514/428-4460

Chapters
1171 Ste. Catherine St. W.;
514/849-8825

Chapters Pointe Claire
6321 Trans Canada Highway, Pointe Claire; 514/428-5500

At Large in the Heart of the City

Chapters Rockland

2305 Rockland Rd., Mount Royal;

514/344-3112

Double Hook Book Shop

1235A Greene Ave.; 514/932-5093

Indigo Books & Music

1500 McGill College Ave., Place Montreal Trust; 514/281-5549

Paragraphe Bookstore

2220 McGill College Ave.;

514/845-5811

Westmount Library

4574 Sherbrooke W., Westmount;

514/989-5300

Yellow Door

3625 Aylmer St.; 514/398-6243

Ever since 1954, some Montrealers have half-suspected that somewhere in this city is a tax-free oasis that municipal authorities are completely unaware of. Here's a description of such a place, called Green Bottle Street:

"On either side of a cobbled pavement were three small houses, six in all, each with a diminutive garden in front, spaced off by low iron palings of a kind that has disappeared except in the oldest quarters."

According to Patrick Waddington's 1954 short story of the same name, all municipal records pertaining to Green Bottle Street were misplaced at the otherwise circumspect City Hall. One day, a bureaucrat finds the missing files and, rather than inform the city, decides to move into this urban Shangri-La.

Waddington, a CBC newswriter and son of a Christian Science faith healer, was the husband of noted poet Miriam Waddington. In the years after World War II, the two circulated in local literary circles, and were often featured in such staple-bound creative-writing magazines as the influential *Preview* and *First Contact*. In 1951, the couple made front-page news after the suburban Hampstead School refused their son. The controversy and skirmish that erupted ended with the overturning of a policy designed to keep Jewish children out of Hampstead schools.

The idea for *Green Bottle Street* was based on a profile of a real-life city official that Waddington wrote about seven years before. The story was translated into many languages and published around the world, perpetuating the legend of an unknown Montreal community.

"Suzanne takes me down to a place by the river" are words that made Leonard Cohen famous. In fact, the song describes a real-life visit he paid to the Old Montreal home of Suzanne Verdal, a dancer, who was then married to the bad-boy sculptor Armand Vaillancourt. Many loft-dwellers in the area are known to claim that their homes are the site of the famous encounter, nobody seems quite sure whose claim is true. As the Suzanne narrative recounts, she offers Cohen tea, which came "all the way from China." The brand was Bigelow's Constant Comment, popular with fans of strong black tea. In a 1992 interview Cohen explained another line in the song, "Jesus was a sailor": "People feel Montreal is the Jerusalem of the north. People who were brought up there have this sense of a holy city, a city that means a lot to us. So, I was able to find a place for that second verse between those two verses about Suzanne and to give it that religious quality that the song has, which is the quality of Montreal." Cohen, who grew up on the hill at 599 Belmont in Westmount, also mentions "the lady of the harbour." As we pointed out earlier, that lady is the statue atop Notre Dame de Bonsecours Church at 400 St. Paul East, whose arms stretch out in a pose welcoming returning sailors, if not Jesus.

FROM FICTION TO FACT

Kathy Reich, forensics expert and bestselling author of Montreal-based whodunits *Déja Dead*, *Death du Jour*, and *Deadly Décisions* , admits that her day job inspires her writing. She conducts autopsies on people who died suspicious deaths, including a Quebec missionary who died a suspicious death in Central America.

THE MAIN MAN

Best cop-who-does-it-his-own-way thriller novel about the St. Lawrence strip: *The Main* by Rod Whitaker, aka Trevanian (1976). Detective LaPointe makes sure to shave only in the afternoon, so he can keep a five o'clock shadow while he rules his domain of St. Lawrence.

CATCHING THE STAGE BUG

Every day, future thespians and spear-holders learn proper intonation, timing, and how to raise one eyebrow at a time at the **National Theatre School** (5030 St. Denis). The lucky ones who make it come to Montreal to learn the essentials of their craft from the faculty at the bilingual institution. But nothing beats real-life experience. So every year, the graduating class form a company to stage eight separate productions — four in English, four in French. The plays range from classic Brecht and Shakespeare to George F. Walker and Michel Tremblay and are staged between October and May at the Monument National (1182 St. Lawrence). Well-known guest directors often direct the plays.

The best part of all: tickets are less than $10. Call the Monument National for details (514/871-2224) or visit the theatre school online (ent-nts.com).

The Best Montreal Novel Never Written

Anton Anghel, 42, was a convicted armed robber living on Queen Mary Road in November, 1990, when cops busted him for the attempted kidnapping of Seagram heir Stephen Bronfman, 26 (pictured, left). According to Anghel's would-be wheelman, who opted to turn informant instead, Anghel was plotting to ambush Bronfman in Old Montreal, confine him, and then ask for at least $8 million in ransom, which would be dropped by helicopter into a remote lake. When the case went before a jury, Anghel denied everything, explaining that the notes he had written describing the plan in Romanian were just scenes from a novel he was working on. He was found not guilty. We're still waiting for the novel.

The Joy of Decoys

When Roger Desjardins was a young boy growing up in Verdun, he often helped his father repair old waterfowl decoys. Soon the strapping lad developed a fascination with the fowl that quacked around on the nearby St. Lawrence River. So what did that get him? Try 17 Quebec Decorative Decoy Championships, no less. Original Desjardins decoys are hotly traded by connoisseurs and collectors, but you can buy reproductions through shop-at-home channels, via websites and at Ducks Unlimited's online shop (ducatalog.com). Desjardins may be cheesily marketed, but this master carver remains among the best in the world at this obscure craft.

Winds of Change, Already

It took a Montreal stage company to crack open a wall of cultural suppression in the former Soviet Union. In June, 1990, Dora Wasserman's Montreal Yiddish Theatre brought a touring production of a comedy, *Sages of Chelm* by Eli Rubenstein, to audiences in the communist country. For three weeks, the troupe performed entirely in Yiddish before about 17,000 Soviet Jews in such places as Moscow and Kiev. During the tour, Wasserman met a sister she hadn't seen in 50 years. A film-production company, Maximage, shot the historic tour to produce a documentary, *Moving Mountains: The Montreal Yiddish Theatre in the U.S.S.R.*, which had its gala American debut at New York's Museum of Modern Art in January, 1992.

Shots at Stardom

Back in the '80s, local photographer Donigan Cumming had a decent job shooting pictures for department-store displays, but he was more interested in the mortality and human nature he saw in ordinary people in their ordinary environments. When it came time to find someone new to photograph, the photographer with game show-host looks would hang around his local corner store and ask the beer-delivery guy if he could tag along. Sometimes the delivery guys' customers would let Cumming shoot them in their modest apartments, sometimes they wouldn't. By 1986, he was exhibiting his work at influential galleries in New York's SoHo district and bagging grants from the Canada Council and Guggenheim Foundation. In 1991, he became an international sensation with his nude photographs of 80-year-old Nettie Harris, a former journalist and movie extra. Cumming's works, which often incorporate sound, video, and installation, have been presented throughout Europe and the U.S. You can see a picture of Nettie curled up on a green carpet in Phaidon's definitive photography survey, *The Photo Book*.

Where the Play's the Thing

Here are some of the local venues where you can catch a play in English.

Photo: John David Gravenor

Centaur Theatre
453 Saint Francois Xavier St., Old Montreal; 514/288-3161; centaurtheatre.com

Espace Go
Home to a women's experimental theatre group, the space also features modern dance and visual arts.
4890 St. Lawrence; 514/845-4890

Le Gesu
This multifunctional theatre has been in operation since 1865.
1202 Bleury St.; 514/861-4036

Monument National
Built in 1893 and renovated in 1993, this complex includes a main stage and two smaller venues.
1182 St. Lawrence; 514/871-9883

That's Entertainment

Mention Orford and a lot of young'uns rush to the closet to fetch their ski pants, but the less Philistine among us (ahem) might also think strings, brass, and wind instruments. The more than 50-year-old **Orford Arts Festival**, held in a provincial park near the ski hills of Southern Quebec, also welcomes world-class talent to an annual summertime event that features master musicians, orchestras, open-air concerts, and opera. The festival also hosts a prestigious eight-week music academy for about 100 promising students from around the world.

The festival was formerly known as the home of the acclaimed Orford String Quartet, which has been disbanded and replaced by the Orford Wind Ensemble. Orford Arts Festival, *819/843-9871*

Rain Buffs

Photo: John David Gravenor

Perhaps one of the greatest public sittings this town has ever seen took place at the ungodly hour of 4:30am on May 26, 2001, when hundreds of volunteers stripped to the bone in the plaza in front of Place des Arts for a Spencer Tunick photo shoot. The New York photographer, known for his depictions of masses of nudes huddled on city streets, snapped pictures of the about 2,500 nudies in attendance, a figure that doesn't include that guy who got shooed for not removing his pants. The rest bared all in the rain and kept cheering madly for some reason whenever Tunick spoke to them over the megaphone.

While the plaza has been an inspired meeting spot for stair-sitters and skateboarders, the complex itself received a little less love, meriting a lemon award from local architects who called the Museum of Contemporary Art building "fragmented" and "collaged," with industrial top-heaviness and a hackneyed blind arcade facing Jeanne Mance Street. The spot across the street to the west is slated as the new home to the long awaited opera house, that will only cost taxpayers a mere $250 million.

Photo: John David Gravenor

You can't judge art by the building that holds it. A case in point: the **Belgo Building** *(372 Ste. Catherine W.)* was built as a manufacturing and showroom centre for local fur traders. (Those were the days: more than 20,000 beaver pelts changed hands in a single day at the 1947 fur auction.) The building once had a bowling alley in the basement, and a vast, much-lamented LP store on the second floor. Now it's thriving as a major hub on the contemporary art scene with about 15 galleries representing young and up-and-coming atists with little exposure, others straight out of art school, and even a few older, established artists. One of the galleries represented Marc Séguin before he made it big on the international art scene. So you could have bought low.

Just a block to the west is another oasis of art. Known as **"The 460"** for its address on Ste. Catherine Street, it houses a half-dozen to a dozen galleries. There are fewer because the rent is higher.

Here are some of the contemporary artists to look out for. You never know where you might find your next treasure.

Newer artists: François Lacasse (painter), Karilee Fuglem (installations, drawings, photography), Emmanuel Galland (video, photography), Nicholas Baier (photography), and Sylvie Laliberté (video installations, performance). Laliberté is one of the most colourful personalities on the scene. Positively eccentric, her naïve persona shows in her refreshing, fun works.

Established contemporary artists: Claude Tousignant, Peter Kraus, Tom Hopkins, Leopold Plotek and Françoise Sullivan (all painters), Geneviève Cadieux (photographer), and Betty Goodwin (paintings, etchings, drawings, multimedia).

The local contemporary art society (commonly known by its French acronym, AGAC) used to hold annual art fairs, a practice that ended back in 1994. But they have been rekindled the past couple of years at an annual spring trade fair. For information about the event: 514/861-2345; agac.qc.ca.

SCHOOL STAGES

Casgrain Theatre

The stage of the John Abbott College theatre department.
21 275 Lakeshore Rd., Ste. Anne de Bellevue; 514/457-6610; johnabbott.qc.ca/webpages/departments/theatre

D.B. Clarke Theatre

This is the main stage for Concordia University drama productions and home to Geordie children's theatre.
1455 de Maisonneuve W.; 514/848-4742

Dome Theatre

Featuring an average of five Dawson College student plays per season, including contemporary works and Shakespearean plays.
3990 Notre Dame W.; 514/931-8731 ext. 7399

F.C. Smith Auditorium

Loyola Campus of Concordia University, 7141 Sherbrooke W.; 514/848-3878

Frank Dawson Adams Auditorium

Part of McGill University.
811 Sherbrooke St. W.; 514/398-3911

Music For the People

The annual **Suoni Per Il Popolo ("Sound for the People")** event, spread out over a number of weeks in June, showcases local and international acts playing hip-hop and dub, free-jazz, improvised music, rock and roll, and something called "beats and blips." You'll hear sound sculptors, techno-composers, and radical poets. Events are held at Casa del Popolo *(4873 St. Lawrence)* and La Sala Rossa *(4848 St. Lawrence)*.
514/284-3804; casadelpopolo.com

Shooting Star

Photo: John David Gravenor

It was the Ides of March, 1977. A Tuesday. Former convict and successful author Hubert Aquin marched into the private grounds of the Villa Maria School, just a few steps uphill from the Metro stop of the same name.

Just 20 years earlier, Aquin was a hopeful middle-class guy from the Plateau Mont Royal, a few good jobs in store and a writing career to look forward to. He took a philosophy degree from a local university and later studied politics in Paris. When he came back home, Aquin wrote articles, produced radio, and hosted shows on TV.

He was already a public figure by the early '60s when he joined a fledgling separatist party. During a stint as the firebrand editor of *Liberté*, the feds suspected him of plotting subversive activities, especially after Aquin announced his intention to join a terrorist cell. He got busted, red-handed, with illegal weapons and ended up behind bars. But he put his sentence to good use, churning out a manuscript for the turbulent and fiery début novel he's remembered for, *Prochain épisode*. Aquin was suddenly famous, influential, and as radical as ever. When the federal government tried to slip him a Governor General's Award, he said, *"Non, merci."*

Now back to the last day of his life. Aquin approached the Roman Catholic girls' school – ironically the ancient home of past governors-general – pulled out a shotgun, pointed it into his mouth, and took his last breath in the bucolic setting of crab-apple trees and fieldstone walls.

Keep It to Your Self

If you're thinking of taking a course to improve your writing, don't hurry, says Montreal's Yann Martel, the 2002 Man Booker Prize-winning novelist who has blasted creative-writing courses for their tendency to homogenize good writing. Martel, the author of the hit novel *Self*, believes that good prose is a product of at least a smidgen of isolation. The Spanish-born Montrealer says instantly showing one's work to fellow students and teachers in search of approval is a sure way of diluting good writing and stunting the creative process.

"You have to be like Solzhenytisin in the Siberian outback, saying 'You don't matter. You are insignificant,'" he said in a CBC interview.

Isolation is no stranger to the hero in Martel's Man Booker-winning *Life of Pi*, which features a guy stranded on a lifeboat in the Pacific Ocean with an injured zebra, an orangutan, a hyena, and a hungry Bengal tiger.

Bound for Glory

Andy Brown had one of those life-changing moments during a screening of *The English Patient* back in the '90s. While his fellow moviegoers were wringing out their handkerchiefs, Brown, then a Master's student in English literature, dwelled on the progress of the novel's author, Michael Ondaatje, had made since being an obscure name printed by tiny publishing houses. With an unheard eureka!, Brown decided to launch his own publishing house, and – voilà! – Conundrum Press was born. In 1996, the former tree-planter published Catherine Kidd's *Everything I Know About Love I Learned from Taxidermy* and had a hit on his hands, which he printed again and again. It hasn't exactly been *cha-ching* ever since but Brown has managed to produce the four perfect-bound titles required for government-grant eligibility and has subsequently blessed CanLit with many titles include poetry collection *Walkups*, a house-by-house salute to the Plateau district by Montreal writer Lawrence Blomgren.

Art to Heart

Here are some of the less obvious places that hold art exhibitions on a rotating basis.

Beaconsfield Library
303 Beaconsfield Blvd.;
514/428-4460

Bonsecours Market
350 St. Paul St. E.; 514/872-7730

Café Bar Farfadet
4108 St. Denis St.; 514/847-1078

Centre de Creativite
1200 Bleury St.; 514/861-4873

Centre de design de L'UQAM
1440 Sanguinet St.;
514/987-3395

The One That Got Away

Photo: Jillian Edelstein © 1997

Mordecai Richler, who always wore a pink shirt when he flew, was promoted to the highest honour within the Order of Canada shortly before his death in 2001, but the awards ceremony was held a few months too late for him to attend. It wasn't the only awards ceremony to give him the slip: there was that elusive Oscar, too. The story goes that back in the late '50s, the taciturn Richler was approached at his London home to rewrite a problematic screenplay for *Room at the Top*, a film based on the best-selling novel by John Braine. Richler was paid for his work, but the way the deal was worded, Neil Paterson kept the writing credit. The movie was a hit, Paterson got all the glowing praise for the script, and ended up taking home the 1959 Oscar for Best Screenplay Based on Material from Another Medium. *C'est la vie!*

Treasure in the Attic

During a visit to Montreal, British novelist and science maven Samuel Butler (1835-1902) spent a few hours checking out the collection at the Montreal Museum of Fine Arts. As he was wandering around, he stumbled into an attic storage area, where his eye was caught by a hidden shape in the corner. The shrouded form turned out to be a statue of the naked *Discus Thrower*, or "discobulus." Curious to know what such a magnificent piece of art was doing in such an out-of-the-way location, Butler collared a passing staff taxidermist and demanded an explanation. The fellow told Butler that the nude was hidden because it was far too vulgar for the public to behold. Bemused and a little perturbed, Butler made light of the incident in one of his well-known poems, which starts like this:

> *Stowed away in a Montreal lumber room*
> *The discobolus standeth and turneth his face to the wall;*
> *Dusty, cobweb-covered, maimed and set at naught,*
> *Beauty crieth in an attic and no man regardeth;*
> *O God! O Montreal!*

War veteran Robert Roussil was rewarded for his combat service with three years of free schooling. When he couldn't decide what to study, somebody signed him up for art, a decision that made the art world and scandal-mongers very happy indeed.

1. In 1949, Roussil unveiled a wooden statue called *Family*, in which a figurative father's genitilia were unashamedly displayed. Complaints ensued and cops moved the sculpture from Sherbrooke Street to a cell at Station 10. Hundreds showed up to see the hastily banned work, which had had its penis covered in cloth. Art lovers could see the statue without its cloth if they paid 25 cents.

2. Within a few years, Roussil had yet another controversial work on the street, inspiring a city lawyer to personally dismember it in the name of the Roman Catholic Ligue du Sacré Coeur.

3. In the '50s, Roussil was working out of a studio, which he dubbed Place des Arts, on Bleury, when police used the controversial Padlock Law (which was innovated by premier Maurice Duplessis to bar restaurauteur Frank Roncarelli from distributing Jehovah's Witness literature) to shut him down. And then they stole his studio's name for the concert hall built near the site.

4. In 1983, Roussil, who by now lived mostly in France, was outraged when four of his sculptures displayed at the Botanical Gardens were destroyed. He sued and was awarded $15,000 from the city.

5. In the early '60s, when discotheques started to open in the city core, club owner William Sofin had Roussil implant a statuesque steel-chain façade in front of his Mountain Street club known as Le Drug. A developer later had it removed. Roussil pursued him in court.

6. Another of Roussil's creations, not unlike the chain-link work, popped up near Beaver Lake. A gang of boys tried to pull it down with a truck.

7. In 1982, when Roussil opened a studio near Mirabel, 200 farmers protested his controversial presence by dumping cow dung outside his barn. A friend of Roussil's berated the farmers and, two days later, the barn mysteriously burned down.

Maison de la Culture Frontenac
2550 Ontario St. E.;
514/872-7882

Maison de la Culture Marie-Uguay
6052 Monk Blvd.; 514/872-2044

Maison de la Culture Notre-Dame-de-Grace
3755 Botrel St.; 514/872-2157

Maison de la Culture Plateau Mount Royal
465 Mount Royal Ave. E.;
514/872-2266

Maison de la Culture Pointe-Aux-Trembles
14001 Notre Dame St. E.;
514/872-2240

Maison de la Culture Rivière-des-Prairies
9140 Perras Blvd.; 514/872-9814

McGill School of Architecture
815 Sherbrooke St. W., 3rd Floor;
514/398-6700

Mile End Library
5434 Park Ave.; 514/872-2141

Verdun Cultural Centre
5955 Bannantyne Ave.;
514/765-7150

Ateliers de Danse Moderne de Montréal

372 Ste. Catherine W.;
514/866 9814

Dance Gallery of Montreal

A ballroom and Latin dance studio offering inexpensive five-week dance courses throughout the year, including swing, salsa, merengue, cha-cha, and rumba.
5159 de Maisonneuve W.;
514/846-8456

Danse Mode Action

Featuring contemporary dancing styles like hip-hop, tap, street dancing, and musical comedy. Geared toward performances, and featuring an end-of-term show.
7507 St. Lawrence; 514/521-9506

École de Danse Louise Lapierre

Performance dance, jazz, tap, classical, Celtic, hip-hop, funk, modern jazz, contemporary, etc. Offers free introductory classes.
1460 Mount Royal E.;
514/521-3456

8. In 1986, Roussil had a deal to put a three-storey-high work in front of the Lavalin Building on Peel (pictured), but the building's architect chose to put it on the side of the building instead. Roussil kicked and screamed but eventually agreed to the switch.

Photo: John David Gravenor

Carving a Reputation

Another source of sculpted scandal can be found at Armand Vaillancourt's workshop on Esplanade Street. Vaillancourt made a splash on the local art scene in 1953, after he took a chainsaw to a dying elm tree at Durocher and Sherbrooke, not far from the Swiss Hut, the legendary hangout of rebels and lefties that is no more. His pioneering Tree of Durocher Street led to a confrontation with city authorities and cemented his reputation as a bad boy of art, a title he confirmed in 1982, when three of his sculptures in St. Louis Square suddenly vanished one night, only to reappear just as suddenly six months later.

Then in 1994, the same year he hopelessly ran for the left-leaning New Democratic Party in a Westmount election, he crossed swords with theatre troupe Carbone 14. After the group won a bidding war to buy an old jam factory on Panet, Vaillancourt neglected to remove his massive Hommage aux amerindiennes from the site. The theatre company then tossed it into a dumpster. Both sides then did the lawyer waltz.

A Little Late to Tittilate

One of the biggest-ever Montreal best-sellers sent shocks not only through the city but also around the world. The full title of Maria Monk's 1836 autobiography pretty much gives you an idea where the book's going: *The Awful Disclosures of Maria Monk as Exhibited in a Narrative of Her Sufferings During a Residence of Five Years as a Novice and Two Years as a Black Nun, in the Hôtel-Dieu Nunnery in Montreal.*

In her tale, Monk details her life as a young nun forced by priests into sex slavery, during which she witnessed all measure of cardboard-collar crime. "One of my great duties was to obey the priests in all things," she writes, "and this I soon learnt, to my utter astonishment and horror, was to live in the practice of criminal intercourse with them." The story struck the right mixture of outrage, piety, and sex to sell 26,000 copies within weeks and 300,000 more worldwide in the years to follow. To this day, many Roman Catholics energetically refute her tale as an attempt by Protestants to smear the Catholic faith. Certain inaccuracies suggested that the story was actually fiction, although judging from some of the subsequent excesses of local Catholic authorities, there might have been some grain of truth in her story. Maria Monk moved to Philadelphia and died at age 33, some time after being arrested as a pickpocket in 1849. Hôtel Dieu moved to its current location at St. Urban Street and Pine Avenue in 1861.

Steeped in Verse and Worse

A revolutionary poet in the strictest sense of the word, Irving Layton's verse collided with the bourgeois romanticism of the 1940s and '50s. After graduating from Macdonald Agricultural College, Layton put pen to paper with a then-shocking brand of subversive and sexually explicit verse, launching to great fame and notoriety. But if the label "dirty" can be attributed to Layton, it's just as much for the level of hygiene he practiced whenever he was in the writing way.

Once when Layton's grown-up son, David, was visiting his father's downtown Montreal apartment, the younger Layton noticed that a filthy layer of grime clung to the surface of the bathtub. Apparently, his father

Egyptian Dance Academy
Lala Hakim teaches belly dancing, or "baladi," as well as Egyptian culture and customs. The Egypt-trained performer has danced in 26 countries, and stages occasional performances around town.
3819 Calixa-Lavallée; 514/523-3316; hometown.aol.com/lalahakim

**Espace Tangente
(Agora de la danse)**
840 Cherrier St. E.; 514/525-1500

Flamenco Dance Centre
Julia Cristina, who was trained in Andalusia, Spain, teaches all levels of flamenco dance, from beginner to advanced.
215 Jean Talon; 514/272-7727

Galerie de danse
*2444 Notre Dame W.;
514/846-8456*

**Piscine-Théâtre
(Agora de la danse)**
*840 Cherrier St. E.;
514/987-3000 ext. 2752*

Spice of Literary Life

Irving Layton, Mordecai Richler, and Leonard Cohen are the obvious examples of how local Jews helped put Montreal on the literary map. And the beat still goes on in the island city, as you can read for yourself in a collection of Canadian Jewish fiction from Red Deer Press. *Not Quite Mainstream* (2002) was edited by Montreal writer Norman Ravvin, who also happens to be Concordia University's chair of Canadian Jewish Studies. Some of the best stories were written by Montreal writers, including Layton, Elaine Kalman Naves, Robyn Sarah, Roma Irena Eisler, Roma Gelblum-Bross, and Claire Rothman. The stories underscore the sometimes quirky, unsettling, and adaptive process of being Jewish in contemporary society.

Bucking and Clicking

Photo: Joshua Radu

JOSHUA RADU

Back in 1995, a 23-year-old photographer named Joshua Radu checked out a rodeo in Laval. He mounted a 400 mm lens to his dependable Minolta camera body and showed up in the morning light just as the cowboys and cowgirls were getting ready. Radu, a half-Cree, half-Scottish guy born in Saskatoon, only shot a single roll of black-and-white film that day, but every frame resulted in a fascinating testament to the sport. Suddenly hooked on rodeos, the former resident of Toronto, Halifax, and London, England, discovered Quebec's circuit of about 20 rodeos, capped by the Festival Western de St. Tite every fall — the biggest rodeo after the Calgary Stampede. Something like 400,000 people from as far as Texas and Alberta attend the two-week St. Tite rodeo, where you can expect to pay $25 for a

THE FESTIVAL THAT RUNS ITSELF

The **Montreal Anarchist Book and Freedom Fair** has managed to attract at least 1,000 people to its event held every May since 2000 and now a move from an obscure east-end venue to the uptown Casa del Popolo promises to increase its appeal.

The event features at least 60 tables hosted by publishers, peddlers, and authors of anarchist literature from all over Canada, the West Coast, Europe, and Central America. Each participant brings a welcome spin to the thought-provoking mix of ideas ranging from globalization and international debt to sexuality and prisoners' rights. The book fair hosts workshops ranging from community gardening to the struggle to address the international debt imbalance to how to build tiny little radio stations that can be helpful in demonstrations.

As a political philosophy, anarchism is about 100 years old, but it's said to be gaining popularity among left-leaning intellectuals and students tired of the old left-right political model. The movement promotes collective decision-making with all members of a society being called on to participate. *Anarchist Book Fair; 514/844-3207; tao.ca/~lombrenoire*

The largest art gallery in Quebec isn't in Montreal. It isn't even under one roof. The annual **Tour des Arts**, held every July throughout the Eastern Townships, is staged in the intimate gardens, studios, and homes of dozens of artists and artisans. Yes, you just ring their doorbells and they'll let you in to peek at the works, with all this explained in their shiny pamphlets that also provide a tour map. With your literature in hand, you just jump in your car or ride your bike along scenic country roads linking towns like Knowlton, West Brome, Sutton, and Mansonville.

The Eastern Townships region begins about 45 minutes east of Montreal – where you'll see a large tourist office just off Autoroute 10 where info on the art tour is happily handed over. For more about the tour, contact the Sutton Tourist Bureau *(800/565-8455)*, speak to an organizer *(450/538-0605)*, or download a tour map *(acbm.qc.ca/tour-des-arts)*.

seat, if they're not sold out already. Radu decided to go all-out, so he applied for a government grant – his first ever – and got it, to spend a couple of full-time months photographing rodeo stops around the province, and making lots of cowboy and cowgirl friends in the process. Seven years later, Radu is to Quebec rodeo what Doisneau was to street kissing near the Eiffel Tower. He's finishing his first book but you can see some of his images online *(pages.infinit.net/joshua)*. For more about the St. Tite rodeo, check out their website *(festivalwestern.com)*

Just Hanging Around

All sorts of institutions have their own little collections hanging on office walls but none are more secret or controversial than the art cache belonging to the English Montreal School Board. This much is known: the collection contains about 100 paintings, including a dozen by Group of Seven master artist A.Y. Jackson, and others by such well-known Canadian artists as Adam Sheriff Scott, Anne Savage, George Horne Russell, Harold Beament, Lorne Holland Bouchard, Thoreau MacDonald, Frederick Simpson Coburn, Douglas Lawley, John Little, and Richard Short.

Most of the paintings were acquired back when the painters were relatively unknown and would often work for the price of lunch or a bus ticket. The estimated value of the art has risen from $650,000 in 1980 to its current $1,039,879. The paintings are believed mostly to be in the Fielding offices of the EMSB but officials, citing fear of theft, won't confirm this.

Technically the paintings don't belong to the board. In 1980, the old Protestant School Board donated them to a separate body controlled by school councillors, for fear that the separatist Parti Québécois might somehow force them to sell them off. More recently, parents of students from the former Catholic school board have made an issue of the art treasures.

The angry Catholic parents noted that the Protestant-dominated EMSB has closed many former Catholic schools since the two boards were forced to merge. So they were effectively saying, "Hey, why don't you do a little sacrificing of your own and sell off the paintings to buy books for the kids."

Montreal: a reader's sampler

There are millions of stories in the city, and quite a few people are writing them down. The only way we could list all our English-language literary talent would be to use microscopic print that might confuse and distress certain non-myopic readers. So we'll have to settle for this eclectic sampler, instead.

Anne Carson

This McGill Classics prof might have a full-time hobby polishing her trophy case, which lately includes the international T.S. Eliot Prize, the Lannan, the Griffin, and a Guggenheim fellowship. And now, to top it off, she's even scored a big mention in an *Unknown City* book! But instead she keeps pumping out the poems that Alice Munro called "marvellously disturbing."

Trevor Ferguson

He wrote a half-dozen novels that were so finely crafted, they didn't make any money. So he changed strategy, adopting the pen name John Farrow, and knocked out *City of Ice*, a 437-page detective thriller based roughly on the gung-ho antics of Montreal's night-squad cops. It took off on international best-seller charts from Japan to Bulgaria, spawning a sequel, *Ice Lake*, and a new sense of direction for Ferguson, who's started writing for the stage.

Elyse Gasco

She inconvenienced a lot of readers of her 1999 debut story collection, *Can You Wave Bye Bye, Baby?* They couldn't put it down. The Plateau dweller and mother of two uses black humour and political incorrectness to explore motherhood, babyhood, parenthood, and adoption. She's adapting her work for the stage.

ISLANDS IN THE STEAM

Some of Montreal's best writers pissed off native Indians in a big way when a pompous plan to honour the fiction-makers turned into a major fiasco. This unnatural disaster started in August 1997, with a government plan to celebrate the 20th anniversary of Quebec's language law, Bill 101. The idea was to name 101 uninhabited northern islands after Québécois literary works and themes. Nicole Brossard's *Le Desert Mauve* would become the name of one of these islands, as would *La Chambre Fermée* after a work by Anne Hébert. The islands were, in actual fact, the remains of mountains and hills that stuck out of the water after the Quebec government flooded traditional land inhabited by Cree Indians to build an electricity project. The Cree objected to the renaming of their territory, which already featured traditional Cree names. So, too, did some of those left off the list of honoured writers, which included just three obscure Anglo nonentities.

A master of plot, voice, and character, Mordecai Richler certainly knew his way around a novel. But when he was writing, he sometimes found the real world challenging and often needed help. For a while he relied on his son, Jacob, to set the videocassette recorder, decipher the channel numbers in the TV guide, and help him fax letters with the print the right way round. Just about the only contraption that didn't give the two-finger typist any problems was his trusty manual typewriter.

During the 1993 Mordecai Richler Roast, Jacob talked about his father's favourite tool:

"A few years ago, a very important day passed for my father, although it was unmourned or even unnoticed in the rest of the world. Olivetti had put together its last manual typewriter. My dad had to go electric.

"These new machines aren't built to withstand his heavy touch. The letters that were stencilled onto the keyboard wore off completely within a week. So every morning he would write them in himself with his supposedly indelible marker.

"Looking at his inky fingers one afternoon, I had to ask him a question. 'Dad, don't you know where the letters are by now?'"

Susan Gillis

She's been publishing her verses since the mid-'90s. In *Swimming Among the Ruins* (2000), the transplanted Haligonian morphs a visit to the Mediterranean into a cat's-cradle of poems inspired by images of Greek ruins. This passage comes from "The Walk": "The sky opened centuries around us: / Roman troops, quarried marble, neighbours. / Animals to market. Blood, / and the olive's long season toward oil."

David Homel

You have to be pretty snappy with words to snag a Governor General's Award. This American expat and Montreal resident has taken home two. As translator of more than 30 French-language books, he's made a lot of Quebec writers more accessible to Anglos. His novels include *Sonya and Jack* and *Electrical Storms*.

David Solway

He's a Hudson-based English teacher, essayist, and poet known for speaking his mind and bamboozling the public with his mind-bending antics. In October 2000, Solway launched a book he purported to be a biographical work of translation titled *Saracen Island: The Poetry of Andreas Kravis*. In fact, Kravis doesn't exist, but *Books in Canada* was sportingly hoodwinked into running a slick spread on the elusive poet. In the real world, Solway is taken seriously for his poems and critical essays on postmodern theories and academic trends.

Andrew Steinmetz

His writing has been likened to a blend of Elmore Leonard and Oliver Sacks. In 2000, he published a memoir of his nine years as a clerk in a large teaching hospital, *Wardlife: The Apprenticeship of a Young Writer as a Hospital Clerk*. His poetry collection, *Histories*, came out the same year. He's still fiddling with new verses, plotting a sequel to his memoir, and forever perfecting an ambitious, semi-autobiographical novel he undertook about a decade ago.

BOUTIQUES

← VÊTEMENTS POUR HOMMES / FEMMES / ENFANTS
SACS À MAIN / MONTRES / LUNETTES DE SOLEIL
BIJOUX / ARTISANAT / CHANDELLES / BIBELOTS / MEUBLES
JOUETS / JEUX / CHAPEAUX / CASQUETTES / MINIATURES
PRODUITS DE LA F-1 / ARTICLES DE PHOTOGRAPHIE

IMPÉRIAL AUTOCAR   TOURS DE VILLE (BILLETTERIE)

CLOTHING FOR MEN / WOMEN / CHILDREN
HANDBAGS / WATCHES / SUN GLASSES / JEWEL
CRAFTS / CANDELS / TRINKETS / FURNI
TOYS / GAMES / HATS / CAPS / MINIA
F.-ITEMS / PHOTOGRAPHY ITEMS

IMPÉRIAL AUTOCAR   CITY TOURS (TICKET OFF

BUREAU DE CH
FOREIGN EXC

AML

Imagine you're standing around naked in a crowded downtown mall. Okay, okay, if you insist, yes – you may imagine Lorenzo Lamas standing there naked instead. Where would he go to get what he needed? These pages would be more useful to him than a humidor to a cigar chomper (we'll tell you where to get yours), a hammer shop to a carpenter (yeh, it's in here), a hot-dog stand to starving man (well, we've got a few problems with that one, but read on and you'll find out why).

To the Bidder
Go the Spoils

Deadbeats who toss out their municipal tax bills along with their Dunkin' Donuts two-for-one coupons will inevitably hear from the tax collectors at the City of Montreal. The debtors' addresses are then advertised on a bulletin board at City Hall and in the classifieds of several daily papers. Then, upon a fixed date, said non-billpayer gets a knock on the door, and a horde of bargain shoppers get ushered in by a city auctioneer with more than a passing resemblance to Brigitte Bardot.

In the old pre-merged city, Montreal scheduled about a thousand auctions a year, although many were – and still are – called off at the last minute, as the debt-ridden miraculously found cash to avert the sale of their TVs, photocopiers, and desks – a frustrating turn of events for would-be bargain-hunters. In 2000, these auctions accounted for about $30 million of the city's $420 million in tax revenues. As for delinquent ratepayers, the city auctions real estate every November. The occasional bargain can be had, but here's the catch: the prior owner has a full year to repay the amount the property fetched at auction. So don't pour big bucks into your best-bid home until you use up at least one full calendar.

Buying—The Second
Time Around

Did you know you can buy things from the government that you already paid for with your taxes? The **Crown Assets Distribution Centre** sells off all kinds of federal government surplus goods – from unopened computer software to never-flushed toilets. They hold regular public sales, auctions, and vehicle liquidations and move everything from clothing to furniture, from cars to livestock. You can occasionally pick up British and United States government surplus at Canadian prices. The bargains change hands in warehouse building 12 North on the Longue-Pointe Military Base (6769 Notre Dame E., enter off Haig Ave.; 514/283-5511; crownassets.pwgsc.gc.ca/text/quebec/quebec-e.htm). All forms of payment are accepted – except cash.

If you've been thinking, "Those Montrealers sure are svelte," the numbers prove you right. According to federal statistics, Montreal's obesity rate (six percent) is well below the national average (15 percent). The reason seems to be that, besides being generally more active, Montrealers like to dress up. And dressing up means fitting two sizes down. But whatever the reason for our innate fashion superiority, you'll find no shortage of places to doll up your gorgeous body – sometimes at a hefty discount.

The best seasons for retail savings come during the slow days of summer and just after Christmas. **Holt Renfrew** has one of the best after-Chrismas sales in town.

Photo: John David Gravenor

Men should check out the clothing stores along Peel, between Ste. Catherine and de Maisonneuve. Anchored by the likes of the mighty **L'Uomo Montreal** (1452 Peel) (pictured) and respected national chain **Harry Rosen** (Les Cours Mont-Royal, 1455 Peel), this strip is a magnet to penny-pinching American businessmen shopping on a good lead. For the price of a couple of suits, such movers can come and flop at a boutique hotel, take in some seedy shows, and flock off back to Boston or Manhattan and still come out ahead – plus get their taxes back. A smattering of high-end men's and women's shops can also be found on the south side of Sherbrooke between Peel and Crescent, such as **Armani**, **Holts**, and **Polo**.

Women should start at **Holt Renfrew** (Sherbrooke and Mountain) and work their way around the corner and turn left down Crescent to Ste. Catherine. **Winners**, in the Place Montreal Trust shopping mall (McGill College and Ste. Catherine) is a great – and cheap – place to spend what cash you have left. For creations by up-and-coming young designers, check out the shopping strip on St. Denis, heading north from Roy.

Stores have adapted to the city's economic ups and downs in past year, so it's never taboo to bargain, and

Duds for a Pittance

Photo: John David Gravenor

There's only one place you have to know if you want to find serious bargains on clothing, footwear and accessories: the shmatte district on Chabanel Street West on a Saturday morning.

The action runs 9am - 4pm on the north side of the street. Start at the corner of St. Lawrence and head west. The garment district is now open for business. The cheaper stores are located closer to St. Lawrence (99, 111, 125 and 133 Chabanel). More upscale goods are available at 433 and 555 Chabanel West.

Just follow the shoppers, look for the sandwich boards and flyers, and prepare yourself to explore the buildings one by one.

You'll find everything from leather goods to babies' wear, from swimsuits to wedding dresses. Prices are usually negotiable; ditto for the tax.

a high-end store is a good place to start. Say you're trying on a pair of $600 shoes. Well, sure they come with nifty felt bags, but can you swing a free pair of $100 shoe trees? It's been known to happen, especially if you're already stocking up on a few other items. And remember that "30 percent off" can usually be pushed as far as half price. Just raise your eyebrows and shoot back, "50 percent off?" You'd be surprised.

Remember, you should never let on that you really dig what you're trying on. As the salesperson describes the product's strengths, just grunt unimpressed and utter the occasional, "Hmph."

And just because you like something you tried on, you don't have to jump at it right away. Ask the store to hold on your selections for a few minutes while you check out an adjoining shop. Chances are they'll try to beat your deal.

Finally, be polite. Although salespeople will bend over backwards to make a sale, they have their professional pride. A few hundred bucks less for the boss won't ruin their day.

Best of all, you don't have to know anybody on the inside, and you won't need introductions. Ever since Canada signed the North American Free Trade Agreement and thousands of garment jobs subsequently went south, all of these merchants are basically starving for cash. So you can walk into anybody's offices and be sure they have something to sell to the public.

Here are a few locations to get you started.

California Avenue
sweaters, summer wear
134-433 Chabanel W.

Concept Aba
leather goods
306-555 Chabanel W.

Corwik Fashions
women's wear
200-225 Chabanel W.

Ambiance Couture
bridal and wedding gear
215-333 Chabanel W.

Clubbers love Claros

Sandra Claros and a multiplying horde of clubbers and scenesters have been berry-berry good to each other. A night-stalking clientele has connected big time with this Paris-trained designer's custom-made and off-the-rack designs, forcing her to move from her first tiny atelier to a storefront/factory with five times the floor size. Nowadays, **Sandra Claros Designer** innovates, produces, and markets cool gear in 1,840 square feet of space-ship silver, glittery red, orange, and gold with unique furniture and plexiglass tables. Some of her hottest stuff includes threads for the after-hours crowd, like signature clubbing pants with ingeniously thought-out water-bottle pockets, safety-minded zippers, and warmth-giving features for the committed raver. Claros is also the first stop for finicky glam types, Goths, and those with a bent for '80s-style rocker fits and fabrics. For women (and discriminating transvestites), Claros makes silk corsets, cocktail dresses, and jeans in an incredible range of motifs, colours, and fabrics. Meanwhile, jeans and pants featuring vinyl, fake fur, and nylon are available for both sexes in discreet and outlandish designs.
1105 de Maisonneuve E., corner Amherst;
514/286-1162

Photo: John David Gravenor

Having grief tying to find shoes or clothing that fits? That should never be a stretch in Montreal. Here are a few local stores recommended by the Tall Club of Montreal.

MEN'S AND WOMEN'S SHOES

Mayfair Boutiques
Place Ville-Marie, Carrefour, Laval and Promenades St. Bruno

Canadian A.B.C. Gennano Petti
Cross-country ski boots up to size 17.
3333 Port Royal West;
514/387-7307

Le Depot Naturalizer
Large sizes.
Metro De l'Eglise, Verdun;
514/768-0642

Tony's Shoe Shop
Men's and women's large sizes.
1346 Greene, Westmount;
514/935-2993

La Bottinerie
Men's large sizes.
6593 St. Hubert St.;
514/276-9022

Every spring and fall, out-of-town antique dealers and film art-department guys jump in their cube vans and head for Montreal. They come for this city's unbelievably amazing rummage sales. If you've never been to one, you'll be amazed how much cool stuff is floating around here, at a fraction of its retail cost.

The larger institutions hold the best sales, like the nun-run, tidy, and well-stocked sale at the **Grey Nuns convent** on St. Marc near René Lévesque. **Westmount's** St. Matthias Church on Côte St. Antoine is a more helter-skelter scene, with all kinds of uptown cast-offs for your haggling pleasure. **The Study** girls' school on Mount Pleasant at Cedar is a crowd-pleaser. Latecomers line up for an entire block, but it's worth waiting to ogle a gymnasium full of Westmount surplus. Any sale in Town of Mount Royal is also worth checking out, while NDG has more than its fair share – like the ones held at **Le Manoir** (*Décarie at NDG Ave.*) (pictured).

Great rummagers follow competitive rules, so memorize and destroy: *The Gazette* carries an announcement of rummage sales on Thursdays in the "It's A Date" section –

WOMEN'S CLOTHING

Grand'heure

4131 St. Denis St.; 514/284-5747, 888/284-5747

Boutique Ambre

201 St. Paul St. W., Old Montreal; 514/982-0325

MEN'S CLOTHING

Bovet

4475 Metropolitain E., St. Leonard; 514/374-4555

M.H. Grover & Son's

4741 Wellington, corner of 3rd Ave., Verdun; 514/769-3771

J. Schreter Inc.

4350 St. Lawrence; 514/845-4231

Photo: John David Gravenor

Giovanni Custom Tailor's

5240 St. Lawrence; 514/274-2427

this is your bible. Most great rummage sales are held just once or twice a year, so show up early. When you get there, check out the art and collectibles. Church folks sometimes overprice stuff you'd never buy, like an Olympic Stadium ashtray, while letting the good items go for cheap. Treasures to be found include: early Celine Dion records still in shrink wrap, silverware picked up at Eaton's before it closed, Quebec Inuit soapstone art, French-Canadian wood carvings, crafts from the Laurentians, Brother André religious mementos, pottery from the old Beauce factory, vintage Danish teak furniture, pre-transistor radios, Fire King glassware, Expo 67 memorabilia, and bone-handled cutlery. Rare-book worms spend most of their time poking through tables of books, while old-school types take advantage of the local flair for fashion and hunt retro duds in pristine condition.

When you approach the cashier to pay, think poor. Highlight the shortcomings of your items. Remember your job is not to overpay for that Rusty Staub wristwatch or first edition Hugh Hood novel.

If you arrive late, you can still check out the corners, where some shoppers dump their cast-off items while trying garments on over their jeans and T-shirts.

Weekly church boutiques, like the one held Thursdays at **St. George's Church** on Stanley, are also listed in *The Gazette*. Although they're often combed-over by local antique dealers, you can never tell when new stock will hit the floor.

The Best of All Possible Orgasms

If you want to liven up your love life but worry that your priest might "tsk-tsk" you for sneaking into a sex shop, then **Joy Toyz** is exactly what the sex therapist ordered. The online sex-accessory supply centre founded by former dancer-choreographer Sebastian Yeung (a woman) peddles all the best gadgets and garments – from leathers and rubbers to beads and vibrators. Joy Toyz also organizes instructive and entertaining home parties, like the ones Grandma used to host to sell Tupperware – minus the plastic kitchen tubs. Last but not least, Joy Toyz runs a sex-educational space on The Main, where you can sign up for workshops like Sexercise, post-natal sexuality, and tantric and strap-on sex. Some of these programs, like Oral Sex and BDSM 101, are also open to men. *415-4200 St. Lawrence; 514/845-8697; joytoyz.ca*

build it and they will shop

In the 1890s, it was hailed as "the finest building in America devoted to the retail business." Others hated it for changing the residential nature of Ste. Catherine Street.

Today, the building is home to **The Bay** department store, across from the hawkers and loiterers of Phillips Square. But from the 1890s through the 1960s, this was the site of Morgan's – the first city department store to abandon its old-town location and risk moving uptown to serve the area's prosperous new residents. The Ste. Catherine Street site had a row of houses before the store was built. They were bought up and torn down.

Other downtown stores soon followed:

Ailes

Goodwins built a store on Ste. Catherine near University. It was later bought out by Eaton's, which demolished it and built from scratch. Eaton's was replaced by the **Les Ailes de La Mode** department store. The ninth-floor restaurant, which was modeled after an art deco steamship galley, is a protected heritage site.

Deals on Heels

Chaussures Super-Prix

If you don't mind shopping at a hole-in-the-wall, this place offers serious bargains with new shoe models arriving daily. Exclusively sells men's and women's overstock from dozens of manufacturers.
4829 Wellington St., Verdun; 514/762-0139

Chaussures Le Sabotier

This downtown establishment has a wide range of casual and chic footwear for men and women.
Complexe Desjardins Shopping Concourse; 514/285-6355

Collins Chaussures de Sécurité

Safety shoes for risky jobs.
7401 Newman Blvd., LaSalle; 514/365-2590

Ciro Shoes

For top-of-the-line men's and women's styles at bargain prices.
288 Notre Dame St. W., Old Montreal; 514/982-9921

Yellow Shoe Store

With more than 100 discount outlets throughout the province, there's one near you. Specialists in their own line of shoes in constantly changing styles.
multiple locations; 514/273-0424

Chaussures Panda

Children's shoes.
Rockand Shopping Centre; 514/737-3910

Dack Shoes

Specialize in Dack and Church shoes for men only.
Place Ville Marie Shopping Concourse; 514/879-5971

Chaussures Pavane-Mayfair Salon

An extensive range of casual and elegant shoes for ladies.
Place Ville Marie Shopping Concourse; 514/866-1123

Birks Jewelers

Birks made the move uptown very early on and for some years were sorry they did. Their new building, expanded staff, and business costs pushed them into the red for the first time. Things eventually turned around.

Simons

John Murphy moved his large store to Ste. Catherine and Metcalfe. Simpson's eventually bought out Murphy's and built their store on the same site. Today, the former Simpson's building houses the Simons department store and Paramount cinema complex.

A Fair View of a Giant

A naked, 17-foot giant greeted shoppers at the **Fairview Pointe Claire Shopping Centre** when it opened in August, 1965. The plaster replica of Michelangelo's *David* was a gift from Simpson's department store, but West Island shoppers weren't quite ready for such advanced concepts of nudity juxtaposed with their grocery shopping. Mothers lobbied to have it removed and the controversy attracted massive crowds of enraptured suburbanites before the likeness was shipped off as a gift to the library of Loyola College, now a campus of Concordia University. On St. Patrick's Day, 1967, pranksters painted it green. It was finally smashed to pieces by vandals who broke into the library on March 20, 1987 and pulled the classical nude down with a fire hose.

When Adam Blechman came to study business in Montreal, he was surprised at how far this city was lagging behind other urban centres in terms of locally relevant Internet content.

"The Internet can be cold," the web developer says. "It's hard to find something that relates to one's own community."

After stumbling across what he saw as a gaping market niche in 1999, the former Torontonian joined forces with business partner Dov Grossmas to develop a user-friendly discount site. Today, **Promogo.com** has signed up more than 200 businesses, each offering printable discount coupons online. The site's ten easy-to-navigate categories list things like automobile goods and services, health and beauty needs, gifts, and professional services. The best part? It's totally free.

Promogo.com is not just for locals, either. The site is listed on major search engines like Google, so prospective visitors can download savings on hotels, restaurants, and local attractions before they arrive.

The service works sort of like an interactive coupon book or weekly sales flyer. But while your average coupons can be used only once, the ones from Promogo.com can be printed as many times as you like.

The site also produces a regular newsletter telling you about all the new discounts. And they give out $100 in gift certificates every week — just visit the site and select "Click Here To Win." Winners are picked randomly, and the odds are significantly better than your average state lottery.

Health Food and Organic Products

A lot of refugees from the hippie and granola days back in the 1970s can be seen rolling their carts through the aisles of this city's many health-food emporiums. But you don't have to be a baby boomer to get what's good for you at one of these places:

À votre santé
A full-range market with organic produce and supplements.
5126 Sherbrooke W. at Vendome; 514/482-8233

Club Organic
A well-stocked health-food supermarket with organic produce, bulk foods, meat.
341 Frontenac, at Marie-Anne; 514/523-0223

Dollard-des-Ormeaux
3827 St. John's at de Salaberry; 514/624-2896

Fleur Sauvage
All sorts of food, natural cosmetics, shampoos, and supplements.
5561 Monkland, near Old Orchard: 514/482-5193

Frenco

Herbs, spices, and organic foods in
bulk. Vitamins and supplements.
3985 St. Lawrence, at Duluth;
514/285-1319

Health Tree

Good range of vitamins, supplements,
cosmetics, and some health foods.
7133 Côte St. Luc; 514/484-1690

Kilo-Naturel

Aisles of natural foods, produce, bulk
goods, skin creams, cosmetics, and
lotions. A naturopath is available in
the store several days a week.
201 St. Viateur W., near Esplanade;
514/278-3377

Tau

Thoroughly well-stocked range of
natural foodstuffs, organic produce,
and specialty items.
4238 St. Denis, near Mount Royal;
514/843-4420

Streets Without Steamies

This city once had a great tradition of curbside salespeople: in the 1890s, Montrealers bought milk, ice, bread and buns, fries, and popcorn from itinerant street vendors. Around the time of World War I, motorized French-fry vans were a common sight on city streets and hot dogs were added around 1930.

But those days ended in 1947, when a certain Dr Hood, in a report to a city subcommittee, slammed street eats as unhygienic. The 200 dog dealers were also accused of impeding traffic, leaving a mess, and competing unfairly with stationary restaurants. One hot-dog wheeler dealer retorted that other dodgy practices were tolerated, such as horse-drawn bread trucks featuring horsemen handling loaves barehanded, or the treats at the Bonsecours market, which included fly-covered meats and shoppers who customarily gobbed all over the place. City Hall threatened the dog dealers with jail time and seizure of their vehicles.

Montreal's draconian ban on street commerce was maintained with an iron fist throughout the Drapeau era, as bans on sidewalk sales of everything from jewellery to newspapers in vending boxes was emphatically policed. Even the eager, entrepreneur, and model to other youths, Eric Langlois, 15, who managed a fleet of 17 ice-cream bikes in 1985, was repeatedly hauled to the cop shop and fined $100. (He reported that more forgiving cops would turn a blind eye in return for "a couple of Fudgesicles.")

The bylaw banning ambulatory tube steaks was reinforced in 1980 and unsuccessfully challenged in 1994 by student Dylan Ritter, 25, whose sidewalk steamies cost him over $1,000 in fines. Mayor Doré, unmoved by Ritter's petition that included 500 favourable signatures, refused to budge on the issue. "I think Montreal has a lot of charm and it doesn't necessarily need hot-dog vendors to add to it," said Doré.

In 1995, Ahmed Trabelsi tried to sell hot dogs in front of City Hall from a $12,000 customized vehicle, but cops put him out of business about 20 minutes into his effort. He repeated his awareness-raising protest two years later, selling (and handing out for free) about 300 hot dogs. Police and inspectors said he'd get a ticket in the mail. Recent promises by city officials to "study the issue" of lifting the hot dog-ban might sound familiar: city officials have periodically promised to do so for over 50 years.

You Say You Want a Health Revolution?

Hung over from paint fumes? Sick of smearing chemicals on your body? You can change your consumer habits with a little help, like free seminars on making your own all-natural products ranging from paint to soap. Every week there's a different lecture at **Le Frigo Vert**, a downtown cooperative affiliated with the English-language Concordia University.

Learn how to make your own tofu and prepare Indonesian foods. Discover the benefits of eating local foods and figure out how to smart-cook meals to retain natural goodness. The back-to-the-earth mission at Le Frigo Vert (which translates to The Green Fridge) is to empower people to cook for themselves and buy smartly in bulk. They have an in-store library where you can learn to prepare your own dishes. They also sell bulk foods and natural produce in season.

A lifetime membership is $15 (free for Concordia students). Non-members are welcome to shop at a nominal markup.
2130 Mackay, near de Maisonneuve; 514/848-7586; lfv@cam.org

skateboarding threads

It was worn loose until Dad caught on. Now it's looking tighter: the right skateboard clothing can make all the difference on the road, ramps, and rails. Just let it be tough. Here are some trusty sk8 shops with a range of T-shirts, caps, helmets, hoodies, shoes, and more.

Alena.mtl
5662 Sherbrooke W.; 514/484-2428

Diz
48 Westminster Ave. N.; 514/486-9123

Spin
2041 St. Denis; 514/288-7746

Underworld
289 Ste. Catherine E., 514/284-6473

Hunka Hunka Burning Leaves

Until recently, last-minute travellers could get $300 flights to Cuba on underbooked charter flights. The dirt-cheap tickets are now scarce but Havana-bound tourists have been known to score rebates on their travels by reselling boxes of stogies on the New England black market. For those who don't want to go all the way to Havana to get Cuban cigars, here are some places offering the world's finest smokes.

La Casa del Habano
Exquisite and loving home to a quarter million dollars in stogies, stored in a walk-in cedar-paneled humidor. Buy 'em and smoke 'em in the smoking lounge, or else scour the selection of lighters, cutters, literature, humidors, and other

smoking accessories — you can even rent a safe to keep your purchases safe, fresh, and ready to burn. *1434 Sherbrooke W.; 514/849-0037*

Blatter & Blatter
Pipemakers since 1907, they also sell tobacco, cigars, and accessories. *365 President Kennedy; 514/845-8028*

C3 International
Specials on boxes of Cuban and non-Cubans, monthly sample packs, and tons of accessories. *9916 Côte de Liesse Rd., Lachine; 514/828-9309*

Casa Habanera Cigars
1229 Metcalfe; 514/876-0057

Davidoff (pictured)
1458 Sherbrooke W.; 514/289-9118

Photo: John David Gravenor

H. Poupart
1385 Ste. Catherine W.; 514/842-5794

Vasco Cigars
1327 Ste. Catherine W.; 514/284-0475

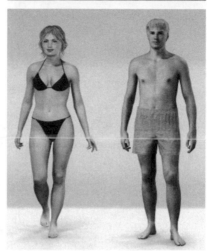

Your Fitting Image

One great thing about shopping at a clothing store is you can always visit the changing room and try before you buy. But how about Internet shopping? How can you try on clothes that you can't actually touch?

A Montreal e-business considered that problem and came up with a profitable solution. **My Virtual Model** is an online program that lets you build a 3D replica of yourself to try on clothing online. Developed by local entrepreneurs Louise Guay and Jean-François St. Arnaud with loads of provincial government cash, the first release of My Virtual Model came out in 1997. The technology has since been made available on leading retail websites like American Eagle, Plus Size, Kenneth Cole, Land's End, FUBU, and Maxim Online. To give the service a free whirl, go to myvirtualmodel.com and click on "create a model," select a gender, give your replica a name, then choose the body features that best match your own. Then sit back and behold the often-eerie likeness of yourself. With a click of a mouse, your virtual version can then be displayed sporting a fetching pair of mauve velvet sweat pants or whatever else you're too lazy or too shy to try on in an actual store.

Photo: John David Gravenor

Books

Just when you thought the city was a homogenous branch plant for international chains, you come across these shopping strips too often overlooked by regular Montrealers.

For the uninitiated, **Wellington** (pictured) can pack a heady buzz as the busy strip belies its undeserved reputation of being a welfare zone full of women with chipped teeth and men with misspelled tattoos. It's actually the bastion of some of the most boisterous and opinionated people in the city. Residents look down from strange inverted balconies and music is often piped through tinny speakers along the road (for some reason "Seasons in the Sun" seems to be in heavy rotation). A couple of perky little cafés can be stumbled into on Hickson, while the strip boasts a hot sporting goods store, as well as the timeless MH Grover clothing shop that has been a landmark for decades.

In the early '80s somebody whipped up a bit of hype for the concept of shopping strips with sidewalks covered by plastic awnings. The shopowners on **St. Hubert** embraced the partial-cover concept and – for a while, at least – the street gained some popularity as a sort of pedestrian mall with cars zooming down the middle. Few show-stopping stores here, but a bargain or two can be had at one of the many shops with perpetual liquidation sales. Known as Bridal Alley, this is a strip where self-respecting women whoul would never shop here descend upon it in droves when looking for that special wedding dress and all things bridal, from shoes to garter belts to tiaras and veils.

NEW

Chapters
While they cut back on the comfy couches, it's still a good place to browse books and check out the crowd. Three floors of books, periodicals, books-on-tape, discount tables, and a Starbucks franchise. Open late.
1171 Ste. Catherine St. W.; 514/849-8825

Double Hook Book Shop
This store championed Canadian literature before it was known as CanLit. This well-heeled location also hosts select readings and launches.
1235a Greene; 514/932-5093

Indigo Books & Music
Well-stocked and lots of author events, the downtown location at Place Montreal Trust is vast and open late.
1500 McGill College Ave.; 514/281-5549
Cavendish Mall, 5800 Cavendish Blvd.; 514/482-2163

McGill University Bookstore

Photo: John David Gravenor

More than textbooks. Bestsellers, curiosities, cybercafé, McGill T-shirts, bags, etc. This big store features a good selection of books from McGill-Queens University Press.
3420 McTavish; 514/398-7444

Nicholas Hoare

Chic surroundings, good selection of new releases, and recherchée music.
1366 Greene Ave., 514/933-4201
1307 Ste. Catherine W., basement of Ogilvy's Department Store; 514/499-2005

Paragraphe Bookstore

Tons of books about Montreal. Exhaustive selection of new titles. Frequent readings, good children's section, and discount program.
2220 McGill College; 514/845-5811

Any dolt knows about Ste. Catherine, but it takes a special dolt to know **Ste. Catherine Street East**. Go beyond the train overpass and hooker hangout at Prefontaine to sample a unique flavour of the city. While several commercial venues have given right up and converted ground-floor businesses into homes, other merchants are fighting the good fight, including a posh little computer store that insists you buzz before you enter. Past Morgan Park, on the north side, check out the health-food store run by aging Catholics in white smocks. This little gem of a shop is a hit with the locals, as customers often outnumber the many crucifixes and prints of popes on the walls.

Before they built a spanking new bridge across the Lachine Canal in 2002, **Monk Street** was the Shangri-La of business thoroughfares – a sort of shoppers' land that time forgot. Well, it hasn't changed much. The auction house beside the church, a liquor commission, and amazingly spectacular thrift shops still line this obscure but bustling Ville Emard strip. And remember while you shop that this proud neighbourhood produced its share of heroes, including hockey legends Mario Lemieux and goaltender Gilles Meloche.

Immigrants came from the Philippines, Caribbean, Eastern Europe, and Asia to set up shops at the two-pronged strip near **Van Horne and Victoria**, and you owe it to yourself to see what they've created. The Filipinas are getting their nails done and renting Tagalog movies. Next door, the Asian merchants tolerate you going wild with their amazing and low-cost imported toys. Across the street, they're lining up for fresh plantain and other West Indian specialities, while a friendly Moroccan bids you to enter his carpet shop. Just try getting bored in this friendly oasis of diversity and cool products.

Just as international, with a strong dash of South Asian and Arabic, is the stretch of **Jean Talon between l'Acadie and Park**. You can haggle for saris, score imported knock-offs, feast on Indian food with Lebanese pastry for dessert, say a prayer at a Hungarian Presbyterian church, and push a shopping cart around the massive Loblaw's market by the historic north-end train station.

Screws Without Getting Screwed

Some of the tools are brand new in the box. Other stuff's damaged and says so. The brands? You never heard of them half the time. But who cares at one-quarter to one-third of retail prices?

Matériaux à Bas Prix *(Low Priced Materials)* is a fast-growing, province-wide chain selling a massive jumble of stuff that renovation-happy home owners dream about at night – things like $40 cordless drills, $13 doors, and $8 gallons of high-end paint. Need a new scuff-proof floor for the imminent Macarena revival? Come on in.

Store founder Christian Richer used to be an antique dealer until he stumbled on this niche. That was more than a dozen stores ago. Matériaux à Bas Prix originally sold damaged stuff, but now carries mostly new items from retail surplus and bankruptcies.

The closest store to Montreal is located in Laval *(1420 rue de Jaffa; 450/624-0204)*.

Mall Down the Line

Carrefour Laval used to be one of those dowdy suburban shopping centres that made you feel like you were in a TV rerun. Now it's more like an indoor village, with 250 or so sidewalk-style storefronts to trick you into thinking you're downtown. It is said that you can buy more than 30 kinds of hairspray at the mall, good news for women of the northern suburbs who like to keep their hair in exactly the same position at all times.

The mall's owner, Cadillac Farview (no, that's not a limo), has poured more than $80 million into the complex, much of it to build a new 300,000-foot addition for upscale tenants like ladies fashion house Zara, department stores The Bay, Sears, and Les Ailes de la Mode, and the big-box renovation store, Rona L'Entrepôt.

And if you've been planning a big career with the Ice Capades, you can practice your skating on the mall's indoor rink.

To get there from Montreal, take Autoroute 15 North to Exit 10, then follow the signs for Le Carrefour.

Stage Theatre Bookshop

Specializing in books pertaining to the stage, dance, visual arts and cinema.
2123 Ste. Catherine W.;
514/931-7466

Photo: John David Gravenor

USED/GENERAL

Academic and General Book Shop

A good place to find out-of-print and new editions. If it's not there, they'll order it.
385 Sherbrooke W.; 514/849-3833

Argo

Small shop with diverse remaindered, new, and nearly-new books and periodicals.
1915 Ste. Catherine W.;
514/931-3442

Cheap Thrills

A nicely cultivated book section with lots of music CDs. Located smack in the middle of downtown.
2nd floor, 2044 Metcalfe St.;
514/844-8988

Diamond Bookstore

Lots of remaindered, scarce, and second-hand stock.

5035 Sherbrooke W.;
514/481-3000

Librairie Astro

1844 Ste. Catherine W.;
514/932 1139

Paradis du Livre

Despite its French name, it's packed with many English titles. Well stocked in science-fiction. Special Star Trek section. Cheap.

5153 Wellington, Verdun;
514/767-2589

Vortex

Hard-to-find, first-edition, and general used titles in painstakingly good condition.

1855 Ste. Catherine W.;
514/935-7869

S.W. Welch Books

Located next to a tombstone maker, a general and used bookstore with a fair science-fiction collection and popular bargain table. They also buy books.

3878 St. Lawrence; 514/848-9358

The Word

Located in a Dickensian space in the McGill Ghetto, it stocks nearly-new textbooks, fiction, poetry, Canadian novels — you name it. Frequently cited as our best English-language used bookstore.

469 Milton; 514/845-5640

Raising the Overhead

When the **Dorval Mall** (now known as the **Fairview Shopping Centre**) opened in 1954, it was a strip mall like all the others in our fine city. But something seemed to be lacking and one day somebody realized what: a roof. So in 1968, the outdoor mall was transformed into one of them fancy interior-type thingies we know so well and love so much today. When the roof was finished, customers started coming in droves, and flocks, and other large groups. More shops opened, fuelled by the bucks of those who liked the feeling of carpet, rather than scrunchy snow, underfoot. Impressed by these results, other malls followed suit — well, it wasn't surprising, considering that they were virtually all owned by the Bronfmans (Cadillac Fairview) or the Steinbergs (Ivanhoe). The **Côte St. Luc Mall**, built in 1956, shed its old open-air form in 1970, and gained a dozen new shops, while the **St. Martin Laval Mall** also went under the roof that same year with similar results. The **Wilderton Shopping Center**, as well as malls in Île Perrot and Beaconsfield, also dropped the word "strip" from their malls within the next two years, and also saw sales skyrocket.

Decking the Malls

Photo: John David Gravenor

The **Rockland Shopping Centre** may just look like a mall to you, but according to the knowledgable folks of the Royal Architectural Institute of Canada, the mall is a work of art. The RAIC went so far as to include the shopping centre in its millennium ranking of Canada's 500 finest examples of architecture.

Photo: John David Gravenor

When American pollster George Gallup visited Montreal in 1947, he told the local Advertising and Sales Executive Club that $20 a week should be enough to secure all the happiness that money alone can buy.

That's not much scratch, but it can still get you pretty far on the "entraide" and second-hand circuits. An entraide, which translates roughly as "shared help," is a non-profit shop where used goods are sold to raise money to help disadvantaged neighbours. There are at least 30 such stores on Montreal Island. The best way to find them is by entering the term "entraide" in the business listings of an Internet phone directory such as *canada411.com*. The local white pages also provide listings for shops whose names begin "entraide" in the business section. You can stumble across them on streets like Wellington, Monk, and Notre Dame.

Numerous Salvation Army and **Village des Valeurs** stores also sell cheap stuff ranging from linens to encyclopaedia to bicycles. You can often find collectable cameras, increasingly desirable ceramics by the likes of Beauce and Laurentian Pottery, vintage clothing, and modern fixtures and furniture. We saw a stack of rare, vintage movie posters snapped up for a couple of bucks a crack.

The central **Salvation Army** depot on Notre Dame near Guy opens at 10 am, Monday through Saturday (it's closed Sundays). If you show up ten minutes early, you'll find an eager queue waiting to get in. The best bargains are to be found in the As-Is section at the rear of the store. Smaller stuff gets wheeled in on trolleys all morning and into the afternoon. Browse the trolley while it's still rolling and get ready to (politely) grab what you want. When you finish paying, ask for the date of the next quarterly half-off sale. As an added bonus, the Salvation Army doesn't tax purchases.

Renaissance *(7250 St. Lawrence, at Jean Talon; 514/276-3626)* is another charity shop like the Salvation Army, but with a decent computer section.

SPECIALIZED

Alternative Bookstore
An "anti-profit" shop run by a mainly English-speaking collective. Featuring black, aboriginal, anti-capitalist, "queer," and topical literature and reviews.
2nd floor, 2035 St. Lawrence; 514/844-3207

Bonder Bookstore
They have been offering a phone-ordering service for decades. "For any book in print." They can order classics, textbooks, computer books, novels — whatever.
52 Westminster Ave. N.; 514/484-3745; bonder.com

Camelot
Computer books, management books, loads of software.
1191 Phillips Square; 514/861-5019
5199 Côte des Neiges; 514/342-2772

Librairie Michel Fortin
Specialists in books and materials for learning languages. Has mostly language books, but also serves as a general bookstore.
3714 St. Denis; 514/849-5719

Photo: Jon David Gravenor

Le Mélange Magique

Books and recordings about the occult, holistic, and metaphysical subjects. They also sell wellness paraphernalia.

1928 Ste. Catherine W.;

514/938-1458

Ulysses Travel Bookshop

Exhaustive range of travel guides, literature, and maps.

4176 St. Denis; 514/843-9447

OTHER LANGUAGES

Abya-Yala Librairie des Amériques

Books pertaining to North, Central, and South America in English, French, Spanish, and Portuguese. Music, magazines, and fair-trade coffee. Loads of book launches and signings.

4555 St. Lawrence;

514/849-4908; abyayala.com

L'Echange

Second-hand books, mostly in French, plus comics and music in other languages.

713 Mount Royal E., 514/523-6389

3694 St. Denis; 514/849-1913

Gallimard

The latest Québécois and French bestsellers with a new-wave flair.

3700 St. Lawrence; 514/499-2012

Slightly downwind from the racetrack at Décarie and Jean Talon sits **Décarie Square**, an embattled mall that, through hardship, dumped its glitzy image and went whole hog to attract bargain-savvy consumers in the nearby area.

One of the two-dozen-plus attractions is the **Winners** store, which stocks end-of-line and surplus designer goods for up to 60 percent off. **Aldo Liquidation** has contemporary footwear for men and women at discounts up to 70 percent. **Baby Tween Furniture Outlet** has furniture for kids and teens at 30 percent savings. **Haya Kova Hats** imports hats from Europe and does made-to-measure, all at a discount. **Handbags Two** stocks designer handbags, evening bags, accessories and garments, while sparing you the tax.

The mall is located on the west side of the Décarie Expressway *(6900 Décarie Blvd., at Vezina Street)* – one block south of the entrance and exit connecting to the expressway.

hip-hop wares

Blaze
Women's and men's clothing, shoes, accessories, CDs.
539a Ste. Catherine W., at Aylmer; 514/845-6787

City Styles
Specializing men's hip-hop/urban clothing. Flyers handed out around town entitle you to a discount.
1445 Bleury, at Ste. Catherine; 514/499-9114

Eastside Fashion Inc
Men and women's gear, hip-hop clothing. Roca Wear, Phat Farm, and Baby Fat. Parasuco and lots of brand names. Shoes by FUBU, Kangol boots, Pelle Pelle, Avirex, Enyce, for ladies and men.
5508 Sherbrooke W., near Girouard; 514/488-1448

Iggy's Hip-Hop Gear
Hip-hop gear, men's and women's, shoes, caps.
6790 St. Hubert St., between St. Zotique and Bélanger; 514/948-8881

N Y C
Like the name says: New York City style. Men's and women's hip-hop/urban clothing and footwear. Accessories including bandannas, jewelery, large crosses, big rings, earrings. Also sells hip-hop music.
1168 Ste. Catherine W., between Drummond and Stanley; 514/874-9494

Off the Hook
Underground/urban gear for men and women. Mixed CDs.
1021a Ste. Catherine W., at Peel; 514/499-1021

Phat Farm
Phat Farm and Baby Fat tops and bottoms, jeans, shoes. Frequent sale promotions.
484 Ste. Catherine W., near Union; 514/861-6565

Sports Fever
Men and women's casual shoes and running shoes. Clothing including Sean John, Phat Farm, Roca Wear, Triple 5 Soul, Johnny Blaze, Academic. Ask about the

Librairie Allemande
German-language literature.
3488a Côte des Neiges; 514/933-1919

Librairie Italiana
All-Italian books, music, and videos (for sale and rent).
6792 St. Lawrence; 514/277-2955

Librairie Las Americas
Literature in Spanish.
10 St. Norbert, off St. Lawrence; 514/844-5994

Middle East Bookstore
Arabic-language books, magazines, music.
877 Décarie, near Côte Vertu Metro; 514/744-4886

discount card – 15 percent off. Good selection of music by local DJs.

1238 Ste. Catherine W., at Drummond; 514/874-0198

Vibes Sports

Self-proclaimed fashion leader of Montreal underground/hip-hop streetwear. Men's and women's jackets, shirts, pants, shoes, etc. Ask for their VIP card to qualify for 15 percent off.

1224 Peel, south of Ste. Catherine W., 514/875-5215

COMICS/UNDERGROUND

Bella Books

Graphic novels, comic books (including works by Montreal's Julie Doucet), literature, and lots of vinyl.

3968 St. Lawrence; 514/228-7730

Fichtre!

Quebec underground comics, underground publications, Fantagraphics, etc.

436 de Bienville, at Rivard; 514/844-9550

Millennium

From *Batgirl* to *X-Men* and lots in between. Action figures galore.

451 Marie-Anne E.; 514/284-0358

Mags and More

Photo: John David Gravenor

No two **Multimags** are exactly alike, and that's probably the secret of their success. Starting in the late eighties with a Spartan location at 1570 de Maisonneuve West near Guy, this made-in-Montreal chain has grown into a newsstand empire of more than a dozen locations here and in Quebec City. Each shop has evolved to suit local tastes, whether in Snowdon (*5236 Queen Mary*) or downtown (*352 and 2085 Ste. Catherine West*) or Westmount (*Sherbrooke just west of Claremont*) or the Gay Village (*1321 Ste. Catherine East*). Some stores have freaky greeting cards, others DVDs, still others sell Cuban cigars and collectibles. But they all have hot-selling books and newspapers from all over the world. The preferred look for the recent stores is shabby-chic, with exposed brick, wood floors, and offbeat furniture. The Mile End shop (*370 Laurier Ave. West*) has a giant garage door that's kept open during the summer. Meanwhile, about 25,000 customers visit the flagship outlet at 3552 St. Lawrence every month, many to thumb swanky architecture, marketing, and design mags – it's one of the busiest nightspots after the clubs shut down. The original store still caters to students, and features scads of reference books which you can pretend to browse before you hit the hottie stands.

Media & Entertainment

Montrealers with an aversion to heavy lifting and other assorted weirdos have flocked to the bright lights of fame like shadflies to a street light in May. In the next pages, we've noted some of the more bizarre interludes in our town's strutting stage — including the madman who beguiled George Lucas, the anonymous menace who made Ringo Starr cower behind his drums, or a certain South Shore mother who entered the annals of fame via the backdoor route ... literally.

Land of the Rising Star

If you see Christy Chung passing by in her native South Shore home town of Brossard, you might not recognize her as one of the planet's biggest movie stars. Chung's serendipitous rise to stardom began in 1992 when she competed at the Miss Chinese Montreal pageant and won. The victory came with an invitation to the Miss Chinese International Pageant in Hong Kong.

Christy had to choose between going to the pageant and accepting a job reading the weather on Radio Canada. She chose Hong Kong.

"It was my first trip away," she said. "I had never left Montreal." She reports being lost onstage amid the gibberish that Cantonese was to her, she didn't even know how she was faring at the competition until a fellow contestant told her: "You just won." Her language skills have since improved.

From 1993 on, Christy has been deluged with opportunities to play leading roles in successful Hong Kong features like *Bodyguard from Beijing* and *Aces Go Places*.

Chung, who was voted the 2000 "sexiest Asian celebrity" by Singapore *FHM* magazine, tells us that her greatest regret was turning down a lead role in Jackie Chan's *Rumble in the Bronx*. But she later got to work with him in *High Binders*, described as the most expensive Hong Kong feature ever. Chung, whose parents still live here, returned to have her first child at the Royal Victoria Hospital — unfortunately it was during the historic Ice Storm of 1998.

From Hong Kong she hankers for poutine and outdoor terraces. "I can't stand the minus-30 degree days," she says, but "Montrealers are so hot. I tell people if you want to go to see the beautiful people, don't go to Toronto or Vancouver, go to Montreal."

The NFB's Tragic Genius

Arthur Lipsett grew up on Hingston in NDG before joining the National Film Board as a 21-year-old in 1957. Four years later, he took footage tossed out by other filmmakers and added a soundtrack of disparate voices, one of which repeats the title *Very Nice Very Nice*. The disjointed short film left viewers with a sense of alienation and most at the NFB dismissed it as the work of an oddball, but many changed their minds when it was nominated for an Academy Award and Stanley Kubrick started writing Lipsett fan mail.

Lipsett's next short *21-87* also displayed disquieting scenes of alienation, showing, for example, a long interlude in which teens dance robot-like without music, something we don't see enough of nowadays. The unsettling work about the relationship between humans and machines had an impact on a young George Lucas, who reported being deeply affected by it although no mention of whether R2-D2 owes anything to the Montreal filmmaker.

Yet Lipsett was hardly the golden boy of the avante garde, as the NFB rewarded his efforts by giving him the tedious job of editing the flies out of scenes from northern fishing movies. Soon he began sawing his furniture, wearing four shirts at a time, and walking down the halls of the NFB with one shoulder pressed against a wall. Lipsett then moved to a tiny decrepit flat in the Clifton Apartments on Côte des Neiges, a building that Friends of the Mountain purchased and demolished amid great self-congratulatory fanfare in 2002. As Lipsett's career and mental health deteriorated, he moved in with his aunt on St. Kevin, as his mother was unavailable, having killed herself when he was 10.

Lipsett took his own life in April 1986, but his films live on. To view Lipsett's work, or any of the other thousands of films produced by the NFB, check out **Robothèque** *(1564 St. Denis St., near de Maisonneuve)*. For three bucks an hour you get a seat at a high-tech visual jukebox where you can punch in and watch your request on a private monitor. (Can you think of a better place to watch his high-tech critique?) It's open noon to nine, but closed on Mondays.

Montreal Film A-Z

Filming in Montreal has grown from a pre-1992 cottage industry into the billion-dollar-plus business it is today. More than $800 million was spent on big- and small-screen projects in 2000, with more than $1.8 billion in economic spin-off benefits to the city. Here is a digested list of featues that were largely shot — although seldom actually set — in Montreal.

The Adventures of Pluto Nash (2002)

Eddie Murphy plays the title character in this story of a nightclub on the moon. Considered one of the biggest bombs in Hollywood history.

Affliction (1997)

Paul Schrader directed this tale of a cop going through a mid-life crisis. Nick Nolte stars in this drama based on a Russell Banks novel. (In a stupid bureaucratic bungle during filming at a Hudson garage in early 1997, an agent with the Quebec French language police ordered the removal of English words that had been legally painted on the movie set.)

😊 Afterglow (1997)

This acclaimed romance starred Nick Nolte (again!) as a troubled maintenance man who falls for a housewife (the forever beautiful Julie Christie) with problems of her own.

😊 Agnes of God (1985)

Canadian Norman Jewison directed Jane Fonda in this story about a naïve nun who's found with a dead infant in her quarters.

😊 The Art of War (2000)

Montreal stands in for New York and Hong Kong as Wesley Snipes plays a framed FBI agent on the run in this thriller, which also stars Anne Archer.

😊 Atlantic City (1980)

Directed by Louis Malle, this watershed Canada-U.S.-France co-production stars Burt Lancaster as a less-than-legendary mobster and Susan Sarandon as a croupier with dreams of working in Monte Carlo. Of special note, Moses Znaimer, the broadcasting tycoon and ex-Montrealer, got a rare acting credit for his portrayal of a character named Felix.

The Ballad of Liz and Dick

Whoever said love is better the fifth time around was probably thinking of Elizabeth Taylor, who tied the knot here with Richard Burton in a Ritz Carlton hotel room in March, 1964. Conducting the services was Reverend Leonard Mason, a minister based at the elegant Unitarian church across the street that, sadly, was later burned down by a frustrated transsexual. The Burton-Taylor wedding made headlines around the world as the fabled union transformed the duo into one of Hollywood's stormiest and most celebrated couples. At the time, the vodka-guzzling Burton was considered one of the world's top leading men and Taylor still enjoyed the dignity of not being associated with Michael Jackson and Bubbles the Chimp. When the reverend's brother, Irving, heard the news back in England, he was quoted as saying, "Our Len marrying her. I can hardly believe it. Mind you, he's not the type who would refuse just because she's been married four times before." At the time, Taylor had just split with singer Eddie Fisher.

Reverse Paparazzo

Photo: John David Gravenor

If you see a familiar figure shooting snapshots of the mansions in the Golden Square Mile, don't bother him; it's just Christopher Plummer and he's busy. The star of countless Shakespearean productions, *The Sound of Music*, *The Man Who Would Be King*, and *The Insider*, Plummer grew up in the West Island village of Senneville. One of the places he likes to visit whenever he comes to town is the Golden Mile district north of Sherbrooke and between Guy and McTavish. A critic of past destruction of the area's heritage properties, Plummer uses his camera to preserve a record of the mansions where he knew people or visited at one time or another. Plummer's grandfather knew a lot of folks here, too. John Joseph Caldwell Abbott was a mayor of Montreal and the first Canadian-born prime minister.

Stand-Up Springboard

When Terry Jones of Monty Python fame calls Montreal "The Cannes of Comedy" he's saluting the **Just for Laughs Festival**, which reigns over all other yukfests as the pit stop that routinely launches chuckle-manufacturers to mega stardom. The first English program launched in 1985 with performances by Jay Leno, Jerry Seinfeld, Kevin Nealon, Mike MacDonald, and Dave Broadfoot.

Here are a few whose appearances were followed by stratospheric fame and fortune.

Just a few moons ago, **Christopher Titus** bummed lifts from guys in beat-up Chevettes to do stand-up comedy in clubs whose upholstery had known better days. His fortunes flipped 180 degrees after a few minutes onstage during the "New Faces" lineup at the 1996 festival, when agents from Fox signed him to play a flawed character in the custom-made TV sitcom, *Titus*, based on his own dysfunctional background. Since then, Mr Titus, as he is now called, still plants his blonde brushcut on backseat headrests as he travels, but now it's in the back of a 2001 Lincoln Towncar Stretch Limousine with twin bars.

The year 1996 likewise smiled on comic **Kevin James**. Shortly after appearing on Jay Leno's late-night show, James came here and impressed a Just for Laughs audience laden with card-swapping agents and talent hunters. He was promptly snapped up for a recurring TV role on *Everybody Loves Raymond*. Later, the square-jawed funnyman morphed into royalty of a proletarian variety, as the star of *The King of Queens* – a witty sitcom in which he portrays an unambitious parcel-delivery guy.

Saturday Night Live's **Jimmy Fallon** was just a little pipsqueak – well, maybe he still is one – when he opened for Penn and Teller in 1996 with an act that included loads of sidesplitting impersonations, like – well, you had to be there really.

A filmmaker who goes by the name of **Mr Lawrence** caught the fancy of suits who saw his film *Hairballs*, which was part of the 2000 "Eat My Shorts" series. The MTV moneymen tabled an offer for Lawrence to develop a 13-episode series. He signed as quickly as he could find a pen that worked. Mr Lawrence, who was also approached by ABC, gives Montreal credit as "indispensable to the boosting of my career and my sexual escapades."

Barney's Great Adventure (1998)

The Newtons drop off their kids, Abby (Diana Rice) and Cody (Trevor Morgan) along with friend Marcella (Kyla Pratt), at the grandparents' farm. A large purple dinosaur (Barney) shows up to play and then everybody chases after a big painted egg.

Battlefield Earth (2000)

This sci-fi thriller was woefully panned, but a small minority described it as an overlooked masterpiece. John Travolta plays the security chief of an alien invasion force bent on enslaving the planet. Based on a novel by Scientology founder L. Ron Hubbard, it features attempted big-budget special effects achieved with a modest budget.

Bethune: the Making of a Hero (1990)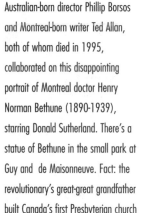

Australian-born director Phillip Borsos and Montreal-born writer Ted Allan, both of whom died in 1995, collaborated on this disappointing portrait of Montreal doctor Henry Norman Bethune (1890-1939), starring Donald Sutherland. There's a statue of Bethune in the small park at Guy and de Maisonneuve. Fact: the revolutionary's great-great grandfather built Canada's first Presbyterian church in Montreal.

Beyond Borders (2002)

Oscar-winning actress Angelina Jolie plays an American living in London in this tale of love and international intrigue co-starring Clive Owen and Linus Roache.

Black Robe (1991)

History buffs will dig this story of love and death featuring a French Jesuit priest (Lothaire Bluteau) in search of a New France outpost in the 1600s. It was based on the novel by the late Montreal writer Brian Moore.

The Bone Collector (1999)

This well-received, suspense-packed thriller stars Denzel Washington as a disabled homicide detective who, paired with a cop played by Angelina Jolie, finds new purpose in a hunt for a serial killer.

Café Ole (2000)

Described by *Variety* as "that rarest of Canadian subspecies, the genuinely sexy romantic comedy," it stars Spanish babe Laia Marull as an illegal Chilean immigrant. A product of Montreal filmmaker Emil Sher, it was shot around the Monkland Village district.

After a 1994 appearance at the comedy fest, local comedian **John Rogers** was lured to Hollywood with a short-lived TV deal that gave way to a writer-producer job on the long-running *Cosby Show*, a gig that apparently didn't involve fetching puddin' pops for Mr Cosby. In spite of what he might tell you, Rogers was not romantically linked to Lisa Bonet.

But the biggest made-in-Montreal comedy success story would have to be **Tim Allen**, who managed to turn bad luck into good after following British comic Chris Lynam onstage at a 1990 show. Lynam, who inserted live fireworks into his derriere, had wrung every drop of mirth from the audience by the time Allen took over the mike. But rather than die a comedian's death by sticking to his practiced routine, Allen ad-libbed about the impossibility of following "Rocket Butt," ending each sentence with the words "up your ass." He smoked 'em, and slayed the house again for the TV cameras at the next night's gala, later bagging an ACE cable-TV award. Soon, fool time turned into tool time for the one-time cocaine dealer, who raked in the bucks with a long running series, *Home Improvement*.

Say What, Monsieur Sennett?

Local boy Mack Sennett was the original King of Comedy. The native of the Eastern Townships attended a Montreal school before heading off to the States for a life in acting. But it was as a producer of silent films that he's best remembered. His studio invented the comic chase and introduced the world to the likes of Charlie Chaplin, Mabel Normand, Fatty Arbuckle, the Bathing Beauties, Buster Keaton, and Gloria Swanson.

Sennett learned to speak French while attending school in the east-end municipality of Pointe aux Trembles, but it didn't always serve him well. At one point late in his life he was invited to go to Cannes, where the French government was to honour him with a lifetime achievement award. After the sumptuous event, Sennett stood up to address the gathering in what he called his best "Sunday patois French." The audience didn't know what he was talking about, but they smiled and clapped anyway. Sennett was philosophical: "My French is of a certain kind – Canuck, laced with Canadian idiom and Irish overtones."

World War Freeb

In the early '80s the city was awash in cheapo, rock-oriented zines with names like *Rear Guard* and *Blow Up*, along with their lower-budget cousins like *Surfin' Bird*, *Going Underground*, and *Red She Said*. But the alternative weekly press as we now know it had yet to grace the bottom of a single Montreal birdcage until 1986, when Julien Feldman, Peter Kuitenbower, Brendan Kelly, Daniel Sanger, Eyal Kattan, and Catherine Salisbury – with the help of a welfare-subsidy program – launched the *Mirror*.

The biweekly immediately dug the dirt, literally: their first edition featured a report on what some influential locals had in their garbage cans. Kattan and Salisbury took over the day-to-day management of the paper, while the rest of the gang soon drifted off into other spheres of journalistic endeavour.

One day, Kattan and Salisbury had the others sign a document purportedly renouncing their claims to ownership of the paper, which by then was offered weekly. Soon, the darn thing was turning a profit and spawned the French-language imitator, *Voir*, which likewise thrived. By the '90s, *Voir's* owner had been spurned in his attempts to buy the *Mirror* off Kattan and Salisbury, so he opened his own English-language competitor called *Hour*. The *Mirror* followed suit by launching a French-language twin called *Ici*.

Soon after, Kattan and Salisbury sold their two alternative weeklies to publishing giant Québecor, but they haven't been able to enjoy their profits. The cash is tied in escrow pending a suit launched by former co-owners Sanger and Feldman, who saw fit to challenge the document they signed in a complex legal case that remains unresolved.

Catch Me if You Can (2002)

Steven Spielberg directs Tom Hanks and Leonardo DiCaprio in this thriller about a con man (DiCaprio) who poses as a pilot, doctor, lawyer, and professor to swindle $6 million in dozens of countries. Shot largely in Old Montreal and Quebec City.

Confessions of a Dangerous Mind (2002)

Based on ex-*Gong Show* host Chuck Barris's autobiography, in which he claims to have served as a CIA hit man, this action comedy marks actor George Clooney's directorial début. Drew Barrymore, Julia Roberts, Sam Rockwell, and Rutger Hauer also appear.

Driven (2001)

When a young race-car driver (Kip Purdue) loses his touch, his boss (Burt Renolds) hires a troubled former champion (Sylvester Stallone) to turn things around. Critics were mixed on this effort.

Enemies: A Love Story (1989)

This amusing postwar drama directed by Paul Mazursky stars Anjelica Houston and a swinging Ron Silver, whose wife catches on to his bed-hopping.

Eye of the Beholder (1999)

Shot largely in Hudson, this whodunit stars Ewan McGregor as a private investigator who trails — and also looks out for — a lethal woman. Also starring Ashley Judd and Canadians Geneviève Bujold, k.d. lang, and Jason Priestley.

Free Money (1998)

Marlon Brando seems to enjoy his role as a megalomaniacal prison warden who's being pursued by a CIA agent (Mira Sorvino). Charlie Sheen stars as a reluctant son-in-law who devises a plan to rob a train.

Grey Owl (1999)

James Bond cypher Pierce Brosnan portrays Archie Stansfeld Belaney, a Briton who famously masqueraded as a native Indian trapper in the first part of the 20th century. Ideal if you enjoy lingering shots of landscapes and furry animals.

The Heist (2001)

Written and directed by David Mamet, this crime drama stars Gene Hackman as an imaginative gang boss and Danny DeVito as a double-crossing fence. Shortchanged by the fence, the gang pursue a shipment of Swiss gold with the help of the fence's son (Sam Rockwell).

Perking Up Pickets

A CBC *Newswatch* crew rolled up in the company van for a none-too-thrilling report about a strike at Moishe's Steak House in October of 1989. Now any ENG team will tell you that picketers usually perk up in a very special way when the news cameras are rolling, but apparently they did so insufficiently for reporter Paul Carvalho, who asked the strikers to liven things up. Moishe's owner wasn't thrilled with these instructions and complained to the CBC, which suspended Carvalho for two weeks following the affair. The situation compromised Carvalho's CBC career, and he ended up leaving the Mother Corporation to produce acclaimed documentaries.

Invitation to Burglary

Prior to becoming the CFCF News correspondent in Quebec City, the now-retired Ralph Noseworthy was a freelance reporter trying to dig up scandals on Robert Bourassa's provincial Liberal government. Sniffing for dirt in 1974, Noseworthy tailed Justice Minister Jerome Choquette, and sat outside his home many a night. The story is that a dismayed Choquette devised a devilish plan to discredit the reporter. The minister got a local cop to try and egg Noseworthy into a break-in at Choquette's home, the idea being that Noseworthy would be caught red-handed and sent to jail. The cop, John Tardif, admitted his regretful participation in the scheme years later. No big deal, however, Noseworthy never took the bait. Choquette has never denied the report.

Shooting Stars

There's always something shooting or at least on the drawing board in Montreal. One of the best ways to develop an immediate expertise on what's filming in town is to visit the Website of the performers' union, ACTRA (actramontreal.ca). The "What's Shooting" section lists the names of the different productions, while the pre-production and post-production sections offer the contact information and basic activities of various production houses.

Searching for Anglo TV

Homegrown French TV attracts so many viewers you'd think they were revealing next week's lottery numbers. In contrast, English-language Montreal programming is sadder than a sentimentalist at the funeral of Patof the Clown. Other than news coverage, the only Anglo programming consists of a couple of shows about Hollywood, a political gabfest, a sports show, and the impossible-to-kill *Travel, Travel*. There's also, apparently, a morning show on Global, but we can't confirm it's still on the air because we usually watch Judge Wapner on another channel.

But nostalgia buffs might peg the '70s as the golden age of local English TV, when productions like George Balcan's game show *It's Your Move* and the sitcoms *Snow Job* and *Excuse My French* enraptured viewers for half-hours on end.

Although Montreal is responsible for such cable network shows as *Dogs With Jobs*, *Student Bodies*, and the dreaded *Caillou*, stations like Canada's Weather Network spurned this city. Prior to going pin-striped in Toronto, the Weather Network beamed out of a Montreal studio until 1999. Theirs was a wacky place, where at least one weathercaster was known to flash her ample assets as a prank designed to distract the male on-air talent, whose eyes were otherwise glued to the teleprompter.

Another lost source of local TV production was cable access. For years, the federal government ordered monopoly cable companies to spend a small percentage of their budgets producing local content. They accomplished this with volunteer-produced shows like *Jim's Eye on Comedy*, and the electrifying *Behind the Scenes* (produced by the very authors of this book).

When the feds lifted the access requirement, Channel 9 productions ended, and the ethnic channel became just about the only game in town for English-speaking Montrealers to express themselves on the square box.

Highlander III: The Magician (1994)

Christopher Lambert resumes his starring role as the immortal Connor McLeod in this contemporary prequel to *Highlander II*.

The Human Stain (2003)

Based on a Philip Roth novel, it stars Anthony Hopkins as a university professor having a bad-luck affair with a troubled janitor, played by Nicole Kidman. It was largely shot on the grounds of the Hovey Manor hotel in the Eastern Townships.

Isn't She Great (2000)

Bette Midler stars in this middling comedy about the life of *Valley of the Dolls* author Jacqueline Susann. Nathan Lane plays her husband.

Johnny Mnemnonic (1995)

Based on a William Gibson short story, this dark sci-fi bomb features Keanu Reeves as a "data courier" with too much on his mind, literally. The lives of millions of people depend on his assignment to carry data from China back to the states, despite the attempts of bad guys to prevent him.

Julia Has Two Lovers (1990)

Prolific Montreal filmmaker Bashar Shbib lucked out by casting a not-yet-famous David Duchovny as leading man in this not-bad, low-budget romantic comedy. Fans of the *The X-Files* snapped up lots of copies of the video from Shbib's website.

Levity (2003)

Hapless bandit Billy Bob Thronton is set free after serving time for killing a youngster during a robbery. Haunted by guilt, he comes to terms with his deeds with the help of a preacher (Morgan Freeman) and a pair of vulnerable women (Kirsten Dunst and Holly Hunter).

😊 The Moderns (1988)

Montreal stands in for the City of Light in this pretentious but fun story about an American painter living in Paris in the '20s. Keith Carradine convincingly plays the painter, whose works are sold by a gallery owner played by Montreal's Geneviève Bujold.

💣 Mother Night (1996)

Nick Nolte plays an American writer recruited to spy on the Nazis. But his cover forces him to spread anti-Semitic propaganda for the Third Reich — a fact that doesn't go down so well after the war.

😊 Mrs. Parker and the Vicious Circle (1994)

Jennifer Jason Leigh portrays world-weary writer Doroty Parker at the height of her social skills in 1920s New York.

But that option, too, was zapped by the corporate world, when in May, 2001, all the ethnic-show producers were convened at the Hôtel Dupuis to learn that their shows had been axed. The makers of *Caribbean Sizzle* and *Hello India!* were sufficiently ticked off that they launched lawsuits against the channel's owner, who in turn sold out to Global. Now called CH, the channel still shows some ethnic programming between inexplicable broadcasts of the very un-ethnic David Letterman.

Since then, local English TV production has drifted into the bogus, with insignificant shows that are barely longer than the old *P.K.'s Video Gold*, a quarter-hour rotation of lacklustre music videos that used to fill what would otherwise have been the dead air between late-night and early-morning programming on Channel 12 in the early '80s.

Late-Night Lunacy

Whether you're having trouble falling asleep or just don't want to, Peter Anthony Holder's late-night radio show on CJAD can help keep your mind off the bogeyman.

Holder Overnight is a refreshingly twisted omnibus of strange news reports, celebrity phoners, visits from a contributing numerologist and a talkative New York cabbie, stand-up comedy clips and more.

Interviews typically included the likes of astronaut Alan Bean, who did a real moon walk, Steve Allen, the first host of NBC's *The Tonight Show*; bar-brawling actor Michael Moriarty from *Law and Order*; comic Jimmie "JJ" Walker, and the skull-smackin' wrestling star, Bret Hart. Holder talks about sex every Wednesday.

He's never afraid to ask the tough questions, but he once picked an unlikely guest to reveal his deepest fear. He was talking with the legendary swimming actress, Esther Williams, when he admitted to having a water phobia. "I won't even get on a boat," he says.

Holder Overnight is heard every Monday to Friday from 11pm to 2am on 800AM.

It's a Guy Thing

Maxim, Playboy, Mechanics Illustrated, Hustler – the world has enough magazines for men. So how did a local upstart turn into one of the world's most-read men's publications in just a few years? Easy: make it a daily, put it on the Internet and stuff it full of advice, sports, entertainment, and more babes than you can shake your stick at. **Askmen.com** cruised by the carcasses of other online magazines that opened and shut in the convergence boom-bust. Three years after it was founded in 1999, the MSN and AOL portals added prominent links to the Montreal-based site. Askmen.com claim that visits soon spiked to 4.5 million hits a month – three times more than its closest online competitor, and six times the circulation of leading magazines, making it the most visited Canadian-based site.

With more than 5,000 articles online at any given time, the site offers candid and practical advice on all kinds of topics relating to men, such as the ubiquitous advice column, travel ideas, "Single Girl of the Week," and undoubtedly stuff on how to properly comb mousse into your hair. Co-founding Con U grads Ricardo Poupada, Luis Rodrigues, and Chris Rovny also write their own stuff when they're not too busy counting their money.

News of the World

One of the most obscure newspapers ever printed in Montreal was *Le Village* – the "official information paper" of the Olympic Village during the 1976 summer Games. There were only 32 editions in total. Published in English and French, it had two editors, John D. Mill and Jean-Luc Duguay, together commanding a team of six reporters and one photographer. A security guard working at the Olympic Village during the Games collected the only full complement known, offering them for sale 25 years later.

Once Upon a Time in America (1984)

Spaghetti western director Sergio Leone and composer Ennio Morricone reunite on this story of friendship and betrayal starring Robert De Niro and James Woods.

One Eyed King (2001)

Armand Assante, William Baldwin, and Jim Breuer star in this drama set in a tough Manhattan neighbourhood where families and friendship often conflict and overlap.

Quintet (1979)

Two plus two equals three in this dreary sci-fi tale shot largely on the former Expo 67 site. Directed by Robert Altman and starring Paul Newman and Vittorio Gassman, it's a story about survival during a new ice age sparked by nuclear holocaust.

The Red Violin (1998)

The history of a 300-year-old violin is traced from Renaissance Italy, through Austria, England, and China, and then back to present-day Montreal, where a collector tries to uncover its past. It won John Corigliano an Oscar for best musical score.

Rollerball (2001)

Set in 2005, this remake of the 1975 James Caan vehicle in which an extreme athlete (Chris Klein) signs up to play the world's most popular – and deadly – spectator sport. It's a sport without rules, a fact the league's boss (Jean Reno) exploits to our hero's peril.

☺ The Score (2001)

A career criminal and nightclub owner (Robert De Niro) goes straight after a close call with the law in this tale that is actually set in Montreal. But he gets pulled back into a last, career-capping caper with friend and colleague (Marlon Brando) with the help of an insider (Edward Norton) at the Customs House in Old Montreal.

The Second Arrival (1998)

A hero played by Patrick Muldoon fights aliens who plan to melt the polar ice caps in this so-so, high-tech sequel to an earlier Charlie Sheen vehicle.

Shadow of the Wolf ☺ (1992)

Set in the north of Quebec in the 1930s, it's the story of Agaguk (Lou Diamond Phillips), an Inuit wrongly suspected of a murder in his small community.

The Turning of the Screw

When there's something wrong under your hood, who you gonna call? Lisa Christensen. This spicy CJAD radio host keeps weekend listeners enraptured with her crafty tips on repairing and maintaining everything from wheel wells to piston rods. After graduating from LaSalle High, Christensen went on to nab a certificate in automotive mechanics and later become the only Canadian female in possession of an American Service Excellence Master's Certificate. This bodacious grease monkey combines a caring and attentive tone with a complete authority over everything automotive. And just because she's a sweetheart, doesn't mean she's a pushover, as her former students will attest, tardiness could lead to sudden execution. Lisa discusses your motorcar woes every Saturday mornings on 800AM from 10am. Call with your car questions: 514/790-0991.

Registered User

Way back in the prehistoric days of the Internet, computer-network whiz Ben Soo learned that the arcane new art of registering a domain name involved tracking down the right bureaucrat, agreeing to a complex set of guidelines, and ponying up hundreds of dollars a year. In 1994, Soo went through those hoops for the name **Montreal.com** and anxious wolves have been crying "Little pig, little pig, let me come in" ever since. The Southam newspaper chain, which owns *The Gazette* and several Canadian city domain names, wanted it, but tried to knock down the price with a tired line about the name losing its value once a wider variety of suffixes come out. The newspaper chain offered a lowball $8,000. Other bidders have included anonymous parties represented by lawyers, and another company that promised up to $250,000 in a dubious profit-sharing arrangement.

Montreal.com's original content, including a great blog, photos, reviews, and a chat room, attracts 30,000 daily hits – three out of four of which originate from outside Canada, but Soo confesses that he's still hoping to turn a profit from the site.

Hollywood Follies

The bombs of Pearl Harbour were no match for leading man Ben Affleck. But as for getting bombed in Montreal, that's a different story. Immediately after he wrapped local filming on *The Sum of All Fears* in 2001, the Academy Award winner checked himself into the luxury Promises drug- and alcohol-rehabilitation centre in Malibu. There were frequent reports of Affleck's extreme partying at places like **Buona Notte** and the **Go-Go**. He was also seen at **Globe Restaurant and Bar**, dancing on top of the bar, buying a round for the house, pouring drinks, and spending time with some rum-and-coke buddies.

Benjamin Bratt was also filming in town that summer, when he was seen having words with his then-fiancée, Julia Roberts. Rumours were going around that the leading man in *Abandon* had been seeing a lot of a certain woman and Julia was none too pleased. They called off their engagement a short time later, although the alleged tryst was never confirmed.

Globe, by the way, is big with Hollywood types. It's where George Clooney hit it off with an actress-barmaid during local filming of *Confessions of a Dangerous Mind* in 2002.

Action Zero

Thanks to a shaky labour situation in August 2001, Montreal lost a shot at being the location for *Daredevil: The Man Without Fear*, which went to Vancouver instead. So nobody got to see Ben Affleck in his shiny red tights. All systems were go for the film to be shot in Montreal, but shortly before cameras were set to roll, 20th Century Fox asked the performers' union for a no-strike guarantee. No way, said ACTRA. The decision led the studio to pack up for the West Coast, where the production union has a separate collective arrangement.

Montreal film heavies reached for the Aspirin and denounced ACTRA for being inhospitable to U.S. productions. ACTRA changed gears and came up with what Fox wanted. Too late, the Hollywood types said they already spent $100,000 in deposits to rent a Vancouver studio. Despite an unusual offer from Montreal studio owners to cover the $100,000, Fox said, "No, thanks."

Snake Eyes (1998)

The Forum is the set for a lavish murder scene in this Brian De Palma flick starring Nicolas Cage as a corrupt Atlantic City detective who gets mixed up in an assassination plot.

The Sum of All Fears (2002) ☺

In an attempt to sow war between Washington and Moscow, a terrorist cell nukes a major sporting event. Young CIA analyst Jack Ryan (Ben Affleck) does everything he can to avert World War III.

Timeline (2003)

Richard Donner directs this adventure story — adapted from Michael Crichton's novel — about a group of students trapped in medieval France.

To Walk With Lions (1999) ☺

George Adamson was a pioneer of wildlife conservation made famous by *Born Free* and his story of Elsa the lion. Richard Harris convincingly portrays this Lion Man of Africa as he risks everything to reintroduce lions back to the wild.

A Walk on the Moon (1998) ☺

This well-constructed chick flick tells the story of a married woman (Diane Lane) who has an affair with a salesman (Viggo Mortensen) during the days of the Vietnam War.

2001: A Space Travesty (2001)

This bomb features Leslie Nielsen in a role reminiscent of Frank Drebin of the *Naked Gun* series. This time, the hapless cop tries to save the U.S. president from captivity on another planet while a presidential clone rules down here on earth.

Waking the Dead (1999)

On the cusp of triumph, a congressional candidate (Billy Crudup) is suddenly overwhelmed with memories of a footloose former lover (Jennifer Connelly) who died years before in a terrorist bombing. Fact: Local CTV news anchor Bill Haugland has a cameo role as — what else? — a reporter.

Where the Money Is (2000)

Paul Newman carries this amusing film about an old-time hood who gets together with an ambitious nurse (Linda Fiorentino) to pull off a caper.

The Whole Nine Yards (2000)

Unlikely characters mix it up in this tale of a bored Montreal dentist (Matthew Perry) who's hungry for money to get a divorce. Soon, a hit man wanted by the mob (Bruce Willis) moves next door incognito.

local humour

"If I do good here, I get to go to Ottawa next."
– Don Rickles

"It's great to be here in Montreal during the annual Pothole Festival."
– Rich Hall

"I grew up in Côte St. Luc and played in a Jewish baseball league. There were no umpires, but there was a lawyer on every base. 'He was out, but I'm sure we can work a deal.'"
– Rick Bronson

"I can't believe they keep turkeys at the Granby Zoo. Why should I pay to see an animal I can find in my freezer?"
– Barry Julien

"There are so many parallels between my life and Christ's. He was born in a stable. I was born in a Quebec hospital."
– Sylvain Larocque

"How could (singer) Garou fall asleep at the wheel of a Ferrari? What, was he listening to his own album?"
– François Massicotte

"When I hear the name Roger, I don't imagine anyone under 50. Gino is a name that comes with hair. I'd never go into business with someone called Tony. And if someone in Quebec is named Steve, Kevin, or Nancy, you know their parents don't speak English."
– Laurent Paquin

"I'm coming back to Montreal — when the Expos win the pennant."
– Don Rickles

"I love being in Montreal. I was in my hotel the first night and ordered an escort, and five snails turned up in my room."
– Allan Havey

SOME STARS ARE BORN; OTHERS PREFER AN ARTIFICIAL WOMB

When she was here in 1985 filming *Keeping Track*, Margot Kidder liked to get away from journalists' questions about her alleged affair with former Prime Minister Pierre Trudeau. Every couple of days, the one-time Lois Lane would visit a local flotation-bath centre. Also known as sensory deprivation chambers, the isolation units are half filled with salty, room-temperature water. Those who spend long periods in such total darkness have reported hallucinations and confusions, something Kidder would learn a lot about later. To give it a try pop over to the one and only **Ovarium** (400 Beaubien E., near Beaubien Metro; 514/271-7515, 877/FLOTTER; ovarium.com).

When the Beatles came to town for their only-ever visit on September 8, 1964, the Fab Four enjoyed some unique local flavour as an undercover member of the local constabulary stood alongside them on stage. The cop was there to protect Ringo Starr, who, upon his arrival in town, had received death threats from the local lunatic separatist fringe who considered the moptops as somehow associated with the monarchy. Starr later told his biographer that the would-be attackers wanted "to get that little English Jew," even though Starr whose real name is Starkey, is not Jewish. He described that night as "the worst gig in my life," and he played with his cymbals tilted upward to deflect any possible gunfire from the crowd. Rather than risk staying the night here, the Beatles flew to Florida immediately after their performance.

The Beatles' top rivals weren't to be outdone. When the Rolling Stones came to town in 1972, a bomb hidden underneath a ramp at the Montreal Forum exploded. The July 17 blast destroyed the cones of 30 speakers in the band's equipment trucks. The bomber's motivation and identity were never determined and the concert went on as scheduled.

Going Up in Frames

Canada is sometimes called Hollywood North because American film companies have taken to shooting here on the cheap. But Montreal's film history can be traced back more than a century to the days when the screening of a 100-foot reel was considered a high-tech sensation.

In the late 19th century, American inventor Thomas Edison's company invented a moving-picture camera called the Kinetograph and a peep-hole viewer called a Kinetoscope. In 1901, he brought his camera to Montreal to shoot a hot action flick, *Montreal Fire Department on Runners*. In the wintertime scene shot in March, Edison photographer William Paley captured a Montreal firefighting crew on a phoney-looking race to the scene of a fire. Crossing the screen from right to left, the chief's sled passes first, followed by a chemical apparatus mounted on a double-runner sled. Next come the horses pulling a hose-bearing sled and, last, a four-horse team pulling an engine.

Edison shot other films in these parts, including a Governor General's war-canoe landing at an ice-logged Quebec City harbour, and the arrival of a British nobleman. The flicks can be viewed online at the website operated by the U.S. Library of Congress (memory.loc.gov).

Lost By A (Chest) Hair

Despite its success luring big-money film shoots, Montreal has a hard time keeping up with Toronto and Vancouver when it comes to U.S. television production. So it was with blubbering joy that local TV types received the news that David Hasselhoff was on his way to shoot his next series in the city.

In *Doublecross*, Hasselhof was going to portray a repentant art forger who's forced to flip allegiances and join a secretive government department. The part did not call for Hasselhoff to appear in his bathing suit but, even more disappointingly, the financing fell through. The show would have been available to four-fifths of the American television market, who were obviously forced to settle for less-interesting programming instead.

Weed Warrior

Some flip burgers, others peddle shoes. A lot of musicians have to moonlight to make ends meet. Not that it helps much with his bills, but the bass player for Grimskunk, a leading local bar band since the mid-'90s, developed a sideline in politics.

The leader of the federal Marijuana Party, Marc-Boris St. Maurice first got into politics following his bust and conviction for possession a decade ago.

After his arrest, St. Maurice was placed in a cell overnight, where he was allowed to keep his tobacco pouch and cigarette papers. Another inmate noticed the papers and borrowed one and, later, another. After the third paper, St. Maurice decided to investigate and found his fellow inmate rolling a hash-oil spliff behind the bathroom stalls. Invited to share a few tokes, Marc-Boris started thinking about a prohibition that police can't even enforce under their own noses.

"I lay back on the bench happily stoned," he said. "That's when it went 'click!' Before, I felt guilty about getting arrested, but when I smoked that joint, I thought, 'This is ridiculous!' And it stuck."

After spending more than $2,000 in fines and lawyer fees, St. Maurice got involved organizing pro-pot events like the Montreal Smoke In. The rocker first stood for office with the Bloc Pot in 1997, which ran 24 candidates in the provincial election and scored 24,000 votes. In 2000, he toured Canada to promote the new Marijuana Party. His 73 candidates took a respectable 66,000 votes in that year's federal election. In his own constituency on the plugged-in Plateau Mont-Royal, St. Maurice tied for third place.

If he could have his way, marijuana "would be readily available to those adults who choose to use it. Would be sold at a fair price and there would be quality standards clearly indicated on the package informing users what they're buying."

Between gigs and recording sessions, St. Maurice also organizes the local Million Marijuana March, held the first Saturday of every May in more than a hundred world cities, including Montreal. For the exact date, check the Marijuana Party's website (partimarijuana.org).

ACTORS OF THE WORLD, UNITE!

Once in a while American film crews will try to sneak up here to illegally shoot on the island, only to quickly have a pitbull firmly gripping their posterior. That canine is named Thor Bishopric, the hardcore chief of the ACTRA performance union who will go after any production that tries to chintz on Canadian talent. Production houses that dare try to duck rules about hiring Canadians will suffer the wrath of Bishopric's union, which has been known to demand the crews get arrested. The scandals often make it to the papers. Eighteen thousand of his peers have twice elected Bishopric — an ACTRA member since the age of four — to his non-paying position. As well as forsaking a paycheque, the presidency has also cost him a once-busy career, in which he provided voices for countless cartoon characters — which fittingly include the voice of Young Hercules.

Armed with $1,200 and the number 1742, you can spend a night in the very suite where John Lennon and wife Yoko Ono staged their famous bed-in for peace in May and June, 1969.

The **Queen Elizabeth Hotel**'s John Lennon Parlour Suite (no mention of Yoko) is where the former Beatle held court for two weeks, made international headlines, and recorded a hit song. The pyjama-clad John and Yoko spoke to about 150 journalists a day and called 350 American radio stations to promote world peace – all from the comfort of their bed.

During a less sleepy moment, Lennon sat up in the sack and composed "Give Peace a Chance" on a table that remains in the room. When he finished writing, he asked acolytes to fetch a tape recorder and a few back-up singers. About 50 fans were hurried in to join celebrities already there like Timothy Leary, Petula Clark, Tommy Smothers, Dick Gregory, as well as a rabbi, a priest, and five local Hare Krishna devotees playing cymbals and drums. This helps explain the verse:

Ev'rybody's talking about John and Yoko,
Timmy Leary, Rosemary, Tommy Smothers,
Bobby Dylan, Tommy Cooper, Derek Taylor,
Norman Mailer, Alan Ginsberg, Hare Krishna,
Hare, Hare Krishna.

Now decorated with gold records and a framed photo of Lennon, the suite has downtown views, conference space, drawing room, parlour, marble bathroom, dining room and kitchen. Two attached bedrooms can be sealed off and rented separately.

Albert Goldman wrote about the Bed-In in his 1988 biography, *The Lives of John Lennon*:

"Lennon envisioned himself at this moment as standing squarely in the tradition of the American civil rights movement. 'In me secret heart,' he confessed, 'I wanted to write something that would take over 'We Shall Overcome.'"

Anonymous Lennon admirers still leave roses outside the room, according to legend. Urban legend, that is. Hotel cleaning staff tell us it never happens.

SOUND ADVICE FOR MODERNS

Sick of the middle of the road? Want to challenge your eardrums with unusual sounds from the Digital Era? Well Montreal has just the festival for you. An offshoot of the annual Festival of New Cinema and New Media, MUTEK – Music, Sound and New Technologies has been showcasing and developing emerging forms of electronic music since 2000. Held every spring, dozens of artists from many countries gather to perform, exchange information with the public and meet industry types. The website (*mutek.ca*) offers direct access to the sounds and photographic archives of past festivals.

514/847-9272

Reeling in the Stars

What do Britney Spears, Bill Gates, the Pope and Queen Elizabeth II have in common? They have all fallen for the notorious on-air shenanigans of Montreal telephone pranksters.

Marc-Antoine Audette and Sebastian Trudel, who call themselves the Masked Avengers (Les Justiciers Masqués), first made news headlines around the world with their on-air cons in 2002. Broadcasting on CKMF (FM 94.3), Audette faked the voice of Celine Dion and got through to Britney Spears, inviting the pop superstar to appear at a celebrity charity event and sing with the likes of Tiger Woods. On April Fool's Day of the same year, the pair succeeded after weeks of trying to reach the world's richest man. Pretending to be Prime Minister Jean Chrétien, they invited Bill Gates to attend a bogus conference and drew him into a 14-minute conversation during which his Microsoft Windows sotware was insulted and he was invited to visit a Montreal strip club.

The pair's earlier targets included Celine Dion and race-car driver Jacques Villeneuve. (You can hear some of their classic prank calls on their website, *radiopranks.com*.)

The duo's routine followed in the footsteps of another nervy radio man, Pierre Brassard of CKOI (FM 96.9), who first imitated Chretien to get Queen Elizabeth on the line in 1995. Brassard managed to keep Her Majesty talking for more than 15 minutes, drawing her into a sensitive conversation about the independence-referendum campaign that was hot news at the time. Brassard's previous successful targets included Bill Clinton, the Pope, and Brigitte Bardot.

Pet Projects

Not only does Amanda Glew help sick and injured animals for a living, she also has her own radio show and fights crime in her spare time. A Hudson-based veterinarian and host of CJAD's *All Creatures Great and Small*, Amanda also provides first aid and behaviour counselling to the Customs Canada Revenue Agency's dope-and-bomb sniffing Detector Dog Team. As if that didn't keep her busy enough, Amanda also finds time to provide basic care to the Laval Police Dog Team and teach natural science at Vanier College. She answers all kinds of animal-related questions on her show, which airs Saturdays at 4pm on CJAD 800AM.

FAMILY DRAMA

Smooth-talking Jack Finnigan has stumped lots of call-in contestants with radio quizzes over the years, but the CJAD trivia king's daughter is the authority on how to make it huge in show biz. Jennifer Finnigan, a five-foot-seven-inch strawberry blond, plays the bitchy Bridget Forrester on soap opera *The Bold and the Beautiful*, an effort that earned her a Daytime Emmy Award in 2001. This Dawson College and Sacred Heart High School grad got noticed after her role in the teeny-bopper local TV production *Student Bodies*.

Another Montrealer making a name in the sudsy daytime dramas is Kelly Kruger, who became the latest Mackenzie Browning on *The Young and the Restless*. The trilingual (English, French, Hebrew) actress reports having made a name for herself through modelling and such shows as *Titans* and *Undressed*, as well as a French-language show called *Sur La Piste*.

FREEDOM WITH A FUNNY ACCENT

Veteran McGill communications professor and culture hound Will Straw regularly regales his students with the tale of how, in his younger days, he bamboozled the world's best known newsgathering team during a great historic moment. As a visiting foreign traveller, he was watching the hordes take hammers to the Berlin wall in November, 1989, when he suddenly noticed that a roving CNN camera crew was having no luck finding Germans able to speak English. Straw – whose German ethnicity runs about as deep as having a passing resemblance to Colonel Klink on *Hogan's Heroes* – stepped up to oblige. Speaking in his best Benny Hill-style German accent, Straw waxed emotional about how the falling of the wall felt to Berliners – a perfomance that was recorded for all the world to see, thanks to the miracle of modern broadcasting.

The News That Didn't Fit

When the *Montreal Daily News* first hit the stands on March 15, 1988, vendors dealt out more than 70,000 copies of the first English-language daily to challenge *The Gazette* since the bandkrupt *Montreal Star*. Along with a bunch of up-and-comers, the *News* (or "the Snooze," as some called it) also attracted such veteran writers as Tim Burke and Nick Auf der Maur. During the début year, the tabloid started by the late Pierre Péladeau of Quebecor, saw staffer Glenn Cole scoop the rest of the Canadian sports media with news of Wayne Gretzky's trade from Edmonton to L.A.

Meanwhile, Auf der Maur leaked that the Canadiens were leaving the Forum, while fellow columnist Albert Nerenberg interviewed the head of the Nationalist Party. The skinhead told Nerenberg, "We're going to put you in a concentration camp."

The Daily News had some of the hottest coverage of the huge PCB fire at a suburban warehouse in 1988, but it also had its weaker moments – like the never-ending series on Turkish immigrants, and an ill-advised exposé on backdoor trends in porno films.

The paper went out of business 20 months later in December, 1989. Perhaps fittingly, it closed almost exactly ten years after the broadsheet *Montreal Star* published its last edition.

Freedom and Suspense

Don't know about you, but when Robert De Niro clung to the underside of Nick Nolte's car just before it sped off in *Cape Fear*, we thought, "Yeah, right."

But in May of 1996, a Montreal prisoner escaped custody in exactly the same way. Proof that art imitates life? The would-be Spider Man was named Camille Levesque. Police had the 38-year-old in custody at the courthouse on Notre Dame Street, but the suspected shoplifter soon saw an opportunity to slip away from his captors. While the cops' heads were turned, he scrambled under a police van, gripped the vehicle's belly and rode off when it pulled away. Said one cop: "It was just like in the movies."

Romancing the Whatever

Courtesy: Abbraxa

With video classics like *Lesbian Fisting Picnic* and *Lumberjack Attack*, Abbraxa has stormed the porn world's ramparts. A native of the South Shore and admitted "black sheep" of her family, she got sick of working the strip-bar circuit a few years ago and went into adult videos. Now she works ten hours a week, pulling down an admitted $300,000 a year.

A proponent of an open, hard-core industry, she sums her view up this way: "We've got to not fear going to the ends of our fantasies."

In some of her features, she has introduced such things to her posterior as four lit candles, a PVC drain pipe, a dozen zucchinis, the big end of a baseball bat, and six ping-pong balls.

"It's like being an athlete," she says. "You have to be well-trained before you try any of this."

Billed as "America's Fisting Goddess," she produces her videos and runs her business and website (abbraxa.com) along with her partner of many years. Her name comes from an album by Santana, with an extra "b" to raise her closer to the top of alphabetical lists.

She receives lots of fan mail in which people sometimes say, "Thanks for making these movies. They make me feel I'm not weird."

One of her most popular videos involves something called "urophilia." Let's just say that to prepare for her role, Abbraxa had to drink a lot of water. "So it doesn't taste bad."

BOXERS, BRIEFS, OR COMMANDO?

During local filming of *The Score*, starring Robert De Niro, Marlon Brando (pictured), and Edward Norton, production insiders claimed that Brando liked to walk around the set without wearing any pants. The story goes that the overweight Brando, who refuses to be photographed from the waist down, was, apart from his shirt, nude. Asked to confirm the story, director Frank Oz said the star actually wore underwear.

The Score, by the way, is one of the few big-budget movies that are actually set — not just shot — in Montreal. The plot surrounds a robbery planned for the Customs House at the bottom of McGill Street, near Wellington.

Bruce Willis also starred in a Montreal-set caper film, *The Whole Nine Yards*. Local critics approved of the way it showcased Mount Royal, Biddle's jazz club and the Old Port, among other backdrops.

BOMB WASN'T THE BOMB

When he visited the downtown Chapters bookstore to promote his 2000 science-fiction flop, *Battlefield Earth*, John Travolta carefully avoided newspaper reporters in favour of "happy" spots on TV and radio. Local press types figured he was just sick and tired of their nagging questions about his support of the controversial Scientology organization. The $100-million thriller went on to become the biggest bomb since *Waterworld* and, arguably, the worst film ever shot in Montreal. One location was decorated to look like the ruins of Salt Lake City eight centuries from now. The $250,000 set was located at the intersection of Notre Dame and St. Jean in Old Montreal. But you won't recognize it from the film, in which it is strewn with burned-out gas pumps, skeletal car wrecks, and trucked-in dirt and weeds.

Guaranteed Pure Dog

Photo: John David Gravenor

It has been called "insane" and "the worst movie of 1974." So, naturally, a lot of people love it, including many fans of that huge Guaranteed Pure Milk bottle sticking out of the Montreal skyline southeast of Crescent and René Lévesque.

The flick was *Sweet Movie*, filmmaker Dusan Makavejev's first international feature. The bizarre plot is an international odyssey of sex, chocolate, postmodern motifs, and unprecedented amounts of male nudity.

Makavejev loved the milk bottle and thought it had great potential for a scene in his film. In a spoof on *King Kong*, an actor wearing a gorilla costume scales the landmark while carrying "Miss Virginity of the World," played by Montreal's Carole Laure. Then they climb in the bottle and do it.

Also starring Saskatchewan-born actor John Vernon, whose real name is Adolphus Raymondus Vernon Agopsowicz (he played Dean Wormer in *Animal House*), the stinker didn't dent Laure's career – she went on to great success in France. But it cast such a black mark on Makavejev's name that the Yugoslav had trouble finding work through the rest of the decade.

But he wasn't washed up yet. In 1981, his film *Montenegro* made loads of cash and received glowing reviews.

Not Just a Pretty Bass

In the days before they moved in stretch limos, the Smashing Pumpkins performed for a punky Foufounes Electriques crowd in 1990. During the show, somebody heckled lead singer Billy Corgan for showing too much "attitude" and hurled a beer bottle at the stage. Corgan leapt off stage to curl his bony fingers around the churl's throat. After the concert, local teen Melissa Auf der Maur approached the relatively unknown Corgan to apologize for the behaviour of Montreal fans, assuring him that his Goth-horror music wasn't really that bad.

A couple of years later, on Melissa's 21st birthday, her father, late journalist-city councillor Nick Auf der Maur, bought her the present she had been longing for: a $700 bass guitar.

Melissa started a band, Tinker, and when she heard that the Smashing Pumpkins were returning to play at Metropolis in 1993, she pestered promoters to include one homegrown act in the lineup – hers. The next summer, the Pumpkins rolled back into town yet again, this time as the headliners of Lollapalooza. Corgan phoned Melissa, took her to dinner, and told her about a new group whose bassist had died of a drug overdose. The band, called Hole, was led by Kurt Cobain's widow, Courtney Love. Corgan offered to recommend her for the job. Melissa thought about it and turned him down – she still wanted to make it big with Tinker. After a few good talkings-to, by friends and folks, Auf der Maur changed her mind, got Corgan on the phone, and got the job in no time. After Hole broke up, Melissa joined the Smashing Pumpkins, but they soon split as well.

offbeat museum

Emile Berliner Broadcasting Museum

Remember those little plastic things you had to clip in the hole of a 45-RPM record so it wouldn't spin all cockeyed on the turntable? Wouldn't you just love to see that kind of stuff again? Okay, well take this down: over in the old RCA Victor record factory, which employed 3,500 in the 1940s, sits the little-known Emile Berliner Broadcasting Museum, where you can listen to old 78s on ancient gramophones marketed as Victor Talking Machines.
1050 Lacasse, near the Saint Henri Metro station; 514/932-9663

TV Scandals

Television producer André Gingras started raving about Jesus and the Mafia and became violent enough to land a year in prison.

Long-time MusiquePlus techie Alain Painchaud confined and tortured a 24-year-old woman in Longueuil for two weeks.

Richard Glenn, host of the TV paranormal show *Esotérisme Expérimentale*, was nailed for sexually touching boys.

Claude Steben, a kiddy-show host, was convicted of assaulting a child backstage during an anti-violence speech at a school.

MusiquePlus Rap Cité host KLMNOP spent a long spell behind bars for sexual assault. He turned down a chance to be set free.

Bruno Diquinzio, star of TV crime series *Omertà*, was caught after 18 months in hiding for having a bomb and massive amounts of drugs in his house.

TV personality Danielle Ouimet was convicted of 22 counts of false advertising.

TQS newsreader Christian Latreille was busted for spousal abuse in the late 1990s after his girlfriend claimed he hurled seven pairs of shoes at her as punishment for wearing a revealing top. A few months later he got mad again and tossed a Labrador puppy at her.

We haven't even mentioned the management of the children's entertainment firm Cinar, which was implicated in various thieving money schemes. Now we have.

Like a cat, William Shatner's career has had many a life. The Montreal native has performed Shakespeare at Stratford, delivered his lines in Esperanto in the cult film *Incubus*, portrayed James Tiberius Kirk of the Starship Enterprise on TV and on the big screen, and out-tumbled the stunt chicks on his series, *T. J. Hooker*. But before his first "Beam me up, Scotty," this bilingual ex-McGill commerce student was forced to take whatever roles he could find, as illustrated in this tale he related to *The Unknown City*.

"When I was starting out in Montreal, I got a job acting on French radio. It being the first radio show in that language that I had ever done, I knew my future jobs in this arena depended on how well I did on this particular show. So it was with great anticipation that I stood in front of a microphone with my script, along with three or four other French actors. There was added tension to the show because the lead actor was late and the show was seconds from starting. Suddenly, through the window of the booth, we saw him run towards us. He came into the booth, grabbed his script, and went to his microphone. With a grand gesture, he flung his arms out wide and knocked my script from my hands. Since a radio show is read, not performed, I had no lines! My script was lying in a heap on the floor. I panicked, choked, and needless to say, was never hired to do another French radio show again!"

Don't Punch Me, I'm Only the Comedian

From Sarah Bernhardt to The Clash, a lot of faces have graced the Saint-Denis Theatre stage over the years. But only one can lay claim to having had his punched out in front of a sold-out crowd.

It was July 19, 1991. The crowd came to see Mary Tyler Moore. What they got instead was a stunning case of audience participation when an irate spectator who objected to Scottish comedian Gerry Sadowitz's routine walked on stage during the show and punched – repeatedly – the comedian in the face.

Turns out he didn't like the comic's punch line. As part of his tongue-in-cheek rant, Sadowitz had asked how Montrealers can stand living among French-Canadians. "Tell them to go back to France," he deadpanned.

Those words were too much for 48-year-old Bernard Fredette, whose attack on Sadowitz lasted about 15 seconds as the confused audience looked on. Security guards had to drag Fredette off stage. The comic, then 31, was sent to hospital and treated for bruises.

Fredette, an architect, pleaded guilty to a charge of simple assault. He received an unconditional discharge in court the next year. Sadowitz went on to be described as "the best comedian in Britain" by *The Guardian*.

Some Police Tabloid Scoops

Escorts from the Chubby Plus agency try to drum up business by flagging down passing cars on a nearby highway.

Bank robbers get nabbed after witnesses read their phone number on the For Sale sign in the back window of their getaway car.

A Laval woman burns down her house and her fiance slaps her with a restraining order on their wedding night.

A Montreal man whose corner store went belly up persuades Celine Dion to pay an exaggerated bill for his daughter's funeral. He then defrauds the workers compensation board with a phony ailment, and finally gets arrested for hanging around downtown bathrooms extorting money from men he accuses of staring at his penis.

A Thetford Mines man was arrested for trying to kill his girlfriend by driving badly.

Marie-Guerta Pierra-Garant, a veteran escort known as "Avale-tout" ("Swallows anything"), hires a stripper to kill her husband, a provincial politician, in his sleep. He wakes up and fights off the attacker.

Cops arrest 13 for organizing chicken fights in Lorretteville.

Bikers who covered their faces at a funeral, in violation of a Beauport bylaw, get off the hook when their lawyer points out that the legislation makes an exception for Halloween. The funeral took place on October 31.

An inmate named John gets released from prison after lying to authorities that he was actually a soon-to-be released prisoner named Corey. Guards let him walk right out, in spite of the fact that his real name, John, is boldly tattooed on the back of his neck.

A 41-year-old Sherbrooke man is discovered on a hospital toilet, his body decomposing after sitting there dead for four days.

Mind Mining with Gary Kurtz

A local newspaper described Gary Kurtz as something out of *The X-Files*, referring not to a character, but to the inexplicable. This Ontario farm boy who has sprouted deep roots in Montreal has become a rare star of the telepathic variety, filling large halls enthralled with his mysterious ability to bend spoons held by audience members or even change the time on their wristwatches without touching said timepieces. In his *pièce de résistance* – and indeed he performs in both official languages – he'll hand out a stack of thick books to volunteers in the audience and ask them to pick out a random passage. From far across the room, he will recite a phrase or two, inevitably flooring the crowd when he recites their chosen text. In another maneuver, Kurtz asks an audience member to merely "think of a card," and then identifies the very same! Whoa, baby! For those hoping to make a few bucks, Kurtz even offers big cash rewards for anybody who can prove that he uses dupes or other underhanded tricks in his show. So far nobody has cashed in.

Waxing Sensational

She has been named the Quebec artist having the most impact outside Quebec, has sold millions of albums around the world, and collaborated on several Hollywood soundtracks. No, we're not talking about Celine Dion.

Lara Fabian moved to Montreal from her native Belgium just out of high school. After establishing herself as a major French-language act, she crossed over with her self-titled English début, producing hits like "I Will Love Again" which led to a sideline on Hollywood film soundtracks.

Now in her early 30s, Fabian has been deemed mature and important enough to join about 500 historical wax figures at the Musée Grévin in Paris. To get her face and figure right, Lara modelled three times for sculptor Michèle Leiser, herself a European-born Quebec artist.

Next time you're in Paris, you can check out Fabian's spitting image in wax between 1-7pm at the Musée Grévin (10 boulevard Montmartre).

Criminal lawyer Adrien Poulin couldn't have known he'd be creating a quintessential bit of Quebec media culture when he set up a publication to drum up business for his practice in 1953. When *Allô Police* hit the stands, it promised that "wounding words or revolting descriptions" would never be found in its pages. Nevertheless, the tabloid soon reported on a drunk driver who ran down a cyclist and kept driving with the victim's face staring right at him through the shattered windshield. This was followed by a report about a 15-year-old Sorel delivery boy being greeted at a door by 30 naked women playing poker.

Allô Police infuriated the clergy, which threatened to excommunicate its readers. Towns passed anti-obscenity bylaws to discourage its sale, and city officials asked cops to pressure vendors not to stock it. As late as 1962, a Montreal street hawker was jailed for selling the offensive publication.

Crime grew exponentially, and by the 1970s the paper was full of soap opera-like coverage of baddies like Richard Blass, a murdering escape artist who survived numerous attempts on his life.

In a bid to expand coverage away from crime – a beat largely usurped by TV and the upstart daily *Journal de Montréal* – *Allô Police* ran softcore porn alongside its gallery of miscreants, which frequently included the names and mugshots of local hookers. In later years, another lawyer bought the weekly and eliminated much of its skin. After it published several exclusive behind-the-scenes photo shoots of Hells Angels members, rival papers accused photographer Richard Tremblay of being personally involved with the gang. Indeed, Tremblay would be caught hiding money for the boss of the city's top escort agency, who was in turn linked to Hells leader Maurice "Mom" Boucher. But *Allô* brass denied the heaviest accusations and pursued libel charges against journalists who linked Tremblay to the biker gang.

In 1968, another criminal lawyer, Raymond Daoust, launched the knockoff *Photo Police*, quickly supplanting *Allô Police* with unheard-of sales of 160,000 copies a week. But after its underpaid writers all quit in unison to open their own crime tabloid, *Spécial Police*, their former editor, Richard Desmarais, had to keep *Photo Police* going single-handed. Soon the breakaway was as dead as one of the blood-splattered mobsters

Richard Tessier, a 76-year-old self-described syphilitic, achieves a landmark 25th conviction for exhibitionism, having shown off everywhere from the Northwest Territories to Roberval, Quebec.

Brothers Robert and Gabriel Hudon, founding members of the FLQ terrorist brigade, are arrested for selling crack cocaine.

A pair of 20-year-old Sherbrooke women dig up a skeleton buried since 1862 and sit it with it while they smoke up.

A father and husband, frustrated by a restraining order, ends up climbing the walls – literally – of his wife's home before crashing to his death.

Simon Marshall, 23, of Charlesbourg, a suspect in 15 sexual-assault cases, was caught looking under the barriers in the women's bathroom at a Ste. Foy Subway restaurant.

featured in its gruesome photo spreads. Desmarais has since taken over at *Allô Police*, and both surviving papers claim to sell 70,000 copies weekly.

An ambitious competitor to this reigning duocracy popped up in the mid '90s, when *Police Plus* published a detailed report on the Rock Machine biker gang written by Robert Monastesse, a loud-talking, apparently fearless reporter. In 1995, Monastesse answered the door of his home and, as his wife and kids stood by watching, two unidentified gunmen shot him in the knees. Monastesse retired from journalism and few journalists have mentioned his name since.

For a few editions in the mid-'90s, crime tabloid *Le Juste Mileu* was a scandalous rag full of vitriol and red herrings penned by the police force's bitterest foes. Former provincial police officer Gaetan Rivest and biker-gang enforcer Robert Savard managed to put out a few issues of what cops came to know as the in-house magazine of the Hells Angels.

Rather than buttering up cops and earning their trust, *Le Juste Mileu* had a habit of publishing the addresses of particularly reviled officers with full-page colour photos of them, surrounded by text suggesting their genealogical proximity to the rat family.

No police misdoing was considered too petty for the paper. When a storekeeper complained that his head had been pushed into a brick wall by cops, the merchant gladly re-enacted the scene for the camera, as did some strippers who complained of rectal searches police apparently laid on them.

Every edition featured a large, colour photo of a statue dedicated to victims of police brutality. The statue, which depicted a prostrate man being kicked by officers from three levels of law enforcement, was obviously a crudely-sculpted bit of modeling clay photographed from below to make it seem larger than it was.

In 2001, cofounder Savard was shot and killed over breakfast at a north-end restaurant. When the chief of police commented on the case, he scored some revenge against the force's old nemesis by revealing details of the editor's many arrests for assault and murder.

Nightlife

When city bedrooms fade to black, the urban air clicks with the spit
and hiss of neon lights, inviting another shift of Montrealers to take to
the darkened streets. So begins another night of carousing in the
tradition of our forefathers and foremothers. Here all the where's and
the hows for your enjoyment of the nocturnal city, with a bunch of
whos, whats, and whens tossed in for good measure.

Ratting Out the Pack

Back in the old days when
Montreal's bustling nigthclub scene
could sustain acts for weeks at a
time, future members of the Rat Pack
made this city their home away from
home for extended working visits.

One of these, a talented young kid
named Sammy Davis Jr., hung his little
hat here. When as an adult he returned
to perform, you could say he wasn't the
best of company – moaning and
whining if 50 hangers-on didn't suck up
to his every gesture. One time, the great Davis walked into a family camera business to
"borrow" a top-of-the-line Leica camera, which he neglected to return. (The store, by the
way, was run by the late Harold Greenberg, who went on to found the multibillion-dollar
Astral entertainment empire.)

Another young performer, Dean Martin, also ruined his local rep and got himself run out
of town by El Morocco club manager Eddie Quinn (who later became a hilariously
cantankerous wrestling manager). Dino's crime? Getting a young Westmount fan pregnant.

Likewise, Vic Damone caused similar misfortune after he cast his seed into the
waiting loins of a young and fertile fan. (Later, the crooner hunk would team up with
fellow Montreal alumnus Burt Bacharach, who learned his licks as a music student at
McGill University.)

So if you see middle-aged spitting images of these big-name performers walking around
Montreal, they just might be their unacknowledged heirs.

Meanwhile, others with long-lasting memories might recall the mopey presence of a
fading Frank Sinatra, who spent several weeks performing here after getting dumped by
Ava Gardner. Little did the Chairman of the Board suspect that his best was yet to come,
shooting back to stardom with his Academy Award-winning supporting portrayal of
Maggio, the ill-fated soldier in *From Here to Eternity*.

Disco Knights

Back in 1985, the Holder brothers – Maurice, Paul, and Richard – rounded up $500,000 and opened **Business**, an industrial-chic disco at Milton and St. Lawrence. The first club in town with apocalyptic lighting and sternum-rattling sound, it also introduced expensive

Photo: John David Grovenor

cover charges. It was the city's coolest place-to-be-seen and helped start a nightclubbing rush to the Main. Business closed in 1991. The Holders and their associates, went on to open **Le Swimming, Sugar**, and the **Royale**.

Bob DiSalvio so liked his family name that he hung it outside his club on the Main – **DiSalvio's**, which was above what's now Shed Café. His son, David, opened **Cafeteria**, the **Mess Hall** in Westmount, **Yoda's Den** on Roy, the **Ginger** noodle bar on Pine, and the **High Bar** on the Main at Ontario. He sold them all off; the High Bar went belly-up after a year. David's nephew, James, became a pop star with his band, Bran Van 3000, which had hits with "Drinking in L.A." and "Move On Up," which had a video featuring sumptuous footage of Montreal.

Twin brothers Marco and Mauro LaVilla were both Concordia University film students when they took over an unremarkable restaurant on the Main near Prince Arthur. They relaunched it as the **Euro-Deli**, serving Italian fast food to clubbers late into the night. In '97, the pair made a film tribute to deejay culture, *Hang the DJ*. The resto remains in the family.

Secret Dance Party

There's a weekly event that's so secret even its participants have never even "heard" of it. **Le Centre des Loisirs des Sourds** *(8146 Drolet)* holds a dance every Friday night that is technically for the deaf, but pop your head in the door and you'll quickly learn that the hearing-impaired can party, dance, and deejay as good as anybody. Friendly people will soon be firing bilingual messages your way in American Sign Language and Langues des Signes du Québec. If you're quick, you'll learn to sign the alphabet or at least how to order a beer without speaking a word.

Nightclubs

Angel's
With the first legal apostrophe on its sign.
3604 St. Lawrence; 514/282-9944

Photo: John David Grovenor

Belmont
Popular with a mostly French-speaking crowd since the mid-'80s.
4483 St. Lawrence; 514/845-8443

Blizzarts
Youngish, retro seats and pop art design.
3958 St. Lawrence; 514/843-4860

Café Campus
In the middle of the pedestrian strip.
57 Prince Arthur E.; 514/844-1010

Cathédrale
3781 St. Lawrence; 514/842-4721

Club Dôme

Gritty downtown scene.

32 Ste. Catherine W.; 514/875-5757

Foufounes électriques

Legendary punk/pop venue.

87 Ste. Catherine E.;
514/844-5539

Jingxi

410 Rachel E.; 514/985-5464

Sona

Open 10pm to 11am.
Rave-style partying.
1439 Bleury; 514/282-1000

Thursdays

Blue blazer and beige pants not
required, but it wouldn't hurt.
1449 Crescent; 514/288-5656

Tokyo

You Only Live Twice meets Studio 54.
3709 St. Lawrence; 514/842-6838

Photo: John David Gravenor

Typhoon Lounge

Enter and exit quietly or suffer the
wrath of the finnicky NDG
neighbours.
5752 Monkland; 514/482-4448

The Local History of Disco

Montreal's reputation as a disco town has been painstakingly earned, night by night, by local dancing fools since the early '60s. **La Licorne** (1430 Mackay) was considered the city's original bona fide disco. This now defunct Anglo-packed nightspot attracted such well-known swingers as Rod Gilbert and J.C. Tremblay of National Hockey League fame. A few doors down was the **Rose Rouge** (1160 Mackay), a snootier place where Pierre Trudeau was known to sip drinks with one pinkie extended. It's still a bar. **L'Orée du Bois** (corner of Dorchester, now René Lévesque) was also big in 1965. Other popular spots in those early days included the **Capricorn** (1451 Metcalfe) and the **Cachot** (1204 Drummond). The big disco breakthrough arrived about four years later when Alfie Wade lured people to the the **Vieux Rafiot**, which was located in the historic **Pierre LeMoyne House** (corner of St. Paul and St. Sulpice) in Old Montreal. The bar was fashioned from an old lifeboat. Wade had just returned from a stay in New York when he noticed Montreal's tiny sound systems weren't cutting it anymore. Soon Wade had every bar in town emulating his booming sound, which remains the standard today.

Waterside Nightclubbing

In 2001, serial club-starter Sylvain Martellino (**Shed Café**, the **Crisco**, the **Cha Cha Club**, **Venus Bar**, and **Piccolo di Diabolo**) launched a weekly Thursday-night summertime bash at the Old Port. **The Belvedere**, as he named it, was such a success that it needed more space, so he moved his event, that attracts as many as 3,000 party animals, over to the Peel Basin at the mouth of the Canal. The 40,000-square-foot space at the foot of Peel is surrounded by water on three sides and is partially covered by raised sections of the Bonaventure Expressway. Unfortunately, this moveable fête was temporarily suspended, but Martellino's has plans for new open-air entertainment.

A Twist on the Twist

According to promoter Solly Silver, who died in 2000, his nightclub helped clean the riff-raff off the Lower Main. The Peppermint Lounge, located inside the Monument Nationale, was home to the Twist, the dance sensation invented by Chubby Checker. "How can anyone plan crimes while they're doing the Twist? They're too busy," he reasoned to city columnist Al Palmer. The club later hosted a young Jimi Hendrix before police, unsatisfied with the owners' refusal to offer payoffs, raided the club for several consecutive evenings. Soon after, the crowds stopped coming. Silver later fell into the bad books of the gay community when his bar Downbeat, one of the few local gay hangouts, inexplicably burned down in October, 1965.

Bar Violence

One sickening, extremely discouraging trend in this town has long been the violence that goes on in and outside of clubs. Bars aren't churches, as demonstrated in December, 2001, when two men were shot at a seedy dive called Bar Ivoire on Notre Dame in front of 50 witnesses — none of whom came forth to offer information. Among the once-rocking clubs that closed down after attacks on their doormen include Business on the Main and the Steel Monkey further up at Rachel. A few years back a doorman was senselessly shot dead at a club on Crescent and Réne-Lévesque, too. In 2001, the madness continued as a 19-year-old was knifed to death outside the Cathédrale; a 20-year-old met the same fate while trying to break up a fight between strangers at the nearby Conga; and a 17-year-old bystander was shot by someone alleged to be a newly-minted Hells Angel who was angry at being refused entry into the Aria nightclub. But perhaps the greatest bar phenomenon to disappear with the shot of a gun was the Thunderdome (1254 Stanley), which employed 50 and hosted 6,000 revelers on its two floors of fun. That all came to a crashing halt when a customer named Presley Leslie, who had a criminal record as long as a Welcome-to-Jamaica-Have-a-Nice-Day tattoo, which included an assault on an officer. Although 21 witnesses gave a remarkably varied description of events, police said — and a coroner's report later agreed — that Leslie started shooting a gun in the club late one night in April, 1990. Cops blasted him four times, including once from only 15 centimeters away.

Pubs & Taverns

Alexanders
First place in town to offer imported beers on tap. Slightly upscale atmosphere.
1454 Peel; 514/288-5105

Au Cepage
The Gazette executive hangout.
212 Notre Dame W.;
514/845-5436

Bar Le Grand Chapeau
The spirit of Park Ex.
570 Jarry W.; 514/273-5901

Bifteck
Rock'n'roll rebel crowd. Considered essential by many.
3702 St. Lawrence; 514/844-6211

Photo: John David Gravenor

Buster Harvey's
An unassuming place east of Décarie run by the son of local hockey legend Doug Harvey.
5175A Sherbrooke W.;
514/483-1663

The city's first-ever nightclub murder took place at the long-gone Dreamland Cabaret *(corner of the Main and Ontario)*, on July 22, 1925. Joe Mauro shot the busboy after nobody took his holdup warning seriously. Mauro, obviously, had many issues to deal with but was hanged before he could really do anything significant about them. Three years later at the same corner, the city's first big nightclub, known as the Frolics, opened up in an old fur warehouse. Serving only beer and champagne and asking a steep cover charge, feature acts included Tex Guigan, who'd greet crowds with, "Hello, suckers!"

Biker Bar Blazes

Roll into just about any bar on the island and you can likely score cocaine and other drugs. In fact, Major Crimes cop Doug Hurley estimates the trade to average a million bucks a year *per bar*. But in 2001, cops discovered that nailing the dealers was more difficult than they anticipated. After snooping around 1,400 of the island's 2,000 licensed liquor establishment in order to bust dealers, the organized-crime division ended up making just nine raids and 32 arrests. Within months, a battle between gangs to control the drug trade in neighbouring bars led to over a dozen arsons, mainly in the southwest part of the island. Although the arsons date back to at least 1997, when bikers burnt down the fabulously popular Eugene Patin at Bernard and the Main, the blazes became more frequent in 2001. In one instance, an innocent man living near one arson target was killed. In another, 50 people could have died had police not luckily noticed a fire at the Two Aces bar. Cops blamed the blazes on the Bandidos, the gang formerly known as the Rock Machine, whose foot-soldiers were paid $1,500 per blaze, in an effort to regain turf lost to the Hells Angels.

Café Sarajevo
The only time we tried to go, a rather large dog was wandering about inside, so we chose another venue, but good things are said about this place, and it's the place Rufus Wainwright started doing his thing.
2080 Clark; 514/284-5629

Carlos & Pepes
Daiquiries and margueritas will wash down your Mexican snacks in this extrovert-friendly haven.
1420 Peel; 514/288-3090

Cheers
1260 Mackay; 514/932-3138

Cock'n'Bull
"The Cock" is an ill lit, poorly laid out place that has somehow won the hearts of weirdos and other colourful characters.
*1944 Ste. Catherine W.;
514/933-4556*

The Unavoidable Bar

Even though it might not be the classiest place in town, it seems that all roads lead to the Peel Pub (or as you might think when you leave this beer parlour, "all ... uhh ... loads read to ... uhh ... what was I saying and where's the bathroom?"). The once-struggling basement establishment on Ste. Catherine at Peel first opened in '62 and, after going through a Bowie-esque gay period, suddenly bloomed in the mid-'80s when owner Jack Weshler had the great idea of hiring young women to serve beer. He boasts of being the first tavern in town to do so.

Since then the Peel Pub's empire has expanded and contracted repeatedly — at one time there were about five franchise around town. That total was brought back down after one now-defunct location was caught pouring unconsumed beer back into fresh pitchers. A good place for cheap, hearty-sized meals, the place can get crowded, and noisy due to its poor acoustics.

The King of Crescent

Until 1967, somebody expressing a desire to go to Crescent Street might have been looking for a dentist or a notary. No bars stood on the strip until a Hungarian immigrant named Johnny Vago, fresh back from a tour helping out his friend Che Gueverra and the Cuban Revolution, changed all that.

Vago opened a basement disco on Stanley called the Don Juan, but digging for the upcoming Metro tunnel damaged the property. He suddenly had a bag full of compensation cash and reopened his discotheque in a cozy basement place on Crescent. The first bar ever on Crescent was an immediate hit, known for its busboys and kitchen staff who were always ready to discuss everything from Kierkegaard to Kant; many were post-grad students working on PhDs.

The bar expanded along with Vago's bar empire, which eventually spanned the entire, well-known block. One holdout was a greasy spoon near de Maisonneuve that resembled a Vago-free bunker. Vago has since sold off his properties and spends his summers at his apartment in the Chateau on Sherbrooke, and his winters in Miami.

Crossroads

Inherited much of the riff-raff jettisoned when the next-door Claremont went upscale. A sociable place where rum and coke buddies hook up.
5028 Sherbrooke W.;
514/484-0401

Donald Duck Tavern

It's always fun to waddle to this spot near St. Michel, where the staff will happily shake their tails and quack open a cold one for ya. Although we suspect that any criticism you might have of this hole-in-the-wall would be like water off a duck's back, the bill won't disappoint, and you won't leave feeling down.
3223 Beaubien East, 725-8058

Else's

An eccentric Scandinavian named Else transformed the Transalpino into a quirky little bistro. She passed on but her essential Plateau watering hole has remained.
156 Roy E. (corner Coloniale);
514/286-6689

Honey Martin

An Irish-style pub. Narrow to the point of being a hazard to claustrophobics.
5916 Sherbrooke W.; 514/484-2999

Mad Hatter

A blaze swept away its original digs but the new Hatter is still packing in the university kids, although some have grumbled about an attitude creeping into the staff lately.
1230 de Maisonneuve W.

Maz Bar

Language law compliant name for Ma Heller's Bar, a unique place in the heart of NDG known as a hangout for war heroes.
5617 Sherbrooke W.; 514/488-0711

Miami

Where filth and dilapidation seem to add up to subversion. With a back terrace that brings Cheech and Chong films to mind, this worlds-apart refuge serves cheap drinks, with Irish whisky permanently on special. Several comical episodes have occurred since customers started complaining about the unwieldy, shin-bashing barstools.
3601 St. Lawrence; 514/845-2300

Photo: John David Gravenor

Woman Beer Pioneers

Until December 1971, women were not allowed in any place where men drank draft beer, and until the mid-'80s, bartenders would look unfavourably upon women trying to enter a tavern. The **Goblet** in the north end was the first to pour beer for women after the 1837 provincial drinking law was amended to fit the beer-drinking needs of both genders.

Legions of Drinkers

Since the entry rules were changed in 1998, non-veterans can pretty much walk into any Legion Hall nowadays and see the bottom of a glass or two. Some say the most joyous day ever in Point St. Charles was the time the boys returning home after the war got off the trains. Some of those boys can still be found in the cozy, red-brick legion on Ste. Madeleine, long run with the greatest of love by war hero Frank Baddely and the help of others like Bill Key and Frank Monroe. Veterans outdo each other with tales of wartime tragedy, but whenever the mood goes the wrong way there's somebody making a joke (watch out for the joker who sadly announces the presence of a DBO, as in "dick blown off").

Here's where you can track down some of the city's legion halls:

543 Ste. Madeleine; 514/932-7586
2272 Viau; 514/256-5335
7771 Bouvier, Lasalle; 514/365-0595
28 Ste. Anne, Pointe Claire; 514/457-9332
5455 de Maisonneuve W.; 514/489-9425
4835 7th Ave., Rosemont; 514/521-5281
1860 Ontario E.; 514/526-5062
575 Jean-Marie Landry, Dorval; 514/631-5786
3015 Henri Dunant, Lachine; 514/637-8002
11500 René Lévesque E., Montreal E.; 514/645-1940
3 4th Ave., Roxboro; 514/684-9575
5433 Laurendeau; 514/768-0106
4538 Verdun Ave.; 514/769-2489
1000 St. Antoine W.; 514/866-7491
4625 Ste. Catherine W., Westmount; 514/931-7798
56 Beach, Hudson; 450/458-4882

A Hostess Awaits

Never will you feel as great a conversationalist as when you're at the **Diamond Gentlemen's Lounge** (1458 Mountain; 514/284-3844), Montreal's only hostess bar. Located upstairs from Wanda's strip club, this place will teach you, real quick, how a $10 drink bought for a fully-clad female employee will gain you her undivided attention and, undoubtedly, endless sympathy and assent (although we haven't tested any contentious view on 'em). Although one might have to have a pretty low opinion of one's conversational skills to opt for such a gimmick, the hostess concept is huge in Japan, and the laid-back, talky, couch-laden décor here is no less agreeable than the dolled-up babes. You might find your conversation ending as soon as your hostess's glass is empty, however.

One Bar You May Never Set Foot In

The seediest joint in town, we think, sits on the second floor at the southeast corner of Mountain and Ste. Catherine. Climb a set of stairs and you're faced with a melamine counter and a few stools on your left. On your right you'll see dozens of small cubicles, with TVs in them displaying all measure of adult fare (at only 25 cents per viewing). God knows what kind of clientele the secretive German owner of this peep show wanted to attract by putting a bar on the premises, but the friendly Sri Lankan staffers are certainly nice folks. No jacket or tie required. Pants might be optional too; we'll get back to you on that.

New Friday's
Loud-talking office crowd.
636 Cathcart; 514/878-3743

St. Sulpice
A huge garden terrace behind this converted mansion always seems to be full of French-speaking students likely from the nearby University of Quebec at Montreal campus.
1680 St. Denis; 514/844-9458

St. James Pub
380 St. Jacques W.; 514/288-1354

Stanley Pub
Picture yourself in a stereotypical Quebec working-class brasserie (yes, there is such a stereotype). Raise two fingers and a waiter in a white shirt and black pants will bring you two glasses of draft. Good cheap meals.
1428 Stanley

Irish

Hurley's Irish Pub

Equipped with fireplaces inside for cold winters days and an excellent terrace for summer nights, this well-situated, friendly establishment has pretty much set the standard for Celtic drinking holes.
1225 Crescent; 514/861-4111

McKibbin's

Ladies night on Wednesdays sees this two-floor woody place rock in a very large fashion.
1426 Bishop; 514/288-1580

McLean's Pub

Once home to the Reimark Tavern, which served the best pig's knuckles in town, this spot has thrived under several names and serves a slightly older crowd.
1210 Peel; 514/393-3132

The Old Dublin

Johnny Assad, Montreal's Persian Publican, will welcome you with good food, and Celtic music after 10pm Nicer inside than out.
1219-A University; 514/861-4448

Photo: John David Gravenor

In the east-end heart of an abandoned storefront city you'll find one or two taverns-turned-neighbourhood-showbar, with none more notable than **Bar Chez Françoise**. You'll recognize it immediately by the photocopied 8x10 publicity shots taped to the windows. Behold the lesser gods of the Québécois pantheon of stars, some of whom might have had a minor French hit on AM radio decades ago and weren't informed of their career expiration date. Here, they belt out their tunes accompanied on the organ by Marcel, the man-for-all-songs. Although the venue is small, the performances seldom lack ambition. Expect to hear generic rock singers doing the inevitable cover of Pagliaro's *J'entend frapper* or women singing Québécois standards about lost love.

Amazingly, there's never any cover charge – not bad, considering that such greats as Martin "Love is in the Air" Stevens performs occasionally, no doubt a show you wouldn't forget soon. Another crowd favourite was the busboy, no less. For a while, the Mexican table-clearer who lived in an apartment upstairs from the bar where he was too poor to own a phone, packed in enthusiastic crowds with majestic singing performances, then returned to the task of cleaning up bottles. On Sundays, free meals are often served, which adds to a warm neighbourhood spirit that's maintained by a melancholic owner who inherited the place from his much-missed parents a few years back. Locals are sensitive to the mockery of city slickers, so best to repress any cynical snickering about the *kétaine*-ness of it all at the risk of your welcome.
3785 Ste. Catherine East

Old Time Rock 'n' Roll

If you thought your nightclubbing days would be over at age 60, you've never been to the **Do Ré Mi Dance Hall** *(505 Bélanger)*, where lucky old-timers can test the moves of more than 20 partners a night. For hour after hour, including weekend afternoons, a friendly array of female-dominated crowds hit the floor for ballroom dancing, while snazzily-dressed men enjoy the ratio. The uninitiated will wonder about the green neon light that causes a geriatric ballroom blitz whenever it's switched on; a green light here means line-dancing time.

Intello-Drinking

Scientists have empirical proof that it's impossible to be too cool. That's great news for the folks at **Casa del Popolo**, a live venue and veggie café that has already made history in the brief time since it replaced the Artishow, the poorly-named – and now defunct – bar at the same locale. As the Bunker was to the Beatles, this place is to Godspeed You Black Emperor! – a publicity-shy intellectual band whose stimulating and very unhummable music has attracted much international attention despite their refusal to do promotion. (In fact, the owner of this club may or may not be one of the furtive band members, but that's between you and us.) As well as hosting their own newspaper full of political commentary, the contents of which are mirrored on the website *(casadelpopolo.com)*, this place, owned by Mauro Pezzente and Kiva Stimac, made the "100 Best Ideas of 2001" edition of the *New York Times Magazine*. It seems the *Times* really like the cigarette machine reworked to distribute artwork, like little sketches and poems packaged in cigarette packs. Shows featuring bands with names ranging from We Are Molecules to Sexhead to the Vapids happen at 4873 St. Lawrence, with bigger acts hosted at a sister stage across the street at 4848. Call 514/284-3804 for anything else you wanna know.

Billiards

Bacci

3553 St. Lawrence; 514/844-3929

4205 St. Denis; 514/287-9331

Le Swimming

With frequent live acts.

3643 St. Lawrence;

514/282-7665; leswimming.com

Photo: John David Gravenor

Metropol

Vast, no-frills hall with 31 tables.
Lots of show-off talent.

1197 St. Lawrence;

514/392-1458

Sharx Pool Bar

Downstairs in the Faubourg mall. Also
has a small bowling alley.

1606 Ste. Catherine; 514/934-3105

Sports Bars

Champs
3956 St. Lawrence; 514/987-6444

La Cage aux Sports
395 Le Moyne St. at McGill;
514/288-1115

Peel Pub-West End
Formerly The Main Event.
6180 St. Jacques W.;
514/485-7665

Karaoke

Karaoke Box
Designed for smaller parties.
2151 Mountain; 514/844-1791

**Resto Bar Quynh
Anh Karaoke**
6104 Côte des Neiges Rd.;
514/731-4339

Vocalz Karaoke Club
1421 Crescent; 514/288-9119

Liberace Owes It All to Us

A promising yet under-performing young pianist kept failing to fill the seats while tickling the ivories at the Mount Royal Hotel's Normandie Roof nightclub in 1943, so a bunch of concerned minds grouped together to brainstorm on the American piano man's inability to drum up impressive audiences. Hotel owner Vernon Cardy, a headwaiter named Victor, soon-to-be magician Tom "Magic Tom" Auburn, publicist Colin Gravenor, caterer Pierre Borbey, and promoter Jimmy Nichols all tried to figure how to reverse the musician's slumping fate. One suggested that the musician drop his first name and pronounce his last name the way it was spoken in the old country. So that night *Walter Liberace* (pronounced: "libber-ACE") switched his handle to the exotic-sounding single name, *Liberace* ("li-bur-AH-chee"). Thus rechristened, fame, fortune, and unbridled sexual excess soon followed.

You Can't Pinch an Inch

We're not sure what happened to the builders of Donald Tarlton's head office. His company, Donald K. Donald Productions, chose to build on the spot where the burnt-out El Morocco showbar once stood on Lambert-Closse. But someone forgot to double-check the measurements. The huge, south-facing wall of the new building was constructed about an inch too far to the south, invading the adjacent property. When the situation was brought to Tarlton's attention, the big guy tried to negotiate with the owner of the adjoining parking lot to compensate him for the lost land. The lot owner, an old-school British immigrant, wouldn't give an inch. Despite negotiating skills that made him the city's top music promoter for decades, Tarlton just couldn't get the old guy to budge. Eventually, Tarlton's contractor had to tear down the trespassing wall and replace it, brick by brick, a tiny bit to the north.

The Black Tradition

After the war, when this city was considered on an even par with New York City as a venue for nightclub acts, many American promoters hesitated to send their popular black performers here. The entertainers could date any receptive woman they chose in Montreal without fear of dirty looks and make their music without having to perform in a clownish, Jar-Jar Binks-like black pantomime. So popular was the city with the black musicians that many chose not to go back. For example, when the Lena Horne film *Stormy Weather* was released, promoters put together a road band for a nightclub tour. Among those who stayed here were sax man Leroy Mason, drummer Walter Bacon, and a bassist named Charlie Biddle. Others, like Louis Armstrong, came as often as they could. Louis was known to casually chat with others while sitting on the crapper extolling the merits of his Swiss laxatives. Dapper tough guy Rufus Rockhead handed out red roses to all women who popped by his Little Harlem nightspot, **Rockhead's Paradise** *(southeast corner of Mountain and St. Antoine)*, a place full of dazzling black chorus girls who would immediately sew needed repairs on their costumes before going home for the night. Developers put an end to it all. They paved over it and put up a parking lot.

But some of that spirit lives on at **Biddle's Rib House and Jazz Club** *(2060 Aylmer; 514/842-8656)*. Possibly one of the great repositories for old time stories of Montreal's jazz era, this styling place features an excellent terrace.

Spanish/ Latino

6/49

A well-dressed, outgoing clientele, marginally older than other clubs. *1112 Ste. Catherine St. W.; 514/868-1649*

Cactus

Slightly cramped, the nonstop salsa fills the floor with perspiring dance maniacs. *4459 St. Denis; 514/849-0349*

Casa Nacho

Wednesday to Sunday from 7pm to 3am, this place is huge with Latin revellers. *90 Jean Talon St. W.; 514/271-5129*

Salsatheque

One of Montreal's oldest, best-known, and most popular Latin clubs, it looks like a '70s discotheque and features dance performances, beauty contests, and live bands on various nights. Wednesday to Sunday is popular with some of the city's professional athletes. *1220 Peel 514/875-0016*

lounges

Acqua Lounge

Comfy downtown spot for laid-back fans of electronic and hip-hop.
1240 Drummond; 514/866-7695

Club 737

Famous for its surly staff, who may brazenly demand you tip them more than you already have, this place offers an unparalleled view of the city. The terrace couldn't be any higher, but it lacks some of the charm of the rooftop bar of the Hotel de la Montagne.
1 Place Ville Marie, Level PH2; 514/397-0737

Gogo Lounge

Retro cocktail lounge everybody tells us is the shit. The cocktail menu is on an old vinyl record. Beware the queues; go early for tables.
3682 St. Lawrence; 514/286-0882

Jello Bar

Rode the martini wave a few years back and hasn't stopped. Couches beckon with a reassuring feng shui. Features '60s kitsch furniture and coloured glass.
151 Ontario E.; 514/285-2621

Raw Bar

On the second floor of the hip St. Paul Hotel in Old Montreal, it serves only raw delights – like tartars, oysters, ceviche, anc capriccio. Wash it down with drinks you can hardly pronounce.
355 McGill St.; 514/380-2222

Sofa Bar

Good after-work joint full of sofas, beautiful people, and port wine.
451 Rachel E.; 514/285-1011

CASK AND YOU SHALL RECEIVE

You know that happy feeling of having a laid-back, nostalgic buzz fused with a smug sense of self-satisfaction? Well, we don't either, but we've heard a lot about it and apparently drinking fine whiskies while smoking cigars can get you there. And "there," in this case, is the **Whisky Café**, poised at the east end of Bernard near the Main. Among the attractions are a urinette, which allows women to stand while they pee. If you're that curious check it out online *(whiskycafe.ca)*. From Glentromie to Glenbeg, if they don't have your whisky, then they don't have it. And they claim to offer cheap lifts home for over-indulgers.
5800 St. Lawrence Blvd., at Bernard; 514/278-2646

gay & lesbian

Agora

A mostly English-speaking clientele frequent this small, friendly bar with nightly happy hour and karaoke.
1160 Mackay St.; 514/934-1428

Bourbon Complex

Not just a club, the Bourbon has been called the world's biggest gay attraction of its kind. Covering a whole block, it has full-service restos, hotel, and bathouse/sauna. Its three bars include a dance club with weekly speicals and themes.
1578 Ste. Catherine St. E.; 514/523-4679

Chez Mado

Every night is a theme night, with visiting DJs, live dancers, live drag shows, and cabaret revues.
1115 Ste. Catherine St. E.; near Beaudry Metro, 514/525-7566

Cleopatra's

Its legendary, outrageous drag shows have been packin' in mixed audiences for the past three decades. Two nightly shows: 11:15pm and 1am.
1230 St. Lawrence, south of Ste. Catherine; 514/871-8066

Club Date Karaoke

Easygoing, fun corner bar, with a mixed clientele, nightly karaoke and occasional invited acts.
1218 Ste. Catherine St. E.; 514/521-1242

GOOD TIMES FOR GOOD CAUSES

Back in the early nineties, a group of friends decided to hold a huge party and donate all the proceeds to a good cause. It was the first Black & Blue event, and 800 people showed up. More than a decade later, the party has grown into a week-long, cultural, social, and sporting event.

The original group of friends now go by the name Bad Boys Club of Montreal, a registered, not-for-profit association which has spun off another handful of events to affirm and celebrate the gay community.

Magnolia Pub

The town's front-and-centre dyke bar features a piano bar, live shows, daily happy hours, and nightly dancing. Open Tuesdays through Sundays. Equally popular with fems, lipsticks, butch — you name it: if she's hot, she's here.
1329 Ste. Catherine E.; 514/526-6011

Parking

Regulars know it as one of the city's top gay hangouts. A vast, stripped-down space that throbs to dance, rock and alternative grooves. Women welcome Wednesdays.
1296 Amherst, Beaudy Metro; 514/282-1199

Sky Complex

A constellation of happenin' attractions, it boasts a cavernous dance hall, deejay club, male strip bar, dinner club, and ground-floor pub. One of the city's most chic night spots, with what insiders describe as a hot clientele to match.
1474 Ste. Catherine St. E.; near Papineau Metro, 514/529-6969

Here's their basic calendar: New Year's — "Bal des Boys"; Valentine's Day — "Red Party"; March — "Bump Gay Spring Ski Weekend"; Victoria Day — "Wild & Wet Weekend"; Gay Pride weekend in August — "Twist"; October — "Black & Blue Festival."

The BBCM Foundation gathers the proceeds from these events to support gay and lesbian community groups and provide AIDS-related health services, social support, and financial relief for people affected by this devastating syndrome.
bbcm.org

Fetish Anyone?

In the heart of the Village, **U-Bahn** is Montreal's kinky underground at its wildest, a leather rubber happenin' for the serious fetishist who has everything in his pervy wardrobe — or do they? Rubber bed sheets and matching pillowcases, rubber socks, and a leather sling complete with bed frame and chains will set you back about three grand but hey, when you've got a dungeon room to furnish you'll know where to go. You can also find more mainstream stuff like leather and rubber jeans, shirts, and chaps. This bonafide European shopping experience features metal flooring and industrial decor punctuating the hard-core, sleazy feel of this real fetish dream store. Don't miss their bi-annual GUMMI NIGHT fetish parties: lots of shiny happy people!
1285 Amherst, Beaudry Metro, 514/529-0808; ubahn.com

Step right up to the freak-show that is life, and learn about the shocking legends of our hand-picked local characters. From the Hollywood starlet whose rapidly stiffening corpse was hurried across a nearby border to the 15-year-old waif whose schtick inspired one of the greatest rock operas of all time. There's no time to lose — let the dirt digging begin!

The Pyramid Was Built Here

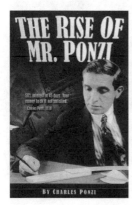

Forget Egypt, the classic pyramid scheme was perfected in Montreal. In 1908, Italian immigrant Charles Ponzi came to town from Providence, Rhode Island, and took a job at the Banca Rossi bank, where he was assigned the task of attracting new customers. This he did by promising amazing interest rates, which he actually paid out to the first few account holders. The business started pouring right in and, as the legal noose tightened, Ponzi's boss fled to Mexico. Ponzi was sentenced to two years in a local jail and eventually returned to his playing field by pulling off a much larger pyramid scheme in Boston. He was eventually exposed when reporters dug up his Montreal mug shot, and ever since his name has been immortalized as a synonym for the classic pyramid scheme.

The Ol' Warehouse Decoy Trick

In the grocery biz there's a practice called diverting, in which you buy loads of grocery products cheap from one place and sell at a higher price elsewhere. It doesn't make much sense to a couple of backwoods boys like us, but a Montreal lawyer moved to Miami and started such an operation under the guise of a company called Premium Sales, soon returning huge profits to a few investors, such as Steinberg grocery magnate Mitzi Dobren. Other backers – 227 of 'em to be exact – also jumped on board with as much money as they could cough up. By 1990, the operation was racking up huge paper profits, while it really consisted of a couple of decoy warehouses with the same few trucks coming and going all the time. The $2-billion annual business was bogus and a check showed that only a tiny amount of legitimate commerce was taking place, as corrupt officials of big grocery firms were rubber-stamping receipts to make the scam look legit. Rather amazingly, a class-action suit launched by the local victims actually resulted in the return of over half of the $116 million local investors lost in the Ponzi scheme.

Despite her squeaky-clean image, Celine Dion (or as some detractors call her for the way they claim she sounds, *Sea Lion Dyin'*) and her husband René Angelil have had a long string of legal mishaps and media controversies.

In 2001, the duo demanded $5 million from the celebrity tabloid *Allô Vedette*, which rehashed a previously-published report stating that the duo rented a large chunk of Caesar's Palace in Las Vegas in order to sunbathe privately in the nude. Angelil cited the September 11 terrorist attacks as the reason he later dropped the suit.

Sept Jours reported that it had destroyed 200,000 copies of a 1998 edition of the magazine because the Dion-Angelil team disliked the headline, "My Son Already Has a Twin." The story reported – correctly – that Dion had frozen identical eggs for later gestation. Still, Angelil demanded all copies of the magazine be destroyed and the brass obliged.

While Dion and Angelil were on a media blitz to let the world know that they were trying to have a baby, the *National Enquirer* announced that Dion was indeed pregnant with twins. Dion figured this was a huge insult worth $20 million – a sum she demanded for invasion of privacy. The magazine settled by making a minor donation to a charity of her choice.

In 1997, Dion requested that Canadian *TV Guide* not run an interview she had granted with the magazine. Dion was likely offended by a question pertaining to a reference to her curious behaviour at a Quebec French-language music awards ceremony in 1990. When awarded the title of Best Anglophone Artist for her debut English-language effort, she bizarrely explained that she couldn't accept the award because she was a Quebecer and not an Anglophone.

In 1994, Dion demanded $20 million from *Photo Police*, which printed the unspeakable rumour that Angelil knew Dion, um, all too well while she was still his underage

Random Sex Tidbits
To Keep You Interested

Deep Undercover

In 1994, suburban Laval's morality squad revealed they regularly subcontracted work to a married man on their payroll to go undercover – in every sense of the word – and have sex with prostitutes in order to gain evidence on practitioners of the skin trade.

Whip Smart

In 1997, a customer at a Beaudry Street S&M dungeon run by professional dominatrix Sylvia Wahl complained that she abused his penis and testicles without his permission. Constitutional lawyer Julius Grey was defending her cause, as she recounted to a court the details of her services, which included offering, uh, fresh liquid refreshments to her customers. Wahl took off to Germany, and Grey would have to wait until 2001 to get another chance to win

protegée. The tabloid crime rag settled out of court.

A Montreal businessman who was sued for producing a line of Celine lingerie, ended up locking horns with Angelil, who said he never granted permission to do so. It soon came out in an interrogation that Angelil had indeed signed a license on the rights, but had apparently forgot about it. Oops. The issue was subsequently settled behind locked doors.

a sex case. That year, Grey convinced a judge that a lesbian stage performance at Les Amazones strip club in which two women lick cherries and whip cream off each other's bodies was, in fact, quite legal (and possibly rather entertaining).

Pole Position

Firefighters aren't always the ones hopping on poles in this town. At the Rachel Street station in August, 1985, two firefighters were busted for having sex with young women from the Starry Night escort service. Cops had been scoping the Cotroni mob-run escort agency because several of the women involved were minors.

Insane Asylum Scandals

Around 1935, the cash-strapped provincial government led by Maurice Duplessis realized that the feds would hand over $2.75 a day for somebody in a psychiatric institute but only 75 cents a day for somebody in an orphanage. Solution? Put the orphans in the insane asylums. This maneuver – blessed by religious, political, and medical officials – netted the church an estimated $70 million in today's terms. The survivors of the horror, the so-called Duplessis Orphans, went uncompensated until 2001 when the Quebec government offered them $10,000 each plus $1,000 per year spent inside an institute. Peanuts indeed, although the lawyer and public-relations officials made millions off the settlement, while bureaucrats in charge of the file were paid $1,000 a day for working on it.

Another story that makes you wonder if the lunatics weren't the ones running the asylums describes the CIA experiments conducted at the Allan Memorial Institute, which was named after shipping magnate Sir Hugh Allan, who owned the Ravenscrag hilltop property that now houses a psychiatric facility attached to the Royal Victoria Hospital. From 1957 to 1961, the CIA paid hotshot psychologist Dr Ewen Cameron to use patients as guinea pigs for experiments that included massive electroshock therapy, the use of LSD, and tape recorded messages like, "You killed your mother." When the American funding ran out, Health and Welfare Canada picked up the slack until 1964, when Cameron walked away from it all three years prior to his death. One of Cameron's close associates in the experiments was Dr Dimitri Pivnicki, who eventually became the prime minister's father-in-law when his daughter, Mila, married Brian Mulroney. Survivors of the incident eventually sued and received settlements of over $100,000 each.

Prog Rockers Can't Fight

Serge Fiori, leader of the legendary '70s Québécois folk-rock band Harmonium, won't forget the night of August 9, 1997 anytime soon. Around 3:30am, he was sauntering down St. Denis with his girlfriend, Marie-Jocèlyne Dion, and a second woman. At the corner of Rachel, the excitable Dion accidentally bumped into one of four young Anglophone women from the tough Park Extension district. Their demands for an apology went unheeded by Fiori, leading to a proliferation of lip-flapping that grew into a good ol' fashioned English-versus-French bitch fight, in which the four Park Ex women proved the more capable pugilists. Fiori would later testify in court of having to "shield himself like a cocoon" as one of the young women beat him "until I was going to die." (While listing their damages, Dion reported having lost a mere button off her shirt, while Fiori complained that his clothes were soiled from cowering on the pavement.) The four Park Ex women were arrested, while Fiori and his girlfriend were awarded $1,300 a month from the victims' criminal indemnity fund (IVAC) for various small ailments, including an aching finger, a sore hip, and depression. Joanne Zergiotis (21), Haddi Doyle (18), Suelynn Taylor (17), and Jennifer Holmes (17), were initially charged with a misdemeanour, but that was inexplicably raised to assault. During the highly entertaining trial in February, 2001, Fiori and Dion's former analyst described the pair as "lunatics." The four young women were acquitted, and a peeved Fiori went on a media blitz to denounce the jury's decision and the media mockery he underwent during the trial.

Pistol Whipped by Leonard Cohen

How inadequate would an *Unknown City* book be without a story about Leonard Cohen and a gun? Prior to the Westmounter's big-time poetry success and subsequent ass-numbing Buddhist crouching, young Lenny was known to pull the occasional odd stunt. When a best friend persisted in behaving recklessly with heroin usage, Monsieur Cohen surprised him with a gift. The *Flowers for Hitler* scribbler presented the man with a carefully wrapped box containing a fully operational gun. The pistol was to serve as a message to the friend along these lines: either get it together now or just shoot yourself and get it over with.

UFO Sightings

The military has a policy of keeping these things quiet, so there must be countless other UFO sightings, but these are the ones we've uncovered for you. If the truth is out there, dagnabbit, then it must be somewhere in these UFO tales as well.

Back to the Big House

In August, 1976, Richard Glenn was called to Mont St. Hilaire, where he had telepathic conversations with little guys with big eyes and tiny noses. Later, the 30-year-old schoolteacher produced an unwatchably-low-budget TV show — at his own expense — called *Ésoterisme Experimentale*. Local cable companies aired the space-mysteries show as cheap filler. He moved to the area near Mont St. Hilaire which, he points out, is known to the Abenaki Indians as "Wigwam Al Ensis" or "Big House (of the People) from the Sky."

Red Ball's in the Sky

When Bernard Guenette reported seeing a UFO near his Laval home in 1979, the authorities he notified responded with condescension and derision. So when, on November 7, 1990, several dozen witnesses noticed a big red ball in the sky over the luxurious indoor-outdoor rooftop

swimming pool atop Place Bonaventure, Guenette started investigating. The sighting lasted two hours, the object could have been up to 4,500 feet across, according to an exhaustive analysis he co-authored about the experience.

A New Airline?

On April 13, 1985, three separate reports arrived at Dorval Airport describing a large, low-flying, oval-shaped object that could have been red or red-and-white. All three witnesses placed the UFO around Park Extension and northern Montreal between 11pm and 1am. A middle-aged Town of Mount Royal couple also reported seeing a slow-moving, low-flying red orb. Wifey freaked out but hubby just plopped his head back on his pillow.

Made in Canada

On April 29, 1991, a number of Montrealers reported seeing a flying saucer above Mount Royal at 9:15pm. And they had indeed seen a 20x10 craft, which was later classed as an Identified Non-Flying Object. Turns out it was just a prop for the shooting of a Labatt beer commercial featuring aliens out to steal the recipe for the beer.

Pete Townshend has repeatedly told interviewers that his Indian guru inspired him to write *Tommy, the Rock Opera*. But could he be deliberately overlooking the Montreal connection? There's significant evidence that The Who's Pinball Wizard character was based on a 15-year-old Montreal waif named Pamela Marchant. After moving to London in the '60s, the Montreal teen misfit gained the attention of rock writer Nik Cohn, who introduced her about town as Arfur, a mute street-urchin and pinball champion. (He didn't want her to speak, fearing her Canadian accent would blow the ruse.) Just after Cohn's novel *Arfur* came out describing the entire tale of the pinball princess, Townshend hooked up with Cohn to get his opinion on a still-in-progress rock opera. Cohn, a rock fan, wasn't impressed. Townshend then wrote a rockier number, in hopes of increasing Cohn's influential support for the upcoming LP. Rather familiarly, the Townshend tune described a "deaf, dumb, and blind kid," who "sure plays a mean pinball." Marchant's pinball-playing persona ended soon after she was featured in a cover story in the Canadian magazine, *Weekend*. Marchant ditched her assumed identity and went on to an ill-fated music career under the guidance of The Who's management team. She eventually returned to Montreal and appeared in the cult film classics *Montreal Main* and *Rubber Gun*. Cohn, who was briefly married to Marchant, also wrote a story that would be adapted as the hit film *Saturday Night Fever*.

The great film-noir femme fatale Constance Ockleman, alias Veronica Lake, spent two years here as a teen while her New York-based stepfather came to be treated for TB. They weren't the best of times for the young lass, as she skipped many classes at her Catholic school and was diagnosed as a schizophrenic. The family moved to Florida, where she won a beauty contest and eventually became a screen legend, thanks to her unruly peek-a-boo hair and sultry voice. After a few years at the top, Lake hit the skids and ended up tending bar in New York. She eventually moved back to Montreal to be with her lover, *Police Gazette* publisher Nate Perlow, who moved here after *Midnight* owner Joe Azaria bought an interest in the publication. Perlow paid for Lake's apartment on Côte des Neiges near St. Joseph's Oratory, where she spent her days in a gin stupor and related incomprehensible stories of her life. When Lake died in August, 1973, Perlow, with the help of two friends, fulfilled her request that her death not appear to have taken place in the drunken squalor of Sin City North. On a hot afternoon, Perlow and *Midnight* reporter Jim Schneider packed Lake's tiny corpse into a gold Oldsmobile station wagon and covered her face with a Spanish doily. As they approached the border, they tensely reported to the border guard that the 54-year-old actress was merely sleeping. The next day it was reported that she died of liver failure after having spent two weeks at the Vermont Medical Center in Montpelier. Few attended her funeral.

BAD JUDGMENT

In recent years, not all Montreal judges have impressed onlookers with their wisdom. Here are a few examples.

In January, 1994, Quebec Court Judge Raymonde Verreault sentenced an unrepentant rapist who had regularly sodomized his young daughter for three years to just 23 months in prison. The light sentence she meted out was in reward for the courtesy the father had shown his daughter by allowing her to maintain her vaginal virginity.

In January 1998, Judge Monique Dubreuil came up with this sentence for two Haitian men convicted of rape: no jail time. And she outraged the Haitian community when she suggested that rape is normal to their culture. "The absence of regret of the two accused seems to be related more to the cultural context, particularly with regard to relations with women, than a veritable problem of a sexual nature," she commented.

Muhammad Ali Helps Montrealer Fight George "Dubya"

Yank Barry, born Gerard Falovitch in 1949 in Ville St. Lawrence, was addicted to cocaine and infatuated with the local Mafia when he pulled a nasty ruse on a business partner. In 1971, Barry enticed a prostitute to seduce John R. McConnell, his partner in a recording company and son of the owner of the daily *Montreal Star*. After McConnell knocked boots with the woman, Barry led on that she was the wife of a Mafia kingpin, who now demanded blood money to repair the offense. Barry defrauded McConnell of $82,000 before being nabbed and sentenced to six years in prison.

A few years later, Barry had mended his ways and became a soy powder magnate, manufacturing a meat-replacement formula in Montreal and selling it throughout the world with the help of mouthpiece Muhammad Ali. After Barry's VitaPro scored a massive, long-term contract to supply soy powder to the Texas prison system, then-governor George W. Bush cancelled the deal. Barry filed a suit for breach of contract. Bush fired back by laying criminal charges that accused Barry of bribing the prison chief. Barry was supremely confident of beating the rap in a case tried in the fall of 2001. Appearing in support of Barry's cause were friends ranging from a former U.S. Treasurer, a second-in-command for the FBI, as well as Muhammad Ali. Barry was found guilty anyway and faced decades in prison. He planned to file an appeal and work on a book.

Superior Court Judge Robert Flahiff would regularly stroll into his bank with loads of crumpled bills. He was eventually questioned and convicted in 1999 of laundering $1.1 million of drug money. He was sentenced to three years but served only six months.

Judge Richard Therrien lost his job when it was discovered that he had neglected to disclose his criminal past: he been convicted for hiding FLQ terrorists at his sister's Montreal apartment in 1970.

Tennis: a Menace

Jim Pierce was born in North Carolina and, after a brutal childhood in which his father beat him regularly, he became a stickup artist. Later he was shot by cops, declared a schizophrenic, and became a part-time vagrant, before eventually gaining status as a tough guy in Sing Sing prison. After his release in 1973, he moved to Montreal where he met Yannick Adjani, a student from France. They had a child, Mary, on January 15, 1975. A few years later, the family moved to Treasure Island, Florida, where his daughter, now 10-year-old Mary Pierce, displayed a startling gift with a tennis racket — an aptitude he helped hone by viciously hitting balls straight at her. Four years later, Mary became the youngest player ever to turn pro and embarked on a string of net-jumping accomplishments. Jim Pierce became the quintessential tennis dad from hell; Mary shunned him, and for several years he was banned from attending her games.

A Perfect Ten for Riding the Bus Through Rosemount

Nadia Comaneci was, of course, the 14-year-old gymnast who stole the world's heart by earning the first-ever perfect 10 score at the '76 Olympics. Local burger-flippers might recall her as the waif who stockpiled as many little packets of ketchup as she could get from the McDonald's near the Forum. (Something 'bout them being rare under Ceausescu's Iron Curtain rule.) After a failed suicide attempt back home, she eventually skedaddled to Hungary and then to Florida, where people frowned upon her tryst with a married man. Then her athletic mentor, Alexandru Stefu, enticed her to move into an upstairs flat in his triplex in Rosemount (at Louis-Hébert and Beaubien). For two years, the gymnastic genius became another anonymous proletarian face on the No. 18 bus to and from the Beaubien Metro — a period that ended in September 1991, when Stefu, 47, was found drowned in a lake he was snorkeling in near Valleyfield. Comaneci soon left Montreal for Oklahoma, where she married gymnastics champion Bart Conner.

COUNTLESS RIOTS

We hate to brag, but if any town is a riot town, this is it. Disorganized scrums of mayhem threaten to arise anytime. Until recently, Victoria Day (May 24) was considered a reason to riot in the Point, and winning Stanley Cups has become a good reason, too — as fans proved in 1986 and 1993 when they tried to outdo the original 1955 Rocket Richard riot. From a list too long to enumerate and broken-heartedly excluding the 1849 riot that cost Montreal its title of nation's capital, these are some of the more riotous displays of civic unrest.

In 1993, Greek-immigrant-dishwasher-turned-restaurant-magnate Peter Sergakis led a procession of the Association of Commercial Building Landlords to City Hall to protest then-mayor Jean Doré's tax hikes. With great gusto, the gang of middle-aged tax rebels smashed down the doors to City Hall. The rebel group was fined $500. The city of Montreal's labour union duplicated the tactic a few months later, only to see two of its leaders tossed in jail for a month and the union fined $32,000.

July 19, 1885 saw the culmination of a series of riots incited by a man who refused to take a compulsory smallpox vaccine. Sadly, while fighting the mayhem, police officer John Malone was killed by a brick to the head.

Sir George Williams University student Roosevelt "Rosie" Douglas (pictured) led a revolt against a professor who had the nasty habit of flunking dark-skinned students. On February 11, 1969, 150 students took over parts of the university's downtown campus (now part of Concordia), keeping the cops out by tossing bottles out a window and spraying them with hoses. Eventually, 97 were arrested and $1.5 million of equipment was ruined. Douglas eventually became the left-leaning prime minister of the Dominican Republic and made a state visit to Montreal in 2000, where, according to his bodyguard, a mysterious gentleman carrying false business cards tailed him. Within days, Douglas complained of stomach pains and soon died of a heart attack.

On August 8, 1992, disappointed fans unleashed mayhem at Olympic Stadium. First, Metallica cut its set short when singer James Hetfield was burnt by pyrotechnics. Hetfield apologized profusely to the disappointed fans. But next up, Axl Rose and Slash showed a less sympathetic attitude as Guns'N'Roses played a few halfhearted numbers before Rose marched offstage. A fansite described the incident: "Fans turned over cars and a bunch of other stuff."

Naked Bonds Girls

A certain San Francisco outfielder not only holds the record for swatting the most home runs in a season (thanks to the maple bats custom-made by an Ottawa carpenter, and whatever secret vitamins he may be taking), but he also holds the unofficial baseball record for wedding local exotic dancers, at two. Barry Bonds' first union was with the Swedish bombshell Sun Rae, previously known to walk the stage of the Chez Parée. They wed in 1987 and separated seven years later. Their long-running divorce became one of the ugliest celebrity splits in American history. It finally ended in 2000, when Sun tried to overturn their prenuptial agreement. Bonds hustled back up here and met a Trinidad-born Marymount High School grad, Elizabeth Watson, whom he wed in '97. The two met at the Sir Winston Churchill Pub and, like her predecessor, Elizabeth had been known to strut clothing-free on stages here and in Ontario.

Bet You Can't Hum It

Bateau dans un bouteille is our city's official song, of sorts. Don't remember the melody? Nor do we, but in 1992, mustachioed Mayor Doré sponsored a song contest – complete with $10,000 prize – to help celebrate the city's 350th anniversary. When the judges were deadlocked over all the fine submissions, big-in-Paris showtune guy Luc Plamondon was called in to choose a winner and – lo and behold! – he picked a ditty submitted by his good friend, *chanteur* Dan Bigras. The melancholic dirge about a boat-in-a-bottle thingy comes complete with lots of generic Québécois-backache-type singing and plenty of emotive strings. The song was energetically panned and in interviews Bigras spoke of it with some embarrassment. Not long after, Christian Roy, who wrote the pithy lyrics, was convicted of beating up his girlfriend.

For a decade after 1963, separatist terrorists with the Front de Libération du Québec wreaked havoc on the city before moving on to middle age and all the great things that come with it. Here's the essential where-are-they-now list on the FLQ.

• Key founding members Gabriel and Robert Hudon were busted selling crack on the Main in 1998.

• Belgian academic Georges Schoeters, who was involved in the early days of the movement, returned to Europe. His current whereabouts are unknown.

• Carole Devault is an informant, author, and perhaps the only woman lucky enough to have experienced beautiful lovemaking both with the hardcore separatist Jacques Parizeau and with hardcore anti-separatist William Johnson. If anybody knows where she is, they ain't tellin'.

• Nigel Hamer, a McGill engineering grad and sole FLQ Anglo, played a key role in the 1970 kidnapping of British Trade Commissioner James Cross. Police repeatedly overlooked tips to arrest Hamer, who ended up serving virtually no jail time, having agreed instead to design tele-medicine systems for the James Bay hydroelectric complex. Now he lives in the McGill Ghetto and designs technical stuff for subway systems.

• Jean Castonguay went out with a blaze of glory. In the mid-'90s the 53-year-old one-time revolutionary walked to the summit of Mount Royal and set himself on fire. His teeth identified him.

• Mailbox bomber Pierre Schneider went on to write for crime tabloid *Photo Police* and now the *Journal de Montréal*. He renounced violence and published an autobiography in 2002.

• Bomber Denis Lamoureux recently retired from a top-level editing post at the *Journal de Montréal*.

• Kidnapper Jacques Lanctôt's father was the right-hand man to Quebec fascist leader Adrien Arcand. Jacques has since gone on to become a respected Outremont-based publisher.

FLQ Terrorist Addresses

3694 St. Christophe
One-time home of Mario Bachand, leader of the deadly Quebec separatist gang.

3775 St. Dominique
Pierre-Paul Geoffroy used to keep his dynamite here.

1279 Redpath Crescent
Where British Trade Commissioner James Cross lived and the scene of his kidnapping.

10945 des Récollets
An FLQ crash pad and meeting place.

3955 St. André
The notorious Cosette-Trudels lived here.

4286 Chateaubriand
Where kidnapper Nigel Hamer lived with a roommate.

5630 Armstrong, in St. Lambert
Where the gang murdered kidnapped politician Pierre Laporte.

3720 Queen Mary, Apt. 12
Where Richard Therrien, his sister Colette, and a roommate harboured fugitive FLQ kidnappers.

COMMUNIST PLOT TO DEMOLISH THE MCGILL GHETTO

Norman Nerenberg and friends were well-known communists of the beatnik era who suddenly developed a taste for old-style capitalist development. Nerenbreg set up Concordia Estates and bought a major chunk of the resplendent neighbourhood east of McGill with plans to demolish six square blocks of greystones and replace them with the $250-million Cité Concordia development. A 20-storey office tower, 500-room hotel, and three apartment buildings would "perhaps" contain some subsidized housing. The developers hired well-known communist agitator Gerry Fortin — who later described himself as "a sucker" — to persuade tenants to move out in favour of a project that Nerenberg described as "a salute to life" and "the kernel of the future."

Eventually, hippies infiltrated Nerenberg's office and scared off many big American investors, but not before much of the Milton-Park area was razed in the early '70s for what would be called La Cité.

• Although his twin brother went into his father's bakery biz, Raymond Villeneuve never kneaded dough. Perhaps the only one of the old gang still battling for separatist revolution, he recently suffered court setbacks for advocating violence. A few years back, Villeneuve ejected Rhéal Mathieu from his extremist MNLQ group after the two differed over political strategies. Mathieu later made the news when he was busted for planting firebombs at a series of Second Cup coffee shops. Mathieu apparently disliked seeing English words on the café's signs.

• Paul Rose, the convicted co-murderer of hostage Pierre Laporte, now works at one of those jobs where you show up and get paid. Or you don't show up and still get paid thanks to the powerful Confederation of National Trade Unions in Montreal; he has also run for office for the provincial NDP and other obscure political groups.

• Jacques Rose, who had a lesser role in the Laporte kidnapping, was last known to be exploiting some of the skills he learned while building false walls do hide members of the gang. He's a handyman and renovator in the Laurentins.

• Francis Simard tells us that everything he has to say about his role in the murder of Pierre Laporte detailed in his 1982 autobiography. He lives in a small town near Three Rivers these days and collaborates with federalist-baiting moviemaker Pierre Falardeau on film projects.

• Fellow kidnapper Jacques Cossette-Trudel also declined to comment on the state of his life these days, although the Montreal resident and professional was one of the few who renounced terrorism in an article discussing the movement in 1990.

• Louise Cossette-Trudel, now long divorced from hubby Jacques seems to be running a photocopying shop in Outremont. She wrote her feminist interpretation of the movement in a book some years back.

when big shots mess up

Bad Cop, Bad Cop

At 2am on February 12, 1992, Detective-Lieutenant Jean Laflêche, head of criminal investigations at Station 53, was weaving down the Décarie expressway. Cops followed and found him idling in a parking lot, asleep, with his pants and underpants at his ankles. He was fined $300 for refusing to blow into a breathalyzer.

Just Stocking Up

City drug czar (and cop) Henri Marchessault was busted in 1983 for raiding the police pantry of 36 kilograms of hashish and 184 grams of cocaine. Future police chief and mayoral candidate Jacques Duchesneau was given the task of apprehending the top-ranking 25-year veteran. Marchessault was sentenced to 14 years.

Department Store Shenanigans

High-flying Parti-Québécois House Leader Claude Charron had a run-in with destiny in January, 1982. Despite being one of the top-ranked, limousine-driven leaders of the would-be new Republic of Quebec, the curly-haired politician was nabbed red-handed trying to make off with a sports jacket from Eaton's department store. As the store had been, perhaps unfairly, associated with English-dominance and French humiliation, irate PQ members chopped up their Eaton's cards, believing that Charron shouldn't have been prosecuted for his kleptomania. Charron never rehabilitated his political career but became a fixture on French TV as a gentle figure popular with grannies.

As if duplicating that script, high-rolling union boss Lorraine Pagé was busted for absconding with a pair of gloves from the Bay department store in Place Versailles in December, 1998. The 51-year-old leader of the CEQ teachers' union tried to wriggle out of the charges with a story of how the gloves accidentally fell into her purse. But the judge wasn't buying, and the woman who ran one of the most powerful unions for a decade was

---

THE STRUGGLES OF OUTREMONT

Park Avenue lawyer Jérôme Choquette, known best as provincial Justice Minister during the FLQ terrorist crisis, had serious ambitions of becoming the mayor of Montreal. But he had to settle for becoming mayor of Outremont, where he quickly banned people from wearing swimsuits in public and hired a crack team of security guards to patrol the city's parks because some of the rich kids were hanging around there. A resident had the swimsuit ban overturned in court.

ANJOU YOU!

Ernest Crépault became mayor of Anjou amid charges of ballot-stuffing in 1960 and quickly made big money by double-dipping as a real-estate agent. By 1968, his suburb had racked up $49 million in debt. The next year his police chief, who was discovered to have a criminal record, mysteriously turned up dead. From 1974 to 1979, the old and ailing Crépault fought various charges of corruption, while repeatedly keeling over in court. The pathetic saga reached its conclusion in 1982, when the city repossessed the ex-mayor's mansion.

THEY PUT UP A PARKING LOT

When the idealistic Montreal Citizens Movement took power under Mayor Jean Doré in the '80s, it was considered a people's revolution, and radical antidemolition types like John Gardiner assumed considerable power. Gardiner, who had once squatted in a condemned building on St. Norbert, soon changed his longtime conservationist colours after local businessmen Robert Landau and Douglas Cohen presented a plan to build a $500-million condo development bounded by René Lévesque and Overdale, and Mackay and Lucien L'Allier. City consultations recommended that the 90 tenants and nine ancient, stately buildings be integrated into the new project. But even downtown city councillor Nick Auf der Maur, rather than defend the tenants, denounced his reluctant-to-leave constituents in newspaper articles and in person. Mayor Doré sent in fire inspectors who — surprise, surprise — condemned the homes in 1987; they were demolished soon after. The would-be condo development never happened, the area became a parking lot, and the MCM was soon turfed out of office forever.

convicted. She quit and launched a successful appeal. So the gloves cost her about $20,000 – the price of a legal odyssey in which she was alternately found guilty and innocent by various judges. But it was too late to save her career, which was touched by the icy hand of fate that decisive day.

Have Car, Will Travel

At 4am on February 6, 1977, the newly-elected separatist Premier René Lévesque was driving home from a party in a car belonging to his mistress. The one-time war reporter might have been hitting the sauce and certainly wasn't wearing his glasses. As a result, he didn't manage to see a man named George Wilson waving him down at McDougall and Cedar. Wilson's friend, 62-year-old Edgar Trottier, had decided to lay down on the road in an attempt to attract an ambulance so he could spend a comfortable night in a hospital. Trottier, a war veteran, was struck and dragged 140 feet by the speeding Premier. Trottier died, and the shaken Lévesque considered quitting politics. Instead, he chose to give up alcohol, although we spotted him buying gin at a downtown liquor store a couple of years later.

Montreal Least

J. Versailles owned most of the hayfields that comprised Montreal East from 1910 to 1931, but later mayors who doubled as real-estate agents bought up the farms and sold them to oil companies. Soon, refineries were stinking up the area. After Edouard Rivert's two-decade mayoral reign started in 1962, the town's population decreased by a third, while those who remained clamoured to join Montreal. Rivert's successor, Yvon Labrosse, managed a city budget that was 90 percent fuelled by the oil companies, which also supported lavish junkets for his councillors. When asked why he encouraged his councillors to bring their wives on the trips, Labrosse replied, "I found out that you spend more when there are only men. You drink more." Labrosse lost his bid to become a councillor in the merged megacity in 2000.

No single tale can describe the various incarnations of Montreal's police force better than the brutal and bizarre story of Bob "Shotgun" Menard, who worked on the force from 1959 to 1985.

1. Menard became an undercover officer on the Social Security Squad, which was nicknamed "the SS." Assigned, by tough-on-crime Mayor Jean Drapeau, to the indelicate task of dismantling evildoing, Menard busted countless gambling dens and whorehouses. In 1973, he assumed the identity of Bob Wilson, an electrician, and moved into the apartment upstairs from gangster Paolo Violi's Café Reggio on Lacordaire. After three years of watching and befriending the Mafia don by discussing their mutual dislike of the Quebec government, Menard dropped the hammer on Violi at a provincial commission on crime. After Violi had finished serving his time, two hit men came and shot the wise guy in his café. "He knew they were coming, but he didn't even move," Menard said with admiration.

2. Menard then joined the legendary Night Squad, a team of about a dozen officers who policed the entire island during the nighttime hours. He was no fan of night owls, as he explained in 2001: "If I see you in the streets, my question is what the hell are you doing out in the city when all of the law-abiding citizens are in bed sleeping?" The Night Squad was a vicious, hard-drinking bunch constantly shaking down club owners and beating confessions out of suspects. The unit practiced such tactics as placing a garbage can on the suspect's head and smashing it with a flashlight until the suspect passed out. In another classic move, an officer would casually offer the suspect a starter pistol to admire. Once handled, the cop would say, "Now I've got your prints. Confess or I'll shoot you and say you came at me with this." Police-friendly judges and misconduct panels disregarded complaints until the squad savagely beat members of the St. Henri-based Dubois gang, who complained, leading the force to be disbanded in June, 1979.

LET YOUR FINGERS DO THE LIBELING

One million copies of Montreal's 1989 *Yellow Pages* listed "Mafia" as one of the languages taught at Platon College on Park Avenue. Apparently, this is how it happened: after the school sent in the ad, some prankster with publisher Tele-Direct monkeyed around with the text and replaced the word "Italian" with "Mafia." Anxious hilarity ensued. The company refused to recall copies of the book.

3. From 1979 to 1985, Menard was the star member of the Holdup Squad, soon earning the nickname "Shotgun" after he developed a preference to avenge robberies, rather than prevent them. His custom was to put on his white gloves and take position, waiting for the perpetrator to exit the robbery zone and then shoot him trying to make a getaway. He won't say exactly how many robbers he shot dead, but one estimate pegs the number at 10 to 15. Menard expressed no regrets. "It costs $75,000 a year to house a prisoner. A bullet costs only 65 cents," he explained. On March 28, 1985, Menard was shot three times by a bank robber in LaSalle. He survived with one lung, damaged hearing, a metal plate in his hip, and braces on both knees. Experts agree that since the introduction of the 1982 Human Rights charter (which really kicked in for good about a decade later), stories like those Menard was involved in aren't likely to happen again.

HELL IN ST. MICHEL

Maurice Bergeron, last mayor of the former municipality of St. Michel, ran a town where you could buy a job on the police force for $500, a zoning change for $375, and a taxi permit for $1,750. A prosecutor investigating the town was warned that "he'd wind up in the river" and, despite the weight of evidence, a 1968 inquiry into Bergeron's stewardship quickly fizzled. Some suspect Bergeron escaped punishment because he was an influential provincial organizer for the governing Union Nationale provincial party. The city of St. Michel joined Montreal that same year.

ST. LAURENT SHAME

Ville St. Laurent was a great town, especially if you had a city councillor in the family. In 1988, an elected representative who scored jobs for family members enthusiastically explained, "If I had a dozen children, they'd all work for the city." Two veteran councillors — including former Montreal Canadiens General Manager Irving Grundman — were charged with taking bribes in 2002.

Mount Royal Hapsburg Fraud

Ever get one of those scam e-mails promising you a share of profits if you send cash to help get money out of a bank? Well, a lifetime ago, Abram Sykowski perfected the scam in this city. Sykowski, a Pole raised in New York's Bowery, first worked as the Human Frog in a travelling freak show. After he got involved with the Capone gang, he toured Europe, peddling fake passports and smuggling dope. In 1934, he realized the potential for a money-liberating scam when he used promises of profit to defraud Mussolini of seven million lira, a fortune back then. Soon after, Sykowski hopped a steamer to Montreal and booked a room at the Mount Royal Hotel under the name Alexander Novarro Fernandez of the royal Hapsburgs, an identity that inspired curious locals to suggest pricking him with needles to test for the famous family hemophilia. The fake prince met a group of local businessmen, suggesting he held a fortune of $350 million in a series of American banks. Of course, he needed funding to get it out and promised investors 10 percent of the cash. In return, the investors gave him $125,000 and a private plane. Sykowski, as collateral, gave them a codebook with information on his various bank accounts. The book was gibberish, and he flew to Venezuela, never to return.

How the Crack Wars Were Won

The name Pablo Palacios still rings in local ears with great resonance, although many can't seem to remember why. Here's the full tale of the controversial cop. In the late '80s, Kirt "Easy" Haywood dealt cocaine from the projects at 865 St. Martin in Little Burgundy. Neighbours would complain and cops would descend, but they could never locate his stash. This continued until police newcomer Pablo Palacios sweet-talked Haywood into becoming a police informant. Using Haywood's information, cops soon managed to take down almost every drug house in Little Burgundy. But Haywood's commerce continued unabated, so the streets were soon abuzz with whispers of an unholy alliance. So one day, when Haywood sought his next batch of cocaine, his suppliers became wary and refused to front him any. Desperate and penniless, Haywood set up a meeting with a Colombian dealer on Park Avenue. But a friend of Haywood's started shooting at the would-be Colombian supplier, who escaped on a southbound bus. The Colombian fingered Haywood, and cops launched a city-wide manhunt for the informant. Early one morning, police spotted a black man with a shaved head (who looked nothing like the dreadlocked Haywood) entering Haywood's home. After seeing the man grapple with a shiny metal lighter, a cop pulled his rifle trigger. The dead man turned out to be Marcellus François, an innocent acquaintance of Haywood's. Palacios arrived at the scene just minutes after the fudge-up and was the first to tell the SWAT sniper that he had shot the wrong guy.

Haywood turned himself in and informed on other dealers, including Osmond Seymour Fletcher, who was arrested and mistakenly released. The fugitive Fletcher went into hiding, from where he bitterly denounced the Palacios campaign. Patrolmen spotted Fletcher on the street a few days later and, when he resisted arrest, a gun went off and Fletcher was dead. Palacios offered to clear the air by inviting TV reporters on his rounds. The cameras caught a minor scoop by displaying him shaking down an apartment after he cleverly identified himself as the "pizza man" – a code word for crack customers. On Labour Day weekend in 1991, Haywood was found shot dead at his girlfriend's West Island home. The murder remains unsolved. Palacios's maverick ways later turned his colleagues against him. In

SOME LOCAL INSTITUTIONS THAT ARE NO MORE

Montreal Home for Friendless Women, Montreal Silent Athletic Club, Junk Pedlar's Union, Invincible Club, Montreal Protestant House of Industry, International Shoe-Makers Protective Society, The Bohemian Club of Montreal, The Independent Pants Makers Union, The Paper Box Makers Union of Montreal, The Sons of Ulster Welcome Club, The Montreal Institution for the Education of Young Ladies, The Fruit Committee of the Montreal Agricultural and Horticultural Society, Institute of Deaf Mutes, Montreal Homeopathic Hospital (1883!), Légion Sanitaire, Independent Operators Basters and Pressers Union, Women's Landlord League of Montreal, The Montreal Dental Club.

LACHINE MEAN MACHINE

During its last years as a separate municipality, Lachine hobbled along as the mayor and his opponents filed legal charges against each other almost every other day. The conflict could be traced back to an incident 30 years earlier, when a previous mayor refused to fill an empty council seat with the runner-up from the prior elections, William McCullock, as had been the prior custom. As the irate opposition boycotted council meetings and ignored a court order to return, the town fell into provincial trusteeship and Victor Timbro, the candidate who got the job McCullock should have gotten, was caught on the take and went to prison. After McCullock died, his son, William Jr., was elected to council, where he tried to even the score with the establishment. When two other candidates split the vote in a 1997 election, William became mayor and immediately sought retribution. A grudge match ensued, as his opponents — unsuccessfully — had fraud charges laid against him. The conflict ended without mercy as island-wide mergers eliminated the municipality.

1997, they testified against the former pizza man in a case of criminal assault, claiming that he had slapped the owner of a Crescent St. bar. Palacios was acquitted and remains on the force.

Black Struggles

Montreal has had a long and proud history of black citizens standing up to discrimination. Here are a few key stories in brief.

In 1709, Intendant Raudot (a colonial governor) confirmed the legitimacy of black slavery in New France, which counted 600 local slaves. One understandbly unhappy person set fire to her mistress's home as a distraction for her escape, but the blaze grew out of control, claiming 46 homes and the Hôtel Dieu hospital. In April, 1734, Marie-Joseph Angélique, 25, was hanged for the affair.

In 1734, Intendant Gilles Hocquart set up a special squad to catch escaping slaves and made it complicated for slave-owners to grant their slaves freedom. When the British took over Montreal in 1760, the former French rulers made sure the Capitulation Agreement guaranteed owners property rights over their slaves.

On March 11, 1898, Queen's Hotel bellhop Frederick Johnson bought two tickets to a play at the Théâtre Français, but the usher refused to seat him and his guest in their seats because blacks were banned from the orchestra section. Johnson sued in Superior Court and won $50.

On January 26, 1919, Sol Reynolds and Norris Augustus Dobson were ordered to move from the orchestra section to the balcony of the Loew's Theatre. They sued and, in spite of fierce opposition from the theatre, won $10.

In 1936, Fred Christie and Emile King were refused service at the York Tavern in the Old Forum. They sued and, this time, the case went all the way to the Supreme Court. Sadly, the plaintiffs lost in a decision that made it legal for merchants to discriminate against whomever they wanted.

lawyer scum

If you want to read nice stories about nice lawyers, you're reading the wrong book, baby.

Divorces 'R' Us

In 1991, Micheline Parizeau was a veteran working on the city's biggest and nastiest divorce cases. She was known for going to any length in order to win big settlements for divorcées, which caused at least one angry husband to plant a bomb in her car. But when she represented a simple housewife who happened to win a $4-million lottery jackpot, things started to unravel. In an attempt to inflate the amount her client stood to gain from her husband, Parizeau advised the woman to suddenly embrace a lavish lifestyle. That advice caused the woman to go broke. A judge eventually disbarred the pompous Parizeau for seven years for exaggerating her invoices and inciting perjury. A journalist later asked the housewife, "Which was worse, losing your $4 million, losing your husband, or meeting Micheline Parizeau?"

"I Didn't Do It"

Lawyer Claire Lortie returned to her home in St. Sauveur one evening in July, 1983, only to find her lover, Rodolphe Rousseau, very much dead. Having had absolutely nothing to do with his death, she did what any right-thinking person would do: she began sawing off his arms and crammed his body into a freezer buried in a wooded lot. Then she forged his name on a dozen cheques and cashed them. Lortie was tried for murder but was acquitted after explaining that she had only mutilated Rousseau's corpse in a panicked attempt to avoid a scandal. She was sentenced to 30 months in prison for that other stuff, and served only 10 months. Lortie eventually chose to return to practicing law in Montreal but was turned down by the local Bar Association.

Strip Clubs

No assignment is too tough when probing the secret underbelly of the Unknown City. So as a duty to you, Dear Reader, we've sacrificed our morals and ventured into the dark demimondaine world of Montreal's strip clubs.

Château du Sexe and Le Chic

Another twin-club situation across from the Paramount theatre complex on Ste. Catherine contrasts the classier Château against the low-rent Chic. Both now feature annoying doormen who seek exorbitant cover charges.

Chez Parée

Considered the city's classiest strip club, high-rent hussies meet high-earning customers in this Stanley Street joint Mario Lemieux described as Wayne Gretzky's Montreal office. One of its dancers was murdered while driving home through the Atwater tunnel after work in 1994. More recently, several violent settling-of-account incidents occurred just in front. Thumbs down for the precious atmosphere, but a salute to the excellent free buffet.

Gotta Give Him a Hand

Gino Boggia, a law student at McGill in the early '80s, had a slight problem passing his courses. In spite of the university's attempts to kick him out for flunking courses, he managed to muddle through and was accepted by the Bar. He went on to an illustrious career, the height – or depths – of which occurred when he convinced moneymen that he was in charge of the financial affairs of a woman who couldn't sign papers for herself, as her arms had been amputated in Cincinnati. He helped himself to $61,000 of her cash until the appearance of a beautifully inscribed cheque signed by the purported armless woman. Investigators tracked her down; she was living happily in France with both arms firmly attached. Busted, Boggia quit the Bar in great haste. At last notice, he was cooling his heels in a California clink.

Infighting

Eric Belhassen became a lawyer in 1978, and the next year had his knuckles rapped for falsifying documents. His subsequent antics led the Bar to condemn him as a "public menace" in 1990, and place him under probation in 1992. Later, he locked horns with Christina Finney-McCullock, a famous hardhead from Lachine. The woman accused Belhassen of grabbing $60,000 from a settlement she was meant to receive. Belhassen responded with a series of harassing phone calls and threats and finally got the boot from the Bar. Finney-McCullock, disgusted that Belhassen had been allowed to continue his practice during the dispute, launched a suit against the Bar of Quebec.

Stolzenberg, Castor's Rip-Off King

Short-tempered sybarite Wolfgang Stolzenberg used to bristle when questioned about his Montreal-based holding company Castor Holdings. On the surface he had no reason to be miserable. He travelled in a $22-million private jet, enjoyed a Westmount mansion, a posh office on McGill College, three downtown penthouses, and a fleet of sports cars. When investors started wondering about a missing $500 million ($200 million from Chrysler Canada alone) ol' Wolfie was nowhere to be found. For nine years, the RCMP conducted an investigation into the matter (their second-longest investigation ever; the Bre-X mining scandal being the biggest). When the Mounties finally presented a 50,000-page report leveling 41 charges against the sneaky German, they took time to praise him as "the Van Gogh of fraud," perhaps in appreciation for the excellent overtime advantages the case offered them. It's widely believed that Stolzenberg lives a life of leisurely skiing and adventure near his native Frankfurt, but there's little hope of getting the Germans to extradite him to face justice here. Meanwhile, no charges have been laid against his local acolytes and associates, although some angry investors slapped a $300-million lawsuit against his accountants, Coopers Lybrand.

Mismanagement with Leo's Boys

The former municipality of St. Leonard had a checkered past of sleaze and scandal, first recorded when Mayor Philias Vanier, known for giving jobs to four of his seven sons, lost power in 1955. During that election, 100 specially deputized police thugs jailed the force's chief and beat up reporters. In 1967, Leo Ouellet was caught paying up to $30 per vote in the kickback-ocracy, and in 1981, Mayor Antonio Di Ciocco was the target of two bombing attempts. After he died of leukemia, a vicious fight for power ensued in which Raymond Renaud emerged triumphant and immediately fired the former mayor's secretary and launched libel suits against a wide variety of his opponents. A judge forced him to rehire his secretary.

Solid Gold

What this place on the Main and Cremazie lacks in intimacy it also lacks in atmosphere. More ain't always better, as proven by the never-ending string of gimmicks — from TV screens featuring cheesy Playboy videos to obnoxious deejays awarding prizes. We're quite fond of the cheap, happy-hour chicken wings though.

Supersexe

We love the garish sign, but the women are cookie-cutter peroxide princesses, and the high-priced couch dance in which the customer stares at a woman on a bed seems like a spectacularly uninteresting way to spend money.

Teazers

This soulless, cavernous space dwarves even the most gargantuan implant-recipients. The general expense also detracts from the experience, although the place merits extra points for its truly gaudy sign.

Naked Lunch

St. Leonard's Gustini Steak House was the city's pioneer nudie restaurant. That's where topless waitresses served ravenous customers as early as 1975, until the eatery was busted by cops, causing owner Esther skin-flaunting naked waitresses serve you grits in several local eateries. Here are some.

What are nice girls doing in a place like **Resto Bar Les Princesses** (4970 Hochelaga)? Last time we supped in this shabby little trailer-like shack in the shadow of the Big O, our waitress was impressive enough to cause us to try using a polished soup spoon as a rear-view mirror. A minor scandal occurred here not long ago when a waitress went out back to have a discussion with a friend without bothering to put her clothes back on. She was fine, er fined.

East of the Jacques Cartier bridge, the Ste. Catherine drag takes on a less spectacular allure but loses none of its character. **Les Courtisanes** (2533 Ste. Catherine E.) is a good appetizer for the bizarre places that lie beyond. These, if you're determined to go, are the other joints on the Essential Sexy-Serveuse Restaurant Tour: **Chez Carole** (2205 Rosemont), **Chez Momo** (3562 Jarry), **Serveuses tenue légère** (7481 de Lorimier), **Rockin 'n C** (4130 Jarry), **Café Fine Gourmandise** (11910 Sherbrooke E.).

BORDELLOS

Just after World War II, young farm girls flooded our city streets, with females as young as 15 years old hanging around the Drummond Café, across from the late Lord Strathcona's downtown mansion, offering to rent their affections for $5. Further east in the Red Light district between the Main and St. Denis, women sitting on pillows on window ledges would offer themselves for $2. Nowadays, brothels are run far more discreetly out of town, under the guise of strip clubs.

Systematically Satisfactory

For those still reeling after learning that the Door Doctor isn't really a doctor, get ready for more devastation. It's about St. Henri's well-loved New System restaurant whose almost-rust-free orange delivery cars drop food to all the right hungry addresses. Brace yourselves: the New System isn't really new at all. In fact, the mouth-watering moniker has hung on the building's shingle for about 50 years, according to staffers — none of whom can recall exactly what the new system is, although they're reasonably confident that it's an improvement over the old one.

A generic office building on Victoria in lower Westmount might not be the first place you'd look for an international man of mystery and intrigue, but Ari Ben-Menashe quacks like just such a duck and walks like one, too. Born in Iran, Menashe – who looks like he'd have trouble doing a dozen push-ups – moved to Israel, where he says he became a high-level political aide to that country's prime minister. From that perch he learned that media baron Robert Maxwell was murdered by Israeli agents; that George Bush Sr. delayed the release of the Iranian hostages so that Reagan could take credit for it; and that America pressured Chile to help Iraq develop chemical weapons. Although Menashe's claims – detailed in his 1992 book *Profits of War* – have been repeatedly denied, much of his story has survived scrutiny. Menashe says he moved here in the early '90s to be with his new wife, and found himself in the eye of an international scandal in December, 2001, when Morgan Tsvangirai, leader of Zimbabwe's government opposition, allegedly came to Menashe's Westmount office and asked him to arrange President Robert Mugabe's assassination. Tsvangirai was really knockin' on the wrong door, as Menashe had been on Mugabe's payroll. Menashe got Tsvangirai to repeat the assassination request before a hidden camera, which was shown on TV news shows around the world. Although many critics considered Menashe's tape as inconclusive, Mugabe was eventually re-elected in a vote many consider rigged.

More Municipal Mayhem

• In 1971, Westmount council – perhaps influenced by their tradition of going for drinks halfway through meetings – decided to revoke the permit of any cab driver who wore long hair, a moustache, or beard.

• In an August, 1966 council session, the Town of Mount Royal passed 20 bylaws in 20 minutes. They boasted that they could have done it in 15, except for the collapse of Mayor Reginald Dawson's chair, which had to be repaired.

• In the '30s, Outremont, for reasons known best to itself, forced its police officers to wear heavy woollen winter jackets – even on scorching-hot summer days.

• In 1966, Verdun doled out $104,000 for "an electronic brain" which, they boasted, "will practically run the city."

• In 1963, an Outremont bylaw forbade gas stations from opening within 200 feet of schools, but no bylaw banned schools from opening near a gas stations, so council okayed a children's school just 25 feet from a set of pumps.

The Eastern Townships welcomes those of the highest breeding, and deepest of pockets. The biggest and best known of the confirmed inhabitants of the lake-strewn bucolic region remains actor Donald Sutherland, who since 1987 has hung his hat at Dunkeld, a country estate near Georgeville. The onetime Expos-game frequenter raised a ruckus in 1997, when he suggested a sewage pipe be rerouted so it would no longer leach dirty water onto his property. First settled by the British, the Townships became the summertime residence of the likes of Mordecai Richler, while other *boyz in da 'hood* include: business giant Paul Desmarais Jr., Liberal politician Paul Martin, Stanley Cup-winning coach Pat Burns, and ex-Quebec premier Jacques Parizeau, who owns a large ranch around Knowlton. Sylvester Stallone and, more recently, Tom Cruise have been rumoured to live part-time in the area, although so far the only evidence of their possible presence was the occasional passing limo with smoked-glass windows. The area has resisted such attempts at development as a proposal to float a casino on Lake Memphremagog and developer Serge Botella's 1987 plan to build a $130-million dome atop twelve blocks of Georgetown.

Model Citizen

Yasmeen Ghauri hasn't let her face go to her head. Ghauri, daughter of a strict family headed by a Pakistani immigrant father and German mother, was launched to supermodeldom after local hair stylist Joseph Del Tortoon discovered the 5'10", 17-year-old, Goth-punk beauty inquiring about "fries with that?" while working at McDonald's. Her parents opposed Ghauri's dreams, but the exotic beauty scribbled her Jane Hancock on a major modelling contract and the rest is history. Well, not history like the Punic Wars and the storming of the Bastille, but history nonetheless as Ghauri skyrocketed to fame by braving flashbulbs and marching catwalks for the likes of Versace, Dior, Chanel, and Jill Sander. The new mother still frequently visits Brossard, where her parents still live in a home on Sauvé Crescent.

- In July, 1968, Roma Foods was convicted of peddling rotten meat throughout the island, but the company appealed and got off on a technicality. Because Roma's headquarters were in Ville St. Laurent, Montreal inspectors had no jurisdiction.

- Following a wave of vandalism in a Lachine park in the 1930s, the town's administration got tough by putting up a menacing sign that said, "Persons of good education and morals are invited in this park."

- In 1988, the Town of Montreal West tried to ban pick-up trucks, motor homes, and commercial vans from streets and driveways.

- In 1962, Verdun tried to tax cable TV.

- Outremont considered a motion to ban the wearing of short pants in 1963.

The Lamb and the Muscleman

Since 1834, revelers in this city have celebrated the good fortunes of the French in the New World by partying down on St. Jean Baptiste Day, June 24. For generations, the celebration's annual parade featured attractions like horsemen decked out to represent past governors of New France, but the showstopper was always a child representing St. John the Baptist carrying a small lamb. The child was meant to appeal to the other young'uns, but moms liked it, too, and dreamed of having their child chosen to carry the bleating beast. But nationalists became disillusioned by such a passive symbol as a sheep. So in 1962, a separatist group that had failed to persuade parade organizers to substitute a black sheep, instead kidnapped the cuddly white animal in protest, returning it just hours before the parade.

In 1963, organizers got rid of the lamb entirely, as well as all open-top cars, which were replaced by 20 "allegorical chariots." In 1964, parade organizer Colonel Yves Bourassa had the child replaced with a muscular statue based on a Rodin sculpture. The parade started unraveling thereafter: in 1968, nationalists pelted Pierre Trudeau, who bravely retained his reviewing-stand spot; and in 1971, cops gratuitously brutalized participants suspected of contributing to unrest. Woodstock-like celebrations were held atop Mount Royal in the mid-'70s, leading to massive park destruction. The Olympic Stadium was the next unsatisfactory locale.

Celebrations later spread to various neighbourhoods. The St. Denis Street party sparked the idea for the Jazz Festival. In recent years, the hoopla has become a laid-back evening in Old Montreal, with a barely political parade.

Ol' Fashioned City Bylaws

Bylaw 1715

Established in 1942, this bylaw forbade children under 14 from venturing outdoors between 9pm and 5am unless accompanied by an adult, or on their way to or from school. Guilty kids were eligible for fines that "shall not exceed $2."

Bylaw 1979

Passed in 1950, it threatened a $40 penalty for "the wearing of indecent clothing" in public places.

Bylaw 1812

This ancient regulation banned hairdressers "affected with a venereal disease" from cutting hair, although it was changed in 1946 to read "affected by any communicable disease or one that causes repulsive appearance."

Bylaw 4176

Professionals practicing the "occult sciences" were banned from their trade in 1970, on pain of a $100 fine. It was overturned in Superior Court on March 24, 1972.

Bylaw 42

"All riots, noises, disturbances, or disorderly assemblages are hereby prohibited in the city," was the wording of this 1870 bylaw. For decades cops used this one to ban everything from megaphones to handing out leaflets at the Santa Claus Parade.

Bylaw 333

This 1905 bylaw empowers officers to arrest "every person strolling or loitering at night ... who cannot satisfactorily account for his presence there or refuses to do so." The one-size-fits-all legislation also banned slingshots and laying down in a state of intoxication.

Bylaw 3416

Established in 1967, this made it illegal for a bar employee to mingle with a customer, on pain of being slapped with a $200 fine or two months in jail. Thus it became *verboten* for a bartender to chat with a customer. This anti-fraternizing rule was enacted at the urging of the police Morality Squad, which suspected bars of duping customers with on-site pickpockets and swollen-price drink scams. The squad also wanted to force bars to remain brightly lit, but they couldn't force that through. The bylaw remained on the books until it was overturned in the mid-'90s.

A Wheelbarrow, a Corpse, and a Snow Bank

Until April 1999, three ultra-religious sect members lived at 6318 Christophe-Colomb, where they consumed no electricity and had no phone. The trio rarely left home, never rode buses, and avoided streets named "Saint" to discourage the devil. They also believed the end of the world was near. Then one day their 80-year-old-mentor, Roland Hamel, suddenly died. Follower Robert Gagnon put Hamel's body in a wheelbarrow and tried to unload it at two funeral homes. Both turned him away for lacking a death certificate. Pedestrians' jaws were presumably agape at the bizarre sight of the religious devotee rolling his dead master around. An exasperated Gagnon ultimately dumped Hamel's body into a snow bank on Bellechasse.

A Tale to Melt Your Heart

The world's first cryogenically suspended child was a Montrealer, but this isn't a particularly happy first. Eight-year-old Geneviève de la Poterie had kidney cancer and spent her final six months receiving treatment in California. After she died and was frozen, Bob Nelson, one-time head of the Cryonics Society of California, tried to reduce costs by placing a second frozen child in her pod in January, 1972. Of course the idea behind suspended-animation is to preserve the body and somehow reawaken the dead person at a later date. But Nelson's crowded chamber was short on liquid nitrogen and it started leaking. The child's corpse thawed in the Los Angeles basement, with highly pungent results. Nelson was sued, successfully, in 1981, and no longer fools around with freezing dead bodies.

banking in Montreal

Banks are where the money is and where there's money, there's mayhem. Here are snippets from some of the action.

Highway Robbery

Six bandits corralled a payroll truck from the Bank of Hochelaga while it passed through a tunnel at Ontario and Moreau on April 1, 1924, fleeing with $142,000 after a shootout that left a bank manager and a robber dead. A phone number in the dead bandit's pocket led the team to a home on Coursol, where the band was divvying up the loot. To everybody's surprise, one of its secret members was a heroic athlete-turned-much-decorated cop, Louis Morel. The dirty cop and three others were hanged.

Merry Christmas

Santa Claus was not in a giving mood on December 14, 1962, when a man wearing Kris Kringle gear robbed the Canadian Imperial Bank of Commerce (6007 Côte de Liesse Rd.) of $142,886. The would-be Santa and two accomplices shot and killed a pair of St. Laurent city police officers. George Marcotte, 29, was sentenced to death but had his sentence commuted. One accomplice was sentenced to life and the other was confined to an insane asylum.

Bomb Squad

André Deblois, 22, walked into a crowded TD bank (near Prince Arthur) on March 8, 1957, sporting a vest made of TNT and a fake nose. His robbery failed when cop shot him in the neck. The Human Bomb was paralyzed and died a few weeks after being condemned to four concurrent 10-year prison sentences.

Machine Gun Molly

Monica Proietti was born near the Red Light district off the Main in 1939, and at 17 married a 33-year-old Scottish gangster. They had two kids and knocked off about 20 banks in their spare time, eventually earning her the nickname "Machine Gun Molly." On September 19, 1967, she and two accomplices robbed a *caisse*

The Critter File

• According to the SPCA, a Laval man drowned 78 squirrels in 1999.

• Distemper killed all the raccoons on Mount Royal in 1989, but they're back now.

• The number of pets Montrealers are allowed to keep varies according to neighbourhood authority. So a Montrealer could move across the street and suddenly be required to get rid of pet cats or dogs.

• English sparrows that were brought here in 1850 to help control insect populations now outnumber pigeons. Their territorial ways have prevented other breeds from proliferating in their airspace.

Photo: John David Gravenor

• Starlings have a Shakespeare fan to thank for their local existence. As a tribute to the Bard in the 1800s, a New Yorker released several hundred of the non-native birds into Central Park. Some of them eventually found their way to Montreal.

populaire (credit union) at 11000 St. Vital Boulevard in Montreal North of $3,000. Police pursued them south on Pie IX Blvd. The car chase ended at the intersection of Villeray Street, where the two male bandits fled as Molly opened fire from her car window with her machine gun. She was shot and killed. Monica would later be immortalized in a theatre musical. Her son, Anthony Smith Jr., also grew up to be a bank robber.

To Serve and Strike

A 16-hour wildcat strike in 1969 saw the City of Montreal's police constables abandon their posts, leading to 50 times more bank robberies and 14 times the average number of commercial burglaries. Sociologists have noted that while crimes against property increased, crimes against people did not.

A Bird's Eye

Linda Marie Snyder, a stripper at Wanda's (on de Maisonneuve), was the lookout for a gang that included five guys from Verdun who knocked off $2 million from banks and jewelry stores in Toronto in 1997. While her accomplices were eventually caught, Snyder remains on the lam and the money has never been recovered.

Negotiation Tactics

On April 17, 1998, Claude Mailhot was doing some banking at a Caisse Desjardins (on de Reims St.) in north-end Montreal, when a gun-wielding bandit demanded a teller open the bulletproof-glass door, threatening to shoot a customer if she didn't. Well, the teller didn't and Mailhot was shot and left paralyzed. The robber ran off empty-handed and now Mailhot is suing the bank for $6 million for their hard-headed, money-grubbing policies.

You're Fired

In his youth, Vincent Meloche had been repeatedly dissuaded from killing himself. But at age 58, he ended up murdering three of his English-speaking bosses at Dupont as they were preparing to fire him in the early '70s. After serving his time, Meloche chose the parking lot of the National Bank (at Papineau and Bélanger) to perform the long-overdue deed. He killed himself by self-immolation in 2001.

• Local gulls were nearly driven into extinction here in the 19th century — an era when their feathers were thought to look good on hats and gowns.

• A 175-pound seal came to the city's old port in 1960, where some workers fed it fish and others pelted it with stones. Authorities put the seal in a public bath, where it went on a hunger strike and died.

• Anybody feeding squirrels, pigeons, or gulls can get nailed with a $60 fine thanks to a Montreal bylaw passed in 1994. But there's no law preventing people from killing and eating them.

• An eagle came into town and hung around the Royal Bank building in Old Montreal in 1931. Cops shot it dead.

Photo: John David Grosvenor

bragging rights for two, please

Add points to your credibility by haunting any of these snack zones.

Momesso's

Son of hard-working Italian restaurateur makes the NHL and wins Stanley Cup with hometown team. That headline might not get Hollywood buzzing but it should be good enough to get you to pop in. Located in that curious little island-within-an-island below the tracks in NDG, this basement place features photos of Sergio Momesso's great moments and satisfies with subs and friendly service.
Upper Lachine and Old Orchard

Policeman's Brotherhood Bar

The Brotherhood, as our police officers' union mystically dubs itself, has long operated its own members-only bar behind smoked glass doors in the basement of its building. Civilians were traditionally welcome only when accompanied by a cop, but now the doors swing wide open, as "café cop" has become a for-all venue. The police motif remains intact.
Berri and Gilford, behind the Laurier Metro

Consenza Social Club

Vedi Consenza e pi mori, as the Romans would say (literally "see Consenza and die"), you absolutely can't refuse checking out this wise-guy hangout nestled in a strip mall. Be subtle, as some patrons might be edgy after one of the better-known regulars, Canadian capo Vito Rizzuto, escaped an attack by gunmen and a car bomb after leaving here not long ago. Strangers are considered a novelty by the dozen sharply-dressed men playing cards and speaking Italian beneath pictures of racehorses and prizefighters.
4891 Jarry, near Viau

Wilensky Light Lunch

You might have seen this place featured in the final moments of the *Duddy Kravitz* flick, and entering this throwback joint you'll know you've entered a parallel sandwich dimension. Doubtless the décor – including eight wobbly wooden stools – is the original deal from 1932. Gooey syrup spooned from a stainless steel vat

• A 42-foot whale swam into the city's east-end port in 1832. Responsible citizens harpooned it. One charged others to see the dead animal in his shed until its smell became overwhelming.

• The 1961 rat infestation saw rats hop into bed with children and gnaw on their milk bottles.

• Three coyotes invaded the city in 1970, with the last being killed on Mount Royal by seven bullets and a cop in a helicopter.

• A cat named Gros Minou fell 20 storeys from a downtown apartment building on May 1, 1973. The flying feline suffered a fractured pelvis and set the unofficial Canadian record for a cat surviving the highest fall.

MAGNAN'S MISCHIEF

Bar owner Yves Magnan was also a top official in the city administration when he helped sculpt a bylaw restricting any bar in Point St. Charles other than his own. In July 1984, his Civic Party banned new bars and the enlargement of any bar in his neighbourhood — with the exception of a narrow stretch where his own time-honoured tavern — **Magnan's** — stands at Charlevoix and St. Partick streets. Magnan justified the favouritism shown his own place by arguing that organized-crime bosses from outside the neighbourhood owned other bars in the area. Although it has enjoyed considerable cache, the last time we visited we pretty nearly choked on the high prices and walked out.

is mixed with carbonated water to make soft drinks, while fried salami sandwiches ($2.55) are served on napkins. Staffers tend to attentively watch you eat, as if readying for further requests. Tips are discouraged and are apparently donated to charity.
Clark and Fairmount

La Maison du Egg Roll

This proletariat Chinese-food joint gained fame when Pierre Trudeau chose this his extremely unlikely venue to give a major constitutional speech. Now it's a hangout for such urban characters as boxer Matthew Hilton and business magnate and tax rebel Peter Sergakis.
Notre Dame W.

Other establishments that might offer bragging rights for wannabe local cognoscenti include **Marvin's** *(Park-Ex)*, **Cosmo** *(on Sherbrooke in NDG)*, **Corner Snack Bar** *(near the old Forum)*, and the **Capri** *(on St. Patrick)*.

East End Gestapo

Mayor Louis-Phillipe St. Pierre was elected mayor of Pointe-aux-Trembles in 1961 and soon ruled the municipality like a tin-pot dictator, quarreling and refusing to sign cheques to creditors for over a year. By 1964, many homes were still without running water and an initiative to dump St. Pierre and join Montreal was ignored. Voters were to get their chance to remove him in 1967; however, somebody made sure the ballot boxes were full even before voting began. As a result, in several districts there were more votes cast than voters. A provincial judge ordered the mayor out of office for three years, but he hung on, pending an appeal. Soon, citizens were burning him in effigy and St. Pierre could only travel throughout his own town with a police escort. It later came out that Mayor St. Pierre had allowed police officers to buy their way onto the squad and that he listened in on his workers through hidden microphones connected to his private car. "I've got the best Gestapo on the island," he once crowed, according to testimony. St. Pierre's successors fared little better, as subsequent mayors Bernard Benoit and Father Maurice Vanier were both later investigated for corruption. By the time it joined Montreal in 1982, P.A.T. had a staggering $55-million debt.

Whether you want to fly kites, hang with transsexuals, or join a cult, there's no better place to do it than in a town with Montreal's libertarian credo, but there are some unwritten rules and other tips that might help. Unwritten, that is, until now.

Famous Last Words

May the soul of John Laird McCaffrey, who died aged 54 back in 1995, rest in peace. His body lies six feet below the verdant slope of the C1300+ section at the Notre Dame des Neiges Cemetery, while above him stands a typical-looking headstone inscribed with these words:

Free your body and soul
Unfold your powerful wings
Climb up the highest mountains
Kick your feet up in the air
You may now live forever
Or return to this earth
Unless you feel good where you are

At first glance, they're uplifting words, brimming with symbolism and imagery. Uplifting, that is, until your eyes wander down the left-hand margin, reading the first letter of every line. After some snoopin', we found the tombstone artisan who inscribed the monument. He told us the verse was brought in by McCaffrey's ex-wife and mistress, and that he didn't even realize the hidden (or was it just coincidental?) message was there until he finished and switched off his sandblaster. His first reaction? "Wow."

brew pubs

Brutopia

Since 1997, this pleasant place has spun its own full-bodied English ales. No bottled offerings are available, so order a Honey Brown if you want to impress the waitress with your devil-may-care *savoir faire*.
1219 Crescent; 514/393-9277

Cheval Blanc

Known to whip up an excellent lager, among other concoctions, this narrow, unassuming, yet stylish spot has licensed its recipes to a brewer that sells bottled versions as far afield as Philadelphia. At 2:30am, a Medusa look-alike with an impressive black mop of hair always seems to saunter in and sit at the bar.
809 Ontario E.; 514/522-0211

Bily Kun

As if one pub named for a pigment-challenged horse – Le Cheval Blanc – wasn't enough for one city, there's actually another one, **Bily Kun**, which also means "white horse," but in Czech. The name was a play on words by the founder, who previously worked at Le Cheval Blanc. But there was no reason to start a trade war over their home-made suds, as the two rival establishments serve different neighbourhoods and even carry each other's products. Packed most evenings with an urbane set of profes-sionals, students, slackers, and hangers-on, consider yourself lucky if you can snag a table after nine. Somehow, the lighting makes everybody look like Euopean film stars, and you expect Charlotte Rampling to walk in at any minute. The walls are festooned with ostrich heads, their necks bent into comical postures – but don't worry, they're not featured on the chalkboard menu.
354 Mount Royal E.; 514/845-3855

Montreal Beer Museum

Several million beers on tap. Restaurant fare as well.
2063 Stanley (Peel Metro); 514/840-2020

• In 1946, J.A. Valois reported the establishment of a committee to work with bathing-suit manufacturers to produce swimwear that was modest enough for the Roman Catholic Church.

• If you hear amazing stories of wanton sex in public parks, well it's nothin' new. It seems sex in city parks was never as popular as it was after World War II. During that period, City Hall second-in-command J.O. Asselin lobbied to close all parks at 11pm to prevent them from being used for "indecent purposes."

• History was made in November, 1971, as the provincial government finally amended the law that gave Montreal's mayor *carte blanche* to ban any demonstration he thought might turn dangerous.

brewin' up a storm

BUT CAN HE SPIN A WEB ANY SIZE?

If you happen to be walking past 505 Sherbrooke East, look up. Way, way up. That's how high Alain "Spiderman" Robert climbed with his bare hands to raise money for sick children in May, 1999. Without the assistance of ropes or climbing equipment, the French climber and daredevil scrambled up the 25-storey tower in less than an hour. At the city's insistence, he was followed up the building by a window-washer's movable scaffold. He celebrated with champagne at the top.

It wasn't his first stunt here. On a tour to promote his autobiography seven months earlier, Robert climbed the 36-storey Place de la Cathedrale (600 de Maisonneuve W.) with nothing but a bag of chalk hanging from his belt. Police arrested him that time, as he hadn't sought the city's approval.

The veteran climber's many previous climbs included the Golden Gate Bridge in San Francisco, and a world record-setting 1,483-foot climb of the Petronas Tower in Kuala Lumpur, Malaysia.

As writers, we like our beer cheap and plentiful. But even we have standards. Luckily, Montreal, is the heart of Quebec's microbrew market. Here are a few of the players.

Brasserie Le Chaudron

Featuring a smooth-drinking hemp beer, they market a handful of brands, including Coeur d'Or and Cobra.

Les Brasseurs Du Nord

Quebec's second-largest microbrewery, they make several styles of additive-free beer under the Boréale label, which features a distinct polar-bear logo.

Les Brasseurs RJ

With popular lines like Belle Geule, Cheval Blanc, and Tremblay, they brew lagers, ales, and Belgian-style beer that's double-fermented in bottles. Taste tours are offered at their Plateau Mont-Royal facility.
5585 de la Roche; 514/274-4941

McAuslan Brewing

Using a special strain of yeast that was smuggled into Canada from England in 1988, they prepare award-winning beer in small batches. The brewery operates an outdoor pub by the Lachine Canal bike path and offers guided tours of their facility.
5080 St. Ambroise; 514/939-3060

Rescousse

A beer with a mission: part of the proceeds of every bottle sold goes to saving the only fish exclusive to Quebec. Available at liquor stores, the red ale's label features a picture of the copper redhorse ("rescousse" in French). If you drink beer like a fish – this is the one!

Unibroue

Adhering to their slogan, "Drink less, drink better," these recipes use all-natural ingredients. The white beer, Blanche de Chambly, was launched more than a decade ago. Some lines are sold internationally.

We Just Can't Win

Montrealers who get hyped about some fantastic contest they see on TV or the 'net will frequently read in small print, "Contest not open to residents of Quebec." The reason we're losers even before we play is Article 58 of the *Loi sur les loteries, concours publicitaires et les appareils d'amusements*, which orders those running a contest to jump through bureaucratic hoops and pay a fee ranging from three to ten percent of the prize to the provincial government. Even *The Gazette* once ran a contest that excluded Quebec residents. The shadowy *Régie des alcools, des courses et des jeux* (RACJ) – an arm of the Public Security Ministry – says the rule is to protect us against fraudulent contests. It seems they also want to protect you from winning the real ones. The phone number for the RACJ is 514/873-3577, just in case you wanted to find out more or, ahem, complain.

Duelling Dudes

Photo: John David Gravenor

There's not much to show for it, but Mill Street has a direct connection to the old tradition of duelling in Montreal. Named for the windmills that once stood along this site by the Lachine Canal, "the windmills" was the preferred place to settle disputes among gentlemen, particularly around the end of the 18th century and beginning of the 19th.

In one of many such contests, Lieutenant Samuel Holland fought Captain Shoedde here in 1795. Holland, just 19 years old at the time, was killed.

HOW TO SCORE AN ICY PAYOFF

If you suspect that sidewalks have become icier in recent years, you aren't on drugs. Or maybe you are, but that's another matter. Until the 1960s, the city blanketed the streets with excess salt to melt ice and snow. But residents complained that the saline crystals were eating up their shoes, fences, and cars. So in the '80s, the city cut back on salt, which had been eroding a serious chunk of a $66-million snow-removal budget. That amount included the operation of 210 sidewalk scrapers whose drivers can make upwards of $80,000 (including overtime) per year clearing 3,500 kilometers of sidewalks. If you slip and fracture a bone on a Montreal sidewalk, write a letter to your municipal authority within 15-30 days (depending on the neighbourhood) and they will generally offer you around $350 to pay you off and drop any potential suit. Not all complaints are rewarded. Among similar claims refused by Montreal bureaucrats: a man sought damages after developing a skin rash after lying on the grass in Lafontaine Park. The city has also refused taxi fares for trips taken on icy days and ~~dry-cleaning bills for slush-covered~~ clothes. And watch out for the snow-clearing trucks: they accounted for a dozen deaths in 1996 and 1997, most of them resulting from reckless driving by city-subcontracted clearers paid extra to work fast.

TURN OFF THE TAP

Montrealers, we regret to report, are the world's biggest consumers of water. Local water-treatment officials say we send 1,287 liters down the drain every day, as compared to just 400 in the U.S., 350 in the rest of Canada and 30 in Africa. It's not that we like lengthy showers more than everyone else; rather, the explanation lies in the fact that 45 percent of our city's water escapes from bursted mains. There are some vague plans to do repairs — at an estimated cost of $371 million a year for several years — but the funding always winds up down the drain, too.

Shakin' All Over

Environment Canada says Montreal's location on the planet's tectonic plates makes it unlikely that we'll be hit with anything more than a magnitude of six on the Richter scale — something that happened in 1935 and 1988. But other experts sing another tune: Risk Management Solutions, a California-based company whose reckoning helps Canadian insurers set their rates, argues that a quake in Montreal could lead to some serious local destruction. In 1997, RMS's top catastrophist warned that Montreal is "vulnerable to low frequency, large magnitude earthquakes where strong ground motion and heavy damage concentrations can lead to fire ignitions and conflagration. Impaired emergency response capabilities and unfavorable winds can quickly aggravate the situation." We say: hide under a doorframe.

Getting Taller in Montreal

Pierre Berthelet leads a small, yet dedicated, subculture of full-grown adults who want to be taller. He published a book that was embraced by a hard-core following of people obsessed with gaining a couple of inches. They take all sorts of drugs and hang upside down for hours to lengthen their spines. Some people are even willing to undergo Izkharov's procedure, an operation that involves breaking leg bones and separating them with clamps, forcing the bones to grow longer. (It's what Ethan Hawke's character had done to rise to Jude Law's height in *Gattaca*.) You can talk to a Montreal doctor who has performed this procedure, although it's only available here for emergency purposes. But doctors in some countries, including South Korea, will do it for cosmetic purposes.

Nothing Like the Raël Thing

Claude Vorilhon was your typical singer, racecar driver, and magazine editor living in France in 1973, when aliens gave him a scoop. The extraterrestrials abducted him and brought him to the planet Elohim in order to explain where humans came from and how they evolved. When he got back to earth, he promptly moved to Quebec to spread the news. Today calling himself Raël, he claims to have 50,000 followers in 84 countries – about 4,000 of them in Quebec. Strippers and devotees of free love make up a good part of his congregation, says respected cult expert Susan Palmer. Those hoping to join the Raëlian movement and cash in on the freedom are asked to pitch in a good portion of their income, while some have been discouraged by the requirement of having to sit through the leader's stupendously boring speeches about aliens. Unlike other cults, Raëlians have welcomed publicity. They've even been known to get believers to "love bomb" inquisitive journalists. (N.B.: The frequent inquiries made by the authors of this book for more information have everything to do with honest reporting and nothing to do with an effort to get "love bombed.") In 1998, aliens ordered Raël to assemble an elite group of beautiful women to entertain them whenever they drop in on earth. Raël's Angels are recognizable by their feather necklaces and might include porn actress Grace Quark. Raël is said to have made her an honorary Angel after he watched her films and recognized her impressive service to humanity. In 2001, Raël made headlines in a big way, testifying before a U.S. Senate Subcommittee about his plans to clone a human child. Apparently, 50 women have already volunteered to participate. The curious can poke their heads in at the group's meetings, which are held on the third Sunday of every month at the Gèsu concert hall and galleries (1202 Bleury).

SCIENTOLOGY WITHOUT APOLOGY

Twenty thousand Scientologists discreetly roam our burgh, according to church spokesman Jean Larivière. But only about 1,000 are considered core members and, no, they don't look anything like the stilt-monsters in John Travolta's tribute to Scientology, Battlefield Earth.

The gang meets every Sunday at 4489 Papineau (corner Mount Royal). What to expect? "Group auditing, special counseling," Larivière says. "You look at the person in front of you, touch their shoulders. It consists basically of very light processes to get your attention on the physical universe around you instead of being in your own mind."

POSTER BOYS FOR MORALITY

In June 1926, 200 religious and social leaders – including the head of the League of Good Morals – protested vehemently against what they thought was a leading factor in the corruption of our young people: movie posters displayed outside of theatres. They demanded that all such posters be banned.

BONES OF CONTENTION

Montrealers are at the cutting edge of a battle against circumcision. One of them is John Antonopoulos, Director of the Circumcision Information Resource, which fields calls from men seeking counsel about matters of circumcision, and is actually a front for the anti-circumcision movement. The group argues that, in the United States, snake-snippers cash in to the tune of $400 million annually for what they consider an unnecessary and harmful practice. Renowned McGill ethics professor Margaret Somerville agrees heartily, describing the removal of baby boys' foreskins as "technically criminal assault." Meanwhile, Antonopoulos won't reveal whether he's circumcized or not.

A CUT-RATE VISIT

Hey guys, why settle for the ordinary when you can plan a different kind of vacation in Montreal? Thanks to modern technology and Dr Yvon Ménard's sharp knife, you can come here and have your penis and testicles removed by experts and have them replaced by female genitalia. Menard's gender-reassignment operations are renowned the world over and happen at the Metropolitan Plastic Surgery Clinic (999 De Salaberry).

Happy, Healthy ... Holy Smokes! Another Montreal Religion

If you see happy, healthy, and holy-looking people sauntering about in white robes and matching turbans, chances are they're members of a religion launched by a Punjabi named Harbhajan Singh Puri, who came to Montreal in 1969. Puri, who was 39 years old at the time, didn't stay long. Depending on who you believe, he was either tossed out of the country or moved because he couldn't stand the local winters. A year later in Los Angeles, he launched a Sikh-like religion called Happy, Healthy, Holy (or 3HO) that promoted Punjabi ways to westerners. At its peak, the religion counted 20,000 adherents in Canada and the States, but these days that number is far lower. Puri now lives comfortably in New Mexico.

Solar Bunk

Rest in peace, little Christopher Emmanuel, whose parents, Tony and Nicky Dutoit, had the misfortune of being members and employees of the Solar Temple cult. Originally from Sheffield, England, Nicky sewed the members' preposterous cloaks, while Tony took care of the ridiculous special effects used by pitchman Luc Jouret. Unfortunately, the French madman and evil force behind the Solar Temple, Joseph Di Mambro, considered young Christopher's name to be proof that the three-month-old was the Antichrist. In 1994, Di Mambro arranged to lure the family into a Morin Heights home, where they were all stabbed to death.

That was only business as usual for the Solar Temple, a cult whose activities and bogus calls to Sirius resulted in 74 of their deaths in Canada and Europe. According to the Quebec Provincial Police, many Solar Temple believers survived the round of suicides and massacres and might even practice their beliefs to this day, although Di Mambro and Jouret were counted among the dead.

The cult was so pervasive that the Hydro Quebec electrical utility investigated its staff for participation in the cult, but said they found no evil-doers. Surviving former members include classical music conductor Michel Tabachnik, who worked in Montreal and took the blame for writing some of the group's literature on suicide.

Back in the early '90s, locals Suzanne Girard and Puelo Deir were fed up. They figured Montreal's gays and lesbians deserved better than the fractious and ill-attended yearly pride parades, which routinely excluded the likes of drag queens and leathermen as some kind of embarrassment to the community. The two friends saw no reason why Montreal's pride march shouldn't rise above its reputation for bickering and take its place among world-class events like those held in San Francisco, New York, and Paris.

Girard and Deir weren't just talking. Risking all the scratch they could scrounge – an almost paltry $15,000 – the pair organized the first Divers/Cité festival, with a wide-open-door policy. The rest is socio-economic history.

Divers/Cité invited everyone: lesbians, gays, bisexuals, transgendered, family, and friends. They even said "come on down" to the city's heteros, and the formula worked. It's now a week-long blast with countless official and off-the-record events generating mountains of tourism cash for the city's perennially bone-dry coffers. So how much frick? Try $40 million in economic spinoffs for the 2000 edition alone (the last year for which figures are available) – an amount that grows larger every year. And merchants love this crowd (studies indicate that homosexual tourists spend 3½ times more than heterosexuals on hotels, restaurants, clothing and souvenirs).

Today, Divers/Cité is one of Montreal's tourism magnets, attracting one million participants from throughout Quebec, Canada, the U.S. and around the world. Its annual operating budget has grown to $1 million – a figure that doesn't take into account the work of armies of volunteers.

Indeed, scarcely a decade after its initial appearance, Divers/Cité has grown to be one of the top ten pride celebrations in the world, and one of the top four in North America (alongside San Francisco, New York, and Toronto). Its parade is even said to be the biggest one-day event in Quebec, drawing a bigger crowd than the St. Patrick's Day Parade in March (but don't say that to an Irishman).

COPS HAVE EARS

Along with the usual Big Brothers monitoring our calls (including Echelon, the RCMP, and whatever dark forces might be hiding under your bed), our own city cops are also avid phone-snoops. At the Montreal police force's Cremazie station, up to 15 cops at a time tap into 45 listening boxes, mostly in pursuit of drug dealers. Under Section 196 of the Criminal Code, authorities need a warrant to snoop and are required to send you a letter informing you that they listened in on you, within three years. But local cops have been rumoured to forget this letter-writing business after one unhappy recipient dragged them through court for many years after they informed him they'd been snooping on him.

Divers/Cité is held every summer, typically at the end of July and early August. From street parties and staged spectacles, to artistic, cultural, commercial and social events – the venues are many, so check out the online schedule (diverscite.org) or call (514/285-4011) for info. Volunteers are always welcome.

TINY TRAIN TOWN

You might have passed that mysterious door under the viaduct and railway tracks that penetrate Place Bonaventure. Well, if you try pulling that door at 891 St. Paul West on any Wednesday night around 7:15pm, you'll be led into a huge underground warehouse laden full of model trains, lovingly cared for by the 30 members of the Montreal Railroad Modelers Association. The club was born in 1950 by frustrated fans of remote-control airplanes who were banned from Fletcher's Field (also called Jeanne Mance Park) after one of their planes smashed through a car windshield. Since that day, the club has amassed a half-million-dollar mini-train collection on 1,000 metres (more than half a mile) of tiny tracks. It features 15 stations and four fantasy cities and has graveyards and detailed nude beaches. Wannabes can become joiners for $15 a month, should they clear a six-month probationary period. The train artists invite the public to an annual open house on the last weekend in October. For details call 514/861-6185.

Pow-Wow Power

Since 1991, the Echoes of a Proud Nation Pow-Wow (450/632-8667; kahnawake.com/events) has been bringing non-Native communities closer to the aboriginal people of Kahnawake. The event began as a gesture of rapprochement one year after the historic 78-day standoff between Mohawks and non-Native authorities at nearby Oka. It's been an annual event ever since — what the native community calls "the best public relations event Kanawake produces." It brings thousands of dollars into the local economy, but it also costs the reserve $100,000 to stage it.

The two-day event has a fairground atmosphere, with upwards of 70 kiosks selling items like crafts, carpets, carvings, clothing, blankets, and dream catchers. There are also several dozen food merchants, offering everything from bison burgers to trout and salmon dishes. There are plenty of fresh fruit juices on sale, but don't bother asking for beer: this is a "dry" event. It matters little, as most folks come to witness the ceremomies, such as the Smoke Dance and the Grand Entry, when Native people perform free-form dances in a circle as, one by one, they are presented. Another attraction is the sight of traditional costumes and headdresses, and just rubbing shoulders with Navajos from Arizona, Ojibwa from Michigan, Cree from the Prairies, and local bands such as Mohawks, Tuscarora, and Montagnais. To drive from Montreal, take the Mercier Bridge and Autoroute 138 West to the Kanawake exit. Head north (turn right) on Highway 207 and follow the signs to the free parking. You can get to Kanawake via the CITSO bus stop at Angrignon Park and, once there, grab a local bus to the pow-wow site (bus information: 450/698-3030). Admission to the pow-wow is under $10 for adults, and even cheaper for seniors and kids.

inventive minds

Some local inventions.

Shake It Up

In 1984, Concordia grad Avtar Pall developed technology to make buildings earthquake-proof. Celine Dion's Laval mansion, the Montreal Casino, the Concordia University library, and the Canadian Space Agency are equipped with these devices that damper the shock of an earthquake.

All Hail

Inventor Gerald Olliver, who moved here from France in 1986, invented a machine that protects crops from hailstorms. The $40,000, six-meter cannon purportedly worked by shooting acetylene gas into clouds, "shocking" water out of its tendency to crystallize.

No Skinny Dipping

In 1989, Emile Génereux, president of Pool-Alert Inc., developed and sold 300,000 pool alarms at $60 a pop. They sound off when somebody sneaks into your pool.

Turbinology

Toss it into a small stream, slap down a bit of concrete, and Robert and Normand Lévesque's water generator noiselessly provides electricity without the need for fuel. Their Boisbriand-based Microturbines Technologies Inc. has been raking in the cash since the mid '90s.

Staple Shagger

Real-estate agent Saheed Khan, who calls himself Alex – "because I look like an Alex" – was pulling staples out of documents when he had his eureka moment. He realized that the world needs a staple remover that pops used staples into a small receptacle attached to the device rather than simply flinging it into your shag carpet. A big American chain bought up his patented staple sucker in 1998 and the world is obviously much the better for it.

A City Flushed With Pride

Photo: John David Gravenor

When Montreal decided to expand its convention centre a few years ago, it ran into a small obstacle. Because the site was located close to several heritage buildings, the Quebec government demanded an exploratory archaeological dig on the site. In addition to finding several old foundations and bits of the old city fortifications, there were the usual domestic articles, like broken bottles, plates, and gunshot. Then they found two wooden barrels that had been dug into the ground beneath outhouses.

Going to the bathroom has come a long way since the old days. Although the city doesn't have the high-tech sidewalk toilets that are so popular in London or Paris, there are countless places to seek relief. Montreal even earns numerous mentions at The Bathroom Diaries

Cannon Fodder

McGill graduate Gerald Bull had a talent for cannons. In '64, the brilliant engineer was rewarded for his cannonating research by being appointed as McGill's youngest-ever full-time professor at age 34. The U.S. government, displeased that Canada didn't share their views on Vietnam, pulled their support for Bull's long-range cannon project, leading Bull to move to Vermont. But the Bronfmans lured him back to develop his cannon at a range near Mansonville, in the Eastern Townships. When he returned to the States, the Americans punished him for doing business with South Africa and put him in prison for a year for dealing with the sanctioned apartheid regime. The debacle cost Bull his health and fortune, and he moved to Brussels in 1981. Meanwhile, Bull's dealings with Iraq displeased Israeli leaders, who reportedly sent two agents into his home to shoot him five times on March 22, 1990. Bull was buried in a cemetery in St. Bruno on Montreal's South Shore and his Mansonville testing range became a marijuana farm, which was busted in 2000.

Hobo History

Back in the golden age of hobos, which lasted from after the U.S. Civil War through the Depression, trying to bum money would likely land you in the clink. Instead, you'd probably get down with the hobos, who always shared their moonshine and held nightlong singing parties.

A leading railway hub, Montreal was far from immune to the phenomenon of hobo living. Camps of itinerant men (hobos didn't let each other keep female company) could be seen on local rail sidings, where they'd scrawl messages to their itinerant friends on the sides of water tanks.

In 1872, Montreal was the scene of a large hobo convention. The celebrated Yorkey Ned had such a fine time, he was inspired to write the popular drinking song, "Moochers Hall."

Next time you happen to be walking near the brick building at the southwest corner of St. Jacques and Peel, check out the plaque on the north side. On this very spot once stood the Grand Trunk Railway's Bonaventure Station. There's little doubt that Yorkey Ned himself walked by this place. He might even have stooped for a freshly-discarded stogie or stuck out his upturned palm in a panhandler's salute.

(thebathroomdiaries.com), a website devoted to postings about public toilets around the world. Here's what some web surfers had to say.

DOWNTOWN

Indigo Books & Music
(Ste. Catherine near McGill College)
Featuring clean, white tiles and lots of paper towels, these bathrooms won an "excellent" rating. And what with the bookstore's late hours, they make a convenient downtown resource.

Peel Pub
(Ste. Catherine at Peel)
One visitor rated the women's facilities "bad" because she found water all over the floor, and "had to pray to God" to find toilet paper.

Pepsi Forum Entertainment Centre
(Ste. Catherine and Atwater)
Self-flushing toilets, automatic faucets, and general cleanliness garnered these commodes an "excellent" rating. The upstairs toilets won special praise for being a place you might want to spend the night.

Photo: John David Gravenor

You've got Dickite (a clay-like mineral), and then there's Moronic Acid (an organic acid), and Fucitol (a type of alcohol). But when it comes to weird names in chemistry, nothing says Montreal quite like the Buckminsterfullerene – a class of molecule inspired by Buckminster Fuller's geodesic bubble on St. Helen's Island.

Before 1985, only six crystalline forms of carbon were recognized. Then a scientific team created this new kind of carbon cluster featuring 60 to 70 atoms.

In awarding the 1996 Nobel Prize for Chemistry to the scientists Robert F. Curl Jr., Sir Harold W. Kroto, and Richard E. Smalley, the Royal Swedish Academy of Sciences noted that the molecule had exactly the same structure "as does the geodetic dome designed by the American architect R. Buckminster Fuller for the 1967 Montreal World Exhibition." The researchers even named their newly-invented molecule, the Buckminster-fullerene, to honour his architectural innovation.

As the American Pavilion, the 20-storey building was one of the big hits at Expo 67. The United States later gave it to the city. Sadly, during renovations a few weeks before the 1976 Olympic Games, the building's transparent acrylic skin was destroyed in a spectacular fire. The hulk of the structure now encloses the Biosphere nature museum.

Presse Café

(Ste. Catherine, across from the Paramount Cinema complex)
Rated "good," these 24-hour bathrooms feature huge, clean, comfortable stalls.

Eaton Centre

(Ste. Catherine near McGill College)
Despite being disability-friendly and featuring changing tables, these toilets were given the thumbs-down for apparently haphazard maintenance and general sloppiness.

Concordia University

(Faubourg Ste. Catherine, Ste. Catherine and Guy)
Located at the east end of the mall, you have to take an escalator up one floor and then turn to your right. The disability-friendly stalls were rated "good" for neatness, size, and privacy.

Queen Elizabeth Hotel

(900 René Lévesque W. at Mansfield)
Located on the ground floor near the bar, these privies were rated "good" for cleanliness and quiet. You don't have to be a guest, but security is always looking out for weirdos, so behave accordingly.

Marilyn Rossner, Ph.D, receives lots of visitors at her laid-back headquarters at 1974 de Maisonneuve – not all of them living. Rossner says she was just four years old when she realized she could see people on the other side of death. To this day, she's grateful that her parents were supportive about her unusual gift, and she grew up to have a well-adjusted life. "Heaven is within," she says. "Hell is a result of fear and anxiety." When she grew up, the petite redhead with the big, shaded glasses became a psychologist, yoga instructor, university teacher, got married, and later took early retirement. Now she heads up the the **SSF-IIIHS Centre** (514/937-8359; iiihs.com), where a spartan faculty instruct other people, most often professionals, on how they can listen to the spirit world, manage stress, read palms, engage in trances and channeling, and practice meditation. On the side, Rossner has contributed her psychological expertise to aid dying children in South Africa and the Soviet Union, work for which she received the blessings of the Pope. Canadians of a certain age will also remember Rossner as the featured handwriting analyst on *Beyond Reason*, a television show based on paranormal phenomena. As one of three panelists competing to guess the identity of a guest, Rossner routinely beat out a palm-reading expert from New York and a clairvoyant from Chicago.

offbeat museum

Dolls and Treasures

If you're the kind of person who likes to play with dolls, combing their hair and putting little dresses on them, well good, because so are we. And if you're looking for creepy, cute, sweet, and cuddly dollies all under one great roof, check out the Dolls and Treasures museum in Old Montreal. You'll find 4,000 of them dating back to 1880. Don't be shy, the owners are pretty much grown, too.
105 St. Paul St. East, 514/866-0110

Biddle's Jazz Club

(Aylmer and President Kennedy)
Rated "good" for cleanliness and celebrity-sightings, these gender-specific bathrooms feature high-tech toilet seats you have to see to believe.

Paramount Cinemas

(977 Ste. Catherine W. at Metcalfe)
Dubbed "very good," these clean and modern bathrooms are open from noon to about midnight, and they say you don't even need a movie ticket.

Sona Club

(Bleury near Ste. Catherine)
These tiny, unisex toilets were rated "good" for the probability of spotting celebrities.

Wyndham Hotel

(Complexe Desjardins, across from Place des Arts)
Open 24 hours and rated "good," these clean and safe toilets feature piped-in classical music.

Movenpick Restaurant

(Place Ville Marie, University and Cathcart)
Clean, safe, and with changing tables, these modern bathrooms were rated "very good." Large, with upscale sinks and hardware, they were also called, "retro, stylish, and sexy."

Feathered Friends Indeed

Located on a sprawling property in the suburban village of Hudson, **Le Nichoir** cares for sick, injured, and orphaned birds. More than 1,000 birds a year are rehabilitated here, 60 percent of which are later released back into their natural habitat. The non-profit centre runs on volunteer power, so if you love birds, you might want to push your observation skills a little and sign up for a volunteer orientation session. The annual half-day workshop combines bird care-and-rehabilitation theory with hands-on practice. There are many ways to help the centre, including fundraising, telephone-answering, bird transportation, construction and repair, food preparation, cleaning, and direct bird care (such as feeding).
450/458-2809; geocities.com/lenichoir

For the Dogs

We did a few dog-in-the-street interviews about a restaurant on St. Denis that opened in December, 2001. It turns out most if not all dogs found the **Cookies** dog restaurant *(3875A St. Denis St.; 514/281-2054)*, quite "ruff." They meant it in a good way, of course. The 1,000-foot eatery carries a dozen flavours of dog cookies, as well as snacks for adults that are wrapped and imported from other places with non-dog oriented kitchens. Leia, an American cocker spaniel, is always on hand, as are the owners, François Champagne and Eveline Morand, to welcome you daily from 11am-6pm (until 10pm on weekends) in a unique city spot, where dogs can happily sniff other dogs, and munch till their tails feel like they'll fall off.

Canine Able

If your idea of the perfect exercise is not doing any, have we got a sport for you. A fast-moving relay game, flyball is the perfect agility exercise — for your dog. Once your canine pal is trained (it usually takes a few hours), the rules are simple. Beginning at a starting line, dogs race across a track and step on a special platform at the other end. Out pops a ball. Then Fido races back with the ball, and it's the next dog's turn to run. There

OLD MONTREAL

Gibby's

(Place d'Youville)

Judged "good," these clean and aesthetically-pleasing bathrooms were considered safe and "chic," with a good mix of classic and modern styling.

PLATEAU

Frite Alors!

(St. Denis and Emery)

Earning an adequate rating, these gender-specific bathrooms feature black lights — which supposedly discourage junkies from shooting up. (It's hard to find a blue vein under black lights.)

Peck Building

(5505 St. Lawrence Blvd.)

Earning an adequate rating, these bathrooms are designed along the lines of "Textile Factory Chic." While the plumbing might leave something to be desired, the toilet stalls can't be beat for the imaginative messages scrawled by previous users.

Whisky Café

(5800 St. Lawrence)

Stand up, ladies, for the only women's urinal in town. The men's urinal is like a waterfall, its steady sheet of water keeping everything clean and odor-free. Rated "good."

are leagues and competitions all over. There's even a flyball "college." **Le Centre Professionnel Canin** offers English-language instruction in the fast-moving relay game. Arrive with your dog and you'll soon be ready to play. *514/745-3200; infochien.com*

EAST END

CBC

(Tour de Radio-Canada, 1400 René Lévesque E.)

Open 24 hours, these modern, gender-specific toilets were rated "good" for general cleanliness and probability of spotting local celebs.

TOWN OF MOUNT ROYAL

Holt Rentfrew

(Rockland Shopping Center)

Located close to the customer-service area, these gender-specific washrooms earned a "good" rating for being weirdo-free and having clean stalls.

VILLE ST. LAURENT

CAE Inc.

(8585 Côte de-Liesse)

While they may be open 24 hours, these gender-specific bathrooms were rated as "bad" for the carelessness of previous users, tobacco smoking, and "irregular" cleaning practices. But maybe the reviewer was a disgruntled employee.

run, don't walk

Visiting a dog run is the canine version of pumping iron, so when it's time to work on Lassie's abs, you've got at least two dozen dog runs to choose from on the island. The majority are open from 7am to 11pm Remember that dog licences are mandatory. They cost $25 per animal.

Some dog runs, by district, starting with our favourite:

Downtown
   Basin and du Seminaire (just west of the Wellington bridge)
   At the back of the Westmount High School athletic grounds near Ste. Catherine and Clarke

Ahuntsic-Cartierville
   Saint Benoit Park and Sault au Récollet Park

Côte St. Luc/Hampstead/Montreal West
   On Mackle across from the Wagar High School field

Mercier-Hochelaga-Maisonneuve
   Liébert, de la Bruyère, and Félix Leclerc Parks.

Notre Dame de Grâce
   William Bowie, Notre Dame de Grâce, Confederation, and Trenholme Parks

Park Extension
   Jarry Park

Plateau Mont Royal/South Central
   De Rouen and La Fontaine Parks

Rivière des Prairies
   Parc de la Polyvalente Pointe aux Trembles

Rosemont
   Père Marquette, le Pélican, and Lafond Parks

Southwest
   Angrignon and Le Ber parks

what you can get away with

We know there are countless laws and if you really tried to know them all you'd go mad wondering if it's legal to breathe in a closed vehicle while shopping for balloons on a Sunday. So here's a vague idea from a police insider about what you can expect to get away with. Note: we strongly advise everybody on our football-shaped island to avoid stupid, annoying, or any other type of behaviour that might seem reminiscent of something you saw on America's-dumbest-criminals, so this section remains strictly for entertainment purposes only.

Giving a Fake Name to Avoid Fines

Canadians are not legally required to carry or produce identification. So if you get busted for a minor bylaw infraction such as jaywalking, riding your bike like a Montrealer, or walking along the railway tracks, you can most likely avoid the penalty by supplying a *nom de plume* and an imaginary address. If the name you give happens to be shared by a wanted criminal, that could pose a problem. The practice is also technically illegal.

Sex in Public

Beat cops will tell you how they come across massive amounts of late-night backseat humping, which they generally ignore. Unless you're doing it in front of minors, police prefer to respond to actual complaints. In the '80s, a rash of gay alley love affairs prompted Tupper Street residents to complain repeatedly. Few complained about the sex but they sure didn't like the used prophylactics lying around.

Smoking Marijuana in Public

A terrible idea that could land you in prison, but in practice, many cops will look the other way. Others will frisk the miscreant and confiscate the drug and give you the ol' don't-let-me-see-you-round-here-again line.

Eat and Runs

One cop estimates that in "four of five cases," managers of low-priced restaurants will not press charges against restaurant customers who don't pay. This favourite trick of the upper-class vagrant set doesn't work as well in pricier establishments, where managers will happily press charges against deadbeat diners.

Food Banks

Where to go when you have more appetite than cash:

La Garde-Manger familiale
For $2.50 they let you jam your knapsack with whatever they have on their shelves. Fridays only 4:30pm-6:30pm
5965 Christophe-Colomb (Paroisse St. Etienne), Rosemont Metro; 514/270-2308

Maison Adrianna
Slightly complicated: one needs to sign up on a waiting list and pay $5 a week to get a wide variety of stuff. Wednesdays only 10am-3pm
2615 Ontario, Frontenac Metro; 514/573-6347

Mile-End Mission
A small place where you show up in the morning and return for your booty in the afternoon. Fridays only, 9am and 12pm
99 Bernard W.; 514/274-3401

Multi-Caf
Free breakfasts for CDN residents, although they try to prevent people from going more than once a month. Tuesdays, Wednesdays, and Thursdays from 9am to 10:30am
5829 Côte des Neiges, Côte des Neiges Metro; 514/733-0554

tattoos you

What better way to pass a quiet day than to have someone mark your skin with ink-filled needles or have holes punctured through your epidermis?

Arts Anciens Tattoo & Piercing

In 1999, the owner, Julio, got into hot water for allegedly doing tattoos and one nipple-piercing on kids as young as 15. He denied everything.
9550 Gouin W., Pierrefonds; 514/421-7408

Derm FX Tatouage

Formerly located at the recently-demolished area near the bridge, these experienced needlers tout their custom work, repair jobs, and Chinese characters that have been perfected over 10 years of practice.
1808 Ontario E.; 514/525-4444

Studio Tatouage West

Since '92 these crazy kids have been inking the Plateau glitterati and have developed a rep for big projects like back-sized jobs.
30 Rachel W.; 514/847-1111

Tatouage Blue Psycho

Named after a blue female figure that proprietor Kate drew one day, this seasoned parlour at the corner of Hickson is known for their tribal and black-shadow designs, as well as repairs of old tats.
3784 Wellington, Verdun; 514/768-2583

Tatouage du Québec

At the corner of Cartier and Ontario sits a 35-year-old father-to-son institution. A guy called Norman heads a staff of eight inkers offering what he considers the best design sheets in town, stuff that he's hunted far and wide to procure. He can draw a mean rock star like Janis, Jimi, Jim, John "anything that starts with J," he says.
1880 Ontario E.; 514/521-5375

NDG Food Depot

NDG residents only. The best in the city. Generous, friendly staff, slightly long waits. Mondays 5-7pm and Fridays 10am-2pm
2121 Oxford, Vendôme Metro;
514/483-4680

The Salvation Army

Food baskets handed out as long as you don't show up too often. Mondays to Fridays from 9am to 3:30pm
2050 Stanley, Peel Metro;
514/288-7686

Sun Youth

Lots of jumping through hoops and filling out forms to get into this place. After the 15th of every month, appointments only
4251 St. Urbain, corner Rachel;
514/842-6822

The Women's Centre

Women only. No ID required, but you must fill out a form, discouraging frequent flyers. Thursdays and Fridays by appointment
3585 St. Urbain, Place-des-Arts Metro, 80 Bus; 514/842-4780

Photo: John David Gravenor

Montreal is without rival when it comes to good bagels. The bagels at **St. Viateur Bagel** *(263 St. Viateur, off Park Ave.)* would be the place aliens would want to land if they were on an interstellar hunt for the perfect bagel. Tourists have been known to drive from adjacent states and provinces just to score a few dozen or so. In fact, many customers have been known just to stand around watching the entertaining display of bagel masters at work, preparing the dough, cutting and rolling the bagels, boiling them in honey water, and plunging them deep into a wood-fired oven. When they're ready, heads up as the baker flips dozens of hot bagels from the oven to the rack. In addition to poppy-seed and sesame bagels and matzo boards, you can pick up smoked salmon, cream cheese, juice, and fresh eggs.

Just south a couple of blocks, the **Fairmount Bagel Shop** *(74 Fairmount W.)* has been selling oven-hot bagels at its so-called factory for more than 50 years. It specializes in a vast array of styles, ranging from cinnamon and raisin to pesto bagels. Assorted fresh toppings are likewise available.

When downtown, you can find reasonably good bagels at the **Faubourg Market** *(Ste. Catherine and St. Mathieu).*

Tip: ask for freezer bags. Uneaten bagels should be sliced and frozen when you get home. To serve, simply remove from the bag, pop in the toaster, and Menachem's your uncle.

Free or Cheap Meals

Accueil Bonneau
Men only. Free. Mon. to Fri. 9:30am-11:15am, 2pm-3pm, Sat. and Sun. 10am-11:30am
427 de la Commune E., Champs-de-Mars Metro; 514/845-3906

Photo: John David Gravenor

Benedict Labre House
Free. Tuesdays 1pm, Wed. and Thu. 1pm and 5:30pm, Sat. and Sun. 12pm
308 Young St., Bonaventure Metro; 514/937-5973

Chez Doris
Women only. Free. Mondays to Fridays at 12pm
1430 Chomedey, Atwater Metro; 514/937-2341

Chez Mes Amis
$2, or 14 meals for $20. Free for kids under eight. $1 for kids eight to 12. Mon. to Fri. 10am-7:15pm, Sun. 4:40pm-7:15pm
5942 Sherbrooke W., Vendôme Metro; 514/482-2210

Comité Social Centre-Sud
$2.50. Mon. to Fri., 7:30am-9am,
11:30am-2pm
1710 Beaudry, Beaudry Metro;
514/596-7092

Les Amis du Plateau
Free. Mon. to Sat.,
12:45pm-1:30pm
4395 Papineau, Mount Royal or
Papineau Metro; 514/527-1344

Multi-Caf
$1. Mon. to Fri. 9:30am-10:30am;
11:45am-1pm
3591 Appleton, Côte des Neiges
Metro; 514/733-0554

Old Brewery Mission
Free dinner served at 5pm daily
beginning on the 15th of the month.
For the first two weeks of the month,
meals go only to those who slept
there the night prior. In 1983, Brian
Mulroney's team loaded a bunch of
'em on a bus to support his bid for
leadership of the Progressive
Conservative Party.
915 Clark, Place d'Armes Metro;
514/866-6591

Resto-Plateau
$2.50. Mon. to Fri.
11:30am-1:30pm
4450 St. Hubert, Mount Royal
Metro; 514/527-5997

in quest of the perfect espresso
– Maria Francesca LoDico

Having my coffee is as close to religious experience as I come. My favorite is cappuccino, equal parts espresso, scalded milk, and a sublime head of cashmere. One teaspoon sugar. No cinnamon. No chocolate shavings.

You should try it. It goes something like this: sit back. Relax. Take your shoes off. Massage your feet. It's time for your coffee break. Contemplate, for a moment, the velvety milk that is like whipped cream, but more supple, a stable, fine foam that holds its shape. Yet it yields, doesn't it?

Bring the cup to your lips, wrap them around the cappuccino's effervescent top hat. Ah, yes, it does yield. The hot espresso and milk rise through the foam, the tiny bubbles pop under your nose as silken coffee and milk blend in your mouth, sweetness with a bitter chocolatey edge.

Amen.

Brûlerie St. Denis
3967 St. Denis, 514/286-9158 and various locations

Café Electra
24 Pine E., 514/288-0853

Caffé Italia
6840 St. Laurent,
514/495-0059

Faema
14 Jean Talon St.
W., 514/276-2671

Java U
1455 Guy, 514/932-5288; 4914 Sherbrooke W.,
514/482-7077 and various locations

Open Da Night (a.k.a. Café Olympico)
124 St-Viateur W., 514/495-0746

Toi, Moi et Café
Buy 250 grams of the Vecchio Napoli espresso beans for home use. I insist! And if you don't have a moka, I'm giving you the evil eye right now.
244 Laurier W., 514/279-9599

Photo: John David Gravenor

index

index

index

index

index

index

KRISTIAN GRAVENOR writes a city column for the *Montreal Mirror*, fathers his four kids, and generally attempts to stay out of trouble.

A freelance writer and book critic whose articles appear frequently in *The Gazette* (Montreal) and *National Post*, JOHN DAVID GRAVENOR has worked as a Tiki-bar photographer, community-TV and video-documentary producer, international telephone operator, door-to-door cookbook salesman, newspaper editor, wedding videographer, translator, and news editor for Southam, Hollinger, and CanWest.